SPC LIBRARY
The code of the West
GR 109 R67 1982

3 6854 00015865 7

P9-CQV-727

THE
CODE
OF THE
WEST

GR
109
R67
1982

THE

OF THE

Bruce A. Rosenberg.

INDIANA UNIVERSITY PRESS

Bloomington

For Ann
Who Makes It All Worthwhile

Copyright © 1982 by Bruce A. Rosenberg

All rights reserved

No part of this book may be reproduced or utilized in any form
or by any means, electronic or mechanical, including photocopying
and recording, or by any information storage and retrieval system,
without permission in writing from the publisher. The Association
of American University Presses' Resolution on Permissions constitutes
the only exception to this prohibition.

Manufactured in the United States of America

Library of Congress Cataloging in Publication Data

Rosenberg, Bruce A.
  The code of the West.

  1. Legends—West (U.S.)—History and criticism.
2. West (U.S.)—Folklore.   3. West (U.S.)—Civilization.
I. Title.
GR109.R67   398.2'32'78   81-47014
ISBN 0-253-31387-2   AACR2
1 2 3 4 5 86 85 84 83 82

CONTENTS

ACKNOWLEDGMENTS

My most heartfelt gratitude goes to the administration and staff of the Henry E. Huntington Library, San Marino, California, who have created the ideal working environment, for two summer fellowships that enabled me to do much of the research that went towards the making of this book, and especially to Martin Ridge, the late Ray Allen Billington, James Thorpe, and that unequalled Reader Services Librarian, who provided me with all that I ever wanted, Virginia Renner. Huntington Reader Sandra Myers was also of great help on the Overland Trail narratives. Much of the research was done at Brown University's John Hay Library, particularly the Eberstadt collection. Peter Balakian and especially Paul Fees, who were then graduate students, were of great help in locating material, Paul in helping to put some of it together. In various phases of my research, students Annelen Archbold, Elizabeth Lawrence, Peggy Martin, and Carl Lindahl taught me a lot about the West. Mr. Thomas Muir of Cincinnati was helpful in locating informants who remembered the great race of the *Lee* and the *Natchez,* as was the Marketing Services Department of the Delta Queen Steamboat Company. Captain Frederick Way, who spent all of his active adult life on the river, has been most gracious in sharing those experiences with me. The Pony Express Museum has been helpful in providing information about the institution it commemorates, as has been the Wells Fargo Bank. Thanks also to three journals that published fragments of essays used here as chapters: the *Journal of the Folklore Institute, Books at Brown,* and the *Huntington Library Quarterly.* Three students and fans of folklore and popular culture have, by their knowledge, patience, and generosity of spirit enabled me to understand a great deal about the American West and how we perceive it: Horace Newcomb, Roger Abrahams, and John Cawelti.

THE
CODE
OF THE
WEST

Introduction

To recompose the past—to give structure, order, hierarchy, and purpose to several events, individuals, and institutions of the American West—is one of the chief purposes of this book. Those irreversible acts that transpired in time may not have had the regularity and coherence ascribed to them, but it is the inclination of historians to want to see causality and patterning. In these pages several institutions prominent in nineteenth-century America (the Pony Express, the Mormon Church, the transcontinental railroads) and events (Custer's Last Stand, the discovery of mineral wealth, the exploitation of the Overland Trail, etc.) are reexamined from the added perspective of folk and popular creations. What I hope will emerge is a fuller, deeper, and broader understanding of American culture in the last century, especially Americans' attitudes toward the West, but also their feelings about themselves and their country as these were projected onto the events and personalities of the West and its unfolding history.

We have often been told, for instance, what President Polk thought and what he publicly declared about the land west of the Mississippi, and we have access to the "official" sentiments of lesser, though still important politicians; but what did the "people in the street" in Tombstone think when the Earps and Doc Holliday gunned down the rival Clantons and McLowrys? Territorial Governor Lew Wallace's response to the Lincoln County range war and Billy the Kid is on record, but what were the people, Mexican as well as American, thinking and feeling about the situation? We have perceived the discovery of gold on the American River in California in terms of demographic shifts, national and even world economy, the political consequences of the rapid colonization of millions of square miles of contiguous (and sparsely inhabited) land, but what were the early prospectors saying to each other and to those back East when they were panning for nuggets in the Mother Lode country, or in the Washoe? How often did the concept of Manifest Destiny enter their thoughts, their letters, their stories, their songs? The corporate histories of the Central and Union Pacific Railroads have been carefully assembled, published, and studied; they tell us a great deal about the difficulty of laying track across an inhospitable prairie, but folklore and the popular arts reveal, in expressive forms, what the men who actually laid the track were feeling. Their responses were different from the motivations of railroad presidents Huntington and Durant, yet are as much a part of that collective American ethos as theirs.

The present book differs, therefore, in this important respect from R. W. B. Lewis's *American Adam,* which describes "a native American mythology" though the author is not interested, as he says, in anthropology, folklore, sociology, or legend. We are both interested in the American myth as a "collective affair"; but while Lewis finds his "representative images" and "anecdotes that crystalized whole clusters of ideas" only in the writings of "articulate thinkers and conscious artists,"[1] I am concerned with a broader spectrum of the American people. Lewis no doubt thinks of most of the people quoted in this book as inarticulate and inartistic, and that arguable point is not germane to this comparison; rather, it should be pointed out that *The Code of the West* finds its representative images in the narratives of people other than the New England elite.

A scrutiny of the folksongs, the tall tales, the personal-experience narratives, rounds out the picture of an entire culture. Folk and popular narratives tell us a great deal about what was happening in the lives of those whose biographies are not in the *Oxford History of The American People;* they tell us not how government publications and church pronouncements depicted the Mormon handcart migration, but how ordinary people saw it; they tell us what it was like to be on the Overland Trail, how it felt to be part of what is now often thought of as merely a demographic movement; they tell us what Custer's Last Stand really meant to the American people—the insulting quality of that sting to their pride—and how they responded to it.

One of the important premises of this book—in fact, of this approach—recently expressed by communications theorist James

Carey, views the commonly shared symbols of our culture as the representations and celebrations of shared beliefs.[2] To understand, to interpret a culture, necessarily involves the researcher in an interpretative exploration of many such commonly shared symbols; the task is cumulative. We may, after a century of analytic scrutiny, have a clear idea of what Herman Melville had in mind in his narrative of a white whale; the interpreter of culture assumes that since thought is public, and so pervasively social, he must come to terms with its commonly shared symbols at all "levels." To understand American attitudes in the second half of the nineteenth century we must know a great deal more than the expressed symbols in *Moby-Dick,* for they are only part of the *Gestalt.*

Henry Nash Smith's *Virgin Land* also takes for its data base much of the popular material of the last century. It anticipated Carey's idea by more than two decades and sees further into the implications of the relations between the collective representations of history and historical processes: "history cannot happen . . . without images which simultaneously express collective desires and impose coherence on the . . . data of experience."[3] *The Code of the West* uses fewer popular materials than did Smith's marvelous book and adds folklore. *Virgin Land* shows how a collective mythology shaped perceptions and evoked acts; the present book tries to interpret what about the West its folklore and popular culture expressed. *Virgin Land* begins with the myth; *Code of the West* begins with the minute particles and fragments of that myth, and others, and works outward.

Those who seek verifiable, immutable "facts" in the swarm of events we term "history" have been suspicious of folklore. Folklore is often thought to be synonymous with "error," even deceit. The folklore used in this book is based on oral tradition (rather than those aspects of culture transmitted by custom) and is subject to entropy. That the human brain does not remember with computer-like accuracy has long been known, and this tendency toward what we pejoratively call "inaccuracy" inclines many people to trust only what is or has been or can be documented. (Not to overstate the case, we also recognize the many and intricate problems in dealing with documentary evidence.) But oral transmission is said to be particularly unreliable. People forget details, add others, change still more. And it is true that while oral traditions are seldom accurate in the positive sense often sought for by contemporary historians (although some traditions are quite accurate, particularly in those cultures where it is of the utmost religious significance to be so), they do often reflect psychological and cultural truths. This is the case with American folklore; nearly all of the legends of Custer's Last Stand, to use just one example, falsify the account of the battle and of Custer's role in it, yet they express the tradition-bearer's attitudes toward Custer, Indian-white relations, and the characteristics of the two races. It is therefore insufficient to talk facilely about and to lightly dismiss the "folk manipulation" of history. It is a commonplace to point out that Custer was a hero to much of white America in the nineteenth century, and decidedly a goat to many in the twentieth century, yet no new revelation about any major portion of the battle or the campaign came to light in the century of this attitude change. History, irreversible and "objective," has not changed; our perceptions have. So too, in almost as dramatic a fashion, has our evaluation of the OK Corral gunfight; largely ignored for nearly fifty years after the Earps and Clantons shot it out, Wyatt became the central figure in the legendary rendering (he was not central in the actual event), due in large measure to the hagiographic biography of him by Stuart Lake (1926), and the subsequent fictionalizing by Hollywood.

Details often become altered in oral transmission; but if this is to have any significance for us we are obliged to push our inquiry further and to ask why such alterations, the "folk manipulation of history" took place, what forms this altered perception assumed, and what both the fact of the alteration and the assumed form mean. The answers to those questions will advance our understanding beyond the unproductive point of merely dismissing oral traditions because they are "usually wrong."

Neither, it should be noted parenthetically, are they necessarily false to that irreversible string of events we think of as history. I remember once telling a class that one of the surest signs of the "fictional" character of an alleged event was its occurrence as a folktale, or its appearance in some form in the folklore indexes. Within two weeks of this fatuous proclamation we all read a newsservice "human interest" story about an army officer in Vietnam who had assigned a dangerous mission to a subordinate in the hopes that he might be killed so that the officer might marry the widow. This southeast Asian lived experience of Aarne-Thompson Type #465, "The Man Persecuted Because of His Beautiful Wife," is best known to us in its Old Testament version, the story of David and Bathsheba.

The relationship between what did happen and what people thought happened (or the "fictions" they wrote about what may have happened) is often hopelessly complex and intricate. In this book what people thought happened is taken to be close to their folklore and popular art, when those feelings are given expressive forms. Custer's Last Stand did happen: on June 25, 1876, more than two hundred officers and men of the United States Seventh Cavalry were killed by a combined force of Sioux, Cheyenne, and their allies. No amount of imaginative retelling of the events of that day—necessarily the creations of the fictionalizing imagination because those who knew best what really happened all died—can de-materialize the fact of that engagement in the Little Bighorn country of what is now Montana. The relationship of events to the public's perceptions of those events is one of the major subjects of this book, as that relationship was (and still is) manifest in about a dozen famous institutions, personalities, and events in the history of the American West.

It is artificial to speak of folklore, popular culture, and elite culture; and while that artificiality makes it possible to deal with each segment of a culture in some coherent fashion, the products of all three have much in common. Richard Dorson pointed out more than ten years ago the pervasive cultural peregrinations of the Davy Crockett legends.[4] Many heroic as well as comic tales were told about him, and they were in wide oral circulation during his lifetime. After his death, newspapers, comic almanacs, cartoons, and comic woodcuts also picked up the tales, giving him an even wider fame. Walt Disney manufactured almost single-handedly a Crockett revival during the 1950s, which was shortly after assisted by a television series. Despite all this popular acclaim, Crockett maintained his position in the elitist view of America, appearing in Parrington's *Main Currents of American Thought.* Such examples are easily extended: the White Steed of the Prairies (subject of the final chapter in this book) is mentioned by Josiah Gregg and George Kendall as having been the campfire topic of conversation of hunters and trappers over the extent of the plains; subsequently, he would appear in *Moby-Dick,* in popular poems of the twentieth century, in the folklore collections of Walter Prescott Webb and J. Frank Dobie, as well as in *Reader's Digest.*

Often it is hard to distinguish between what is popular and what is more "serious" art. The products of all cultural levels usually share a certain believability. That is, for at least the moment of performance (hearing or reading a story) belief is involved. The operative critical cliché has it that fiction creates its own world. What happens seems real, a part of us wants it to be real, or at least possible, if we are to enjoy it. Such are the dynamics of the reader/-listener-text relationship, even when we know that the basic premise of the narrative is false. A recent best-seller, Len Deighton's *SS-GB,* is set in England, which has been defeated by the Germans in World War II. At every moment, then, on every page, we know that what Deighton is narrating could not have happened. Yet the novel is full of suspense, we still empathize with the characters (the positive ones anyway, while we hope for the confusion and demise of the evil), and it has been one of this author's most successful works. The situation is much simpler in narratives—elite or folk—of the American West: there was such a region, Davy Crockett and Jim Bridger and Buffalo Bill and George A. Custer did really live, gold was actually found there, etc.

We want to know not only that tales about these men/institutions/events were believed, and why, but the forms in which such beliefs were expressed: legend, anecdote, tall tale, and so forth. Form may be related to belief, but in ways that are not yet precisely understood. All of these forms occurred in the West, and about the West, and all have been used in one way or another in the present study. Each genre, each specimen, has had to be evaluated for its contribution to our understanding of the phenomenon it describes: whether it is to be taken literally, hyperbolically, symbolically. Legends are commonly believed by their transmitters, and told as "true"; other kinds of narratives are told for entertainment only, but once we know what was thought to be less than serious—often funny—we have a good clue to those subjects that were to be taken quite seriously. Personal-experience narratives are also ostensibly true accounts of "real" events, but all too often become gradually transmuted by the techniques of fiction in which they are clothed: nearly all of our accounts of unusual or otherwise eminently repeatable "real-life" experiences take on a dramatized texture, so that it is sometimes, for one who was not "there," indistinguishable from invented stories. As with fictions, we give our anecdotes, our legends, our personal-experience narratives direction, point, timing, and a punch line.

Several of the topics scrutinized in this book seem almost inevitably to be related in a limited number of narrative forms: certain events—particularly repetitious ones, such as the Overland Trail experiences or the Pony Express rider's route—have inherent forms. Travelers on a journey from point A to point B have the form of their description determined for them, though details may differ, especially when their experiences have been radically different: those caught in snows in the Sierras will tell a somewhat different story from those who got through relatively safely and comfortably. Yet many of the actual details of the Overland Trail are surprisingly uniform: the experience of guard duty, the encounter with buffalo, prairie storms, fording of rivers, encountering Mormons or Indians, reaching California or Oregon. Stories of the Pony Express share this predictability. The rider traveled from one station to another, and given that fact of his occupation, no great variety in Pony Express narratives should be expected. He encountered dangers, decidedly limited in number, and may have had to extend his normal route because of unusual circumstances. Beyond these variables, not much flexibility should be expected if the story is to retain any sense of verisimilitude.

So too with events and the attitudes they embody. Very little is known of the last moments of Custer and the five companies with him, so we are all free to reconstruct those last moments according to our predilections. If he is brave—a hero—then his motivations will be noble (as in "They Died with Their Boots On"), he will be greatly outnumbered, probably betrayed as well, and will be among the last to die, if not the very last. If he is a coward or a fool, then he is entrapped by the enemy through his folly; he and his men will not kill many of their foe at all, his defense will not be orderly, but a rout, and his death may be ignominious. He may even be said to have committed suicide. In either case it is crucial to know, if possible, what did happen and what cannot be known so as to determine, secondly, what has been invented. Once we know that, we are in a strong position to decide why the narrative has been given its particular form and what meaning is intended by that construction. Interpretation, however, will be at least as slippery a matter as with literature.

To bring an interpretation of culture closer to the methodology of literary criticism, following philosopher Paul Ricoeur and some sociolinguists, we will want to treat a social event as though it were a text. A literary text is created for us; the social counterpart is interpreted by us and those who share the experience with us. The social "text"—the event—also has its beginning, middle, and end; it too has contents, usually in which characters, though they are real

rather than fictional, perform; and social events as well are subject
to interpretation, necessarily by rules which are part of our culture,
but which are privately implemented.

Every time a narrative is told it may have different meanings,
each version valid for speaker and audience; ideally we will want to
discuss meanings with the teller—the tellers—rather than have to
decide for ourselves without any "hands-on" experience, but in the
case of oral narratives of the past that is extremely difficult. What
was communicated is as evanescent as a cloud, unless it was written
down. And if that happened, other interpreters—writers, editors,
and the like—may come between us and the storyteller, the tradition-bearer.

We always run the risk in secondhand, analytic analyses of
imposing our own structures, our own hierarchies on historical
texts, rather than revealing what those events meant to contemporaries. It is important to understand as much of their world as
possible, to see why certain events were possible then, how they were
interpreted by those who "read" these event-texts at the moment of
experience, and then responded as they did. In some cases their
interpretations were made explicit, and we are the more fortunate
for that. But in many instances we do not positively know their
interpretations—"native" interpretations—and our analytic perceptions will have to do.

The folklore of the West that survives today, the (printed) popular culture of that time, even conventional interpretations based
upon documentary sources, may not enable a scholar today to make
an interpretation of the events of the day that will match the understanding of people a century ago. We feel gratified when, after feeling that certain gold rush stories suggested that many prospectors
thought the West's mineral wealth was inexhaustible, one of the
men at the early diggings is quoted in print as saying that "there was
always more where that came from." But in other instances the
interpreter is on his own, with only the material and a knowledge
of the apposite history to guide him. For example, the laying of more
than ten miles of track in a single day: no contemporary said that
the event encapsulated the spirit in which the entire transcontinental railroad was built. Still that one day does symbolize the preoccu-
pation with speed that characterized the construction of the road,
even though that symbol was first verbalized by this writer; yet it is
not the less real or any the less expressive for that.

Ray Billington's *America's Frontier Heritage* concluded that speed and its adjuncts—haste, mobility, impatience with obstacles to advancement, and opportunism—were characteristically American traits: they were an important, defining, aspect of the American national character. So too are an inner-directedness, a fierce competitiveness, and a predilection for the individual;[5] *The Code of the West* supports Billington's findings from a data base and a point of view that amused him—when a portion of this book was read at the Huntington Library during the summer of 1979.

A more exclusively folkloric study of this historical "period" would have involved intensive interviewing of many people over an extensive range of land, stretching from St. Joseph, Missouri (the eastern terminus of the Pony Express route), as far south as New Orleans (where the *Lee* began its race against the *Natchez*), through Tombstone, Arizona, and Lincoln County, New Mexico (Billy the Kid country) to the gold fields of California—north and south, it's a very big state—and then into the Rockies and the haunts of the mountain men, along the track of the Union Pacific, the Overland Trail (to California as well as to Oregon), and along the route of the Mormon handcarts. If such an extensive and exhaustive study were possible, the results would still not be entirely satisfying because the cultural evaluation that would emerge would only be partial, since, as in the case of the folklore about the handcarts, it is important to compare what the migrants were saying with the official statements (and "folksongs") of their church elders in Salt Lake City. As with Custer's Last Stand, it is crucial to know, as much as that is possible, what did happen on the Little Bighorn that day (June 25, 1876), to gain a more useful perspective about what people thought, or said they thought, happened. And there may be instances when we will want to examine what has been called "fakelore," material invented and transmitted through modes decidedly not folkloric: the classic example is Paul Bunyan, invented by an advertising firm to be a lumber company logo. But even the persistence of fakelore can reveal to the careful researcher some quality of mind and imagination of the believer or the bearer of this spurious tradition. The purity of lineage that is of such importance to the academic folklorist will probably matter little, if at all, to the people who tell and listen to fakelore.

In this book, written sources as well as oral have been used throughout; the number of written sources actually far outnumbers the oral, as one would expect when the subject had its life more than a century ago and so much of its lore survives only in writing.

Popular magazines of the nineteenth century were full of folklore
(though it was not thought of as such by their reporters and editors):
Harper's, Leslie's Weekly, Niles Weekly Register, and the *Police Ga-
zette* continually published, in the name of "human interest" no
doubt, barely reconstituted and unregenerated folkloric material.
The legend of Wild Bill Hickok as a marvelous marksman and an
even more marvelous human being probably had its beginnings in
the pages of a *Harper's* feature article. The Western newspapers of
the day printed the most fanciful tales of gold strikes because it was
in their own best interests, and those of the areas they served, to do
so. Popular histories and biographies, whose targeted readership
was usually children, are another rich source of fables and legends,
often intended to instruct, often printed simply because the story
they told was interesting. Autobiographers were by no means above
using imaginative fictionalizing flourishes, often enough for self-
aggrandizement. And the dime novels were (and still are, of course)
veritable repositories of folklore and legend, though usually in a
form and with a quality distinctively their own, which set such
products of popular culture off from those of a genuine oral tradition;
they must be approached warily to decide what about them expresses the ethos of their consumer-minded writers and editors, but
must nevertheless be approached.

The productions of all "levels" or "spheres" must be sifted and
evaluated when interpreting an historical event. For the bottom line
of (my) interest in these events, institutions, and personalities of the
West is an understanding of what folk narratives and other, more
consciously created fictions, mean: why did people make up the stories they did or, hearing them, find them of sufficient interest to
want to repeat them? Why have certain stories about the American
West during the last century gained an imperishable currency? And
what do all of these tales, of many kinds and from sources as varied,
tell us about the culture that produced them? It is the attempt of this
book to define a portion of the ethos of nineteenth-century America
as it was expressed about and toward the West by the stories Americans told each other.

Such was the methodology of *Custer and the Epic of Defeat;* its
success there has encouraged me to continue its use, and in the
present volume to expand its cultural implications, to examine not
merely Custer and his last battle, but a larger chunk of our Western
experience.

At least two important subjects have not been treated in this book. A superficial look at women in the West did not reveal very much: the "whore with the heart of gold" (Julia Bulette in Virginia City, "Silverheels" in Montana, Mattie Silks in Colorado, Martha Camp in Panamint, etc.) and those women who attained their immortality because they could do masculine things and do them better than most men could: Annie Oakley, Calamity Jane, Belle Starr. But just beneath this surface are the stories and legends of a great many women—the martyred Narcissa Whitman, the sentimentalized "Baby Doe" Tabor, even Willa Cather, or the thousands of women whose names are not known to us but who commanded the "deference universally paid" them[6]—and the roles women played in the history of the West were so varied and so full that it would be unfair to try and discuss them in a single chapter.* The method of this book has been to construct composite narratives or to search for representative stories; either method would do a great injustice to women, especially if they were to be discussed only in a chapter on, say, "The Whore With The Heart of Gold." And the cattle drives, particularly those that began in Texas, and which seem to those of us who know the West chiefly through the movies as the quintessential "Western" event, are also absent. On this subject I felt that I could add little that was new to the work of Austin and Alta Fife's critical edition of Thorp's *Songs of the Cowboys;* and that the pattern of meanings expressed by this lore was somewhat similar to those already discussed in other chapters.

European friends have pointed out to me that much of the lore which I have cited is "merely" transplanted from the Old World. And, of course, that is true. It is freely acknowledged that such quintessential songs of the West as "Streets of Laredo" and "Garry Owen" are borrowings, but in the United States they acquired a new, "characteristic" garb. Many of the stories told by and about the prospectors at the Mother Lode and Comstock Lode regions may have foreign analogues, but the stress on certain aspects, the particular combination of tales, marks them as American; for instance, the folklore of Europe does not suggest that the mineral wealth of the land is inexhaustible. Europe has its Pocahontas-figures and its Custers and, of course, its Robin Hood, but the mountain men (or "Wild

---

*Different approaches to the West have evoked several books on the women there; among them are Dee Brown, *The Gentle Tamers: Women of the Old West* (New York: Putnam's, 1957); Helen Beal Woodward, *The Bold Women* (New York: Farrar, Straus and Young, 1953); John M. Faragher, *Women and Men on the Overland Trail* (New Haven: Yale University Press, 1980).

Men") of Europe are not the same, nor did that cluster of civiliza-
tions ever produce the solitary gunfighter; Grettir is not much like
Billy the Kid. Borrowings and adaptations were certainly made, and
those wholesale, but in their new environment and new setting that
lore became identifiably and expressively American. To that were
added those ingredients usually conceded to be American originals,
particularly narratives of the Overland Trail. Even if every single
detail of each song, story, legend, or anecdote had its analogue in
Europe or among Native Americans—and that is not the case—in
combination, and in their new American clothing, they can be said
to be "ours." Collectively and compositely they are American folklore.

The chapters are ordered, roughly, by the "message" expressed.
If this were a conventional history of the West, the arrangement
would probably be chronological. But I have chosen to begin with the
lore of those earliest of pioneers, the mountain men, because the
stories about them express such wonderment and extol their resourcefulness and endurance in overcoming the privations and dangers of living in that fabulous land west of the Mississippi. Tales of
prospecting for gold and silver, and the characteristic thrust of those
narratives belong next, expressing as they do something in the
American grain that is with us still.

To live on the prairies and beyond the mountains demanded
endurance, and the next two chapters, on the Overland Trail and the
Mormon handcart migrations, extol endurance. They are of somewhat different kinds, though; the Mormons were driven by an astonishing religious fervor, the gentile Overland Trail travelers by a
variety of motives more secular. Whether boredom and discomfort
or suffering and the everyday prospect of death had to be endured,
both these groups persevered. Both arrived, finally, in their own
versions of the Promised Land.

Custer, as I have shown, has his counterparts throughout the
world, and in all times. He is the exemplar of bravery, and as such
is not the property of any one culture. Yet he has become in our
sentiments one of the most American of soldiers.

The institution of the Pony Express, the race of the steamboats
Rob't E. Lee and the *Natchez,* and the laying of ten miles of railroad
track in one day—all express the desire for and the cultural value
of speed. Yet they are not ideological analogues; a different kind of
speed is suggested by each. The swiftness of the lithe pony rider is
nothing like the steam-powered force of a Mississippi riverboat; and

neither has much to do with the compulsion to finish one's task in a hurry, even if at the expense of quality of workmanship and efficiency.

The chapter on that most Western of characters, the gunfighter (in his role of pistoleer and as Robin Hood), and the chapter on that recurrent and haunting lady, Pocahontas, might logically have appeared elsewhere in the book. Both she and Robin Hood are rather baldfaced cultural thefts, probably from Europe. Yet both have become Americanized, and in their adaptations say something about the American mind in that they are also more universal expressions of human sentiment.

The chapter that was not detachable from its present position, could not be free-floating or interchangeable, describes the folklore and literary observations about the White Stallion of the prairies. Solitary white horses roaming freely in defiance of all attempts at subjugation may possibly exist in the lore of other nations (I could find no analogues), but stories about the White Steed seem to me to epitomize the attitudes of many Americans toward the West. The White Steed is liberty and independence personified; it is in large measure what we think—and what the nineteenth century thought —the West was all about. The White Stallion subsumes, encompasses all; the chapter about him must conclude any discussion of the lore of the West.

The Code of the West offers no major new understanding of that vast and nebulous region we call the trans-Mississippi West, either historically or folklorically. The data base has been taken from recognized historical sources, and a great deal of new oral material has not been used. Rather, the present book examines nearly a dozen old standbys of the mass media's rendering of the period and region and evaluates the continuing popularity of these cultural symbols. Why are they still popular (though often transmuted), why do they almost immediately come to mind when "the West" is spoken of? Not as focused thematically as, say, Leo Marx's *The Machine in The Garden,*[7] *Code* deals with the West's symbols fragmentarily. The results are neither complete nor coherent as a cultural description or interpretation; but no regional culture is so monolithically consistent as to lend itself to easy summation. The focus here is, diachronically, on the lore and ideas of our century as much as on those of the past. I interpret several frequently used symbols of the West as cultural expressions with meaning for our ancestors and for us.

Mountain Men
Narratives

ROBABLY no first-generation pure folklore about the mountain men exists anymore; there may be some in the hills of Montana, Wyoming, Colorado, or Idaho but at this moment in our history one cannot imagine any narrative about them that has not been influenced by the many written popular accounts of their exploits. Some of these enduring, adaptable men drifted west around the turn of the (nineteenth) century, where they became—or were—trappers, hunters, guides, or traders, and by 1843 their heyday was over. During that year the most famous of the mountain men, Jim Bridger, decided to build "Fort Bridger" to trade with Indians and settlers, and to give up trapping. But even then, after only a few decades, the lore about mountain men was extensive. It was simultaneously popular and folk, though precisely what that difference was can never be recovered now.

Nevertheless, from this contaminated lore—some would call it "fakelore"—we can learn quite a bit about attitudes toward the West. Most of the materials appear to be exoteric, and we have almost no evidence of what stories the mountain men told among or about themselves. But in several respects, and on several subjects, outsiders (Easterners mainly) have internalized Western attitudes; probably, as in the case of many of the printed anecdotes and legends of the mountain men, the writer empathized with the Westerner for the moment, and the resulting stories reflect that literary pose. Whether tellers and listeners believed these tales is, in this instance, almost unknowable.

Very broadly speaking, mountain man narratives seem to be of two types, those that exclaim over the topographic and climatic wonders of this strange and wonderful land that was so full of marvels for nearly all Americans—most of whom lived east of the Mississippi—and those that warn of the dangers of life in this new land for those who first came to it and exalt the ability of the veteran, the mountain man, not only to cope with this often inhospitable environment, but to thrive in it.

That first class of stories—about the topographical and other natural marvels of the frontier—was likely to find a receptive audience among readers in seaboard cities who had only heard about Yellowstone Park, the Petrified Forest, or the vastness of the American plains. These were experiences only to be imagined; then why not an alum creek so bitter that it puckered time, petrified birds in petrified trees singing petrified songs, or a canyon so long that one could shout a wake-up call in the evening and not have it bounce back till eight hours later, when it was time to get up?

That the land was dangerous everyone knew, even in those years preceding the decade of mass migration that followed the discovery of gold on the American River and silver in Virginia City. But how dangerous, and in what ways? Mountain man narratives are full of close encounters with wild Indians and wilder animals. Related kinds of stories tell of the Westerners' ability to deal with these dangers and conversely, others tell of the inept greenhorn's brushes with danger, and even death. The hairbreadth escape is a staple of mountain man and greenhorn tales—in mountain man tales, escape is effected by cunning and craft; in greenhorn stories, by sheer dumb luck.

A great many of the tales that deal with the marvelous Western landscape have at one time or other been attributed to Jim Bridger. Whether or not they are his inventions does not seem particularly important, since many of them are also ascribed to others, such as Moses Harris or James Meek. More important is their currency. One of the most popular of the Bridger stories is about the "obsidian cliff"; this version, told by Charles Francis Adams (in *What Jim Bridger and I saw in Yellowstone National Park*) purports to be a first-person telling:

> Coming one day in sight of an elk, I took careful aim and fired at the animal, but to my surprise, the animal was not wounded, and apparently did not hear the report. I fired again and again with the same result; exasperated, I took my rifle by the barrel and rushing at the animal, crashed into an immovable wall, which proved to be a moun-

tain of transparent glass, on the other side of which was that elk grazing, that mountain was not only of pure glass, but was a perfect transparent lens, and that elk was twenty-five miles away.[1]

Hiram Chittenden told the story much the same way, the major difference being that he told it in the third person, and his version may even have preceded Adams's. The Chittenden version has more drama. The elk is "magnificent" and "unsuspecting." For the second shot Jim "drew considerably nearer and gave the elk the benefit of his more deliberate aim," but to no avail. "Utterly exasperated," he "rushed madly" toward it, only to crash into the mountain wall of glass.[2] Besides exaggerating the size and extent of obsidian formations, the story exalts the mountain man's legendary marksmanship, assuming that once "Old Gabe" had aimed and fired at the elk, he would of course hit it.

One of the most famous of tall tales is the encounter with the petrified forest, the wonder of which is heightened (in this tale) because the mountain man enters it for the first time, and is caught off guard. In this version, related by George Ruxton (*Life in the Far West*) in 1849, the narrator is Moses "Black" Harris, and the narrative situation is one in which he is playfully gulling some greenhorns:

"Well, Mister Harris, trappers are great travelers, and you goes over a sight of ground in your perishinations, I'll be bound to say."

"A sight, marm.... I've seen a putrefied forest.... A putrefied forest marm, as sure as my rifle's got hindsights, and she shoots center. I was out on the Black Hills.... The snow was about fifty foot deep, and the bufler lay dead on the ground like bees after a beein'.... One day we crossed a cañon and over a divide and got into a peraira, whar was green grass, and green trees, and green leaves on the trees, and birds singing in the green leaves, and this is February, wagh! Our animals was like to die when they see the green grass, and we all sung out, 'hurraw for summer doins.'

'Hyar goes for meat,' says I, and I jest ups old Ginger at one of them singing birds and down comes the crittur elegant; its darned head spinning away from the body, but never stops singing, and when I takes up the meat, I finds it stone, wagh! 'Hyar's damp powder and no fire to dry it,' I says, quite skeared.

'Fire be dogged!' says Old Rube. "Hyar's a hos as'll make fire come"; and with that he takes his ax and lets drive at a cotton wood. Schr-u-k—goes the ax agin the tree and out comes a bit of the blade as big as my hand. We looks at the animals, and that they stood shaking

over the grass, which I'm dog-gone if it wasn't stone, too. Young Sublette come up. . . . He looks and looks, and scrapes the trees with his
butcher knife, and snaps the grass like pipe stems, and breaks all the
leaves asnappin' like Californy shells.

    'What's all this, boy?' I asks.

    'Putrefactions,' says he, looking smart, 'putrefactions'."[3]

Stories attributed to Bridger usually lack the narrative fullness that
Ruxton gave to his version of Harris in Arizona, but with brevity
they advance this theme logically. Folklorist and raconteur J. Frank
Dobie "quotes" Bridger as saying,

Yes, them putrified trees stand up natural like any other trees. They
are simply monstrous. You can ride all day and not get acrost the forest.
And all up in the limbs there's putrified birds, some of 'em blue and
some of 'em red and all other kinds of colors. And them putrified birds
is act'ually singing putrified songs.[4]

But the most imaginative Petrified Forest story is told by Hiram
Chittenden, again attributed originally to Bridger:

Quite unexpectedly he came upon a narrow, deep precipitous chasm
which completely blocked his way. Exhausted as both he and his horse
were with their long march, he was completely disheartened at this
obstacle, to pass which might cause him several hours of strenuous
exertion and carry him far into the night.

    Riding up to the brink to reconnoiter he found that he could not
stop his horse, which kept moving right along as if by its own momentum out over the edge of the precipice, straight on at a steady gait and
on a level line, as if supported by an invisible bridge. Almost before he
realized it he was safe on the other side, and in his desired camp. His
utter amazement at this miracle soon abated when he remembered the
strange character of the country he was in, and he concluded that this
chasm was simply a place where the attraction of gravitation was
petrified.[5]

Yet another variant, retold by Gene Caesar, combines this version
with an Indian escape story: Bridger, attacked by too many Blackfeet, was able to ride off through the air since gravity was petrified.[6]
The Indians did not pursue. So much for the petrified forest. But that
is not all that we shall have of the violation of natural laws. Companion piece to the petrified-law-of-gravity story is one about an alum-
dense creek, told again by Jim Bridger—as Charles Adams would
have it:

I forded the creek one day and rode out several miles and back, and noticed that the return journey was much shorter, and that the horse's feet had shrunk to mere points, so that the animal could hardly hobble. Seeking the cause, I found it to be the astringent quality of the water saturated with alum to such an extent that it puckered even distance.[7]

Told with dry wit, no doubt.

So famous had yarns attributed to Bridger become that Stanley Vestal, in a biography of Kit Carson (Happy Warrior of the Old West), tried to depict life in winter quarters with several of the boys huddled around a fire, and Kit and his comrades listening to Jim Bridger competing "with the best in telling the whoppers beloved by the mountain men."[8] This particular story, of the stream that is ice-cold at one end but steaming hot just a bit away, is not one of the biggest of the "whoppers." Nor can it ever be established that Kit once heard Bridger tell tales. But again, it is the recurrence of this tale and not its historical authenticity that is most important:

I war trappin' in the Black Hills. It war cold that day, fit to freeze yore breath in chunks. And up on the peaks where the snow had been a meltin', the water purty nigh froze my feet off. But as I come a-wadin' down hill, purty soon I noticed that the water war gettin' warm, and swift as all get out. I looked ahead and seen steam. Boys, I tell ye, I jumped out o' that crick quicker'n scat—and jest in time. Why, damn my hind-sights if that water hadn't run down hill so fast it was a-bilin' at the bottom.[9]

Hiram Chittenden, as much a defender of Jim Bridger's reputation as he was of the extraordinary beauty and natural aspects of Yellowstone, does not want his readers to disbelieve the icy/boiling spring story; he explains it in terms of "an immense boiling spring" which flowed directly into Yellowstone Lake and which floated, "owing probably to the expansive action of heat" in a stratum a few feet above the cold water. "When Bridger was in need of fish," Chittenden tells us, "it was to this place that he went. Through the hot upper stratum he let fall his bait to the subjacent habitable zone, and having hooked his victim, cooked him *on the way out!*"[10]

Bridger could exploit other aspects of the natural to his advantage as well. For he was, with many of his comrades, resourceful and skilled in the ways of the West, at home in this magical fairyland world, dealing with the life it offered as though he were one of nature's children, while the tenderfoot and the greenhorn were continually baffled and endangered by it. We are told, for instance, by Gene Caesar (and many others) that when Bridger camped for the night in "Eight-Hour-Echo Cañon" he would shout, just before retiring to his bedroll, "Time to get up!" And, sure as the laws of nature, the echo would rebound to Bridger and his friends eight hours later when it was in fact "time to get up."[11]

Why Bridger got to be the subject of so many of these tales cannot be known. It seems unlikely that he really invented or told all of them either to entertain his friends or to green the horn. Yet in the folklore of the West he is more famous for these tales than for the really important work he did in opening up that region; "Jim Bridger's lies" was almost a household word in the last century and at one time was the title of a column in *Ned Buntline's Own* weekly. Perhaps he was the mountain man par excellence, and his status as a titan made him the obvious target of humor. He was heroic in the everyday conduct of his life, but because he was not dramatically slain—as was Custer, for instance—he could be made the victim of gentle whimsy. Belittling Bridger, making him seem slightly ridiculous by attributing absurdly ridiculous stories to him, eased the anxieties that men feel when in the presence, however remote, of one who has been advertised as a giant.

The fierce climate of the West also figures in stories; the most interesting anecdotes and one-liners come from the Southwest and are complaints of homesteaders; as such, they are stories whose protagonists have given up life in the West or else are remaining under protest, like the "Lane County Bachelor." Mody Boatright tells one about the horse that was nearly lost in a sandstorm because its owner tied him to some sagebush; as the sand gathered, the sage, which is not rooted, settled on top of the accumulating sand. The horse was found several hours later atop a dune, still tied to the bush.[12] General Sherman is once supposed to have said, after all, that "If I owned hell and Texas, I'd rent out Texas and live in hell.[13]

To show how tough life is out West, one of Boatright's informants tells of the grasshoppers that "were especially fond of onions, which they ate down into the ground, leaving only a thin shell. One man reported that as they passed his door, their breath smelled." Another complained that "when I came here fifty years ago, I had sixty-five cents and the asthma. I still have the asthma." A sign on the side of a wagon, which Boatright dates around 1874, announced,

> From Sodom where it rains grasshoppers
> Fire and Destruction
> Going back east to visit my wife's relatives

Less pathetically resigned was the sign reported on a door in Abilene, 1886:

> One Hundred miles to water
> Twenty miles to wood
> Six inches to hell
> God bless our home
> Gone to live with the wife's folks[14]

Of course it wasn't all drought, starvation, heat, and grasshoppers. A placard in a Van Horn (Texas) hotel read,

> COME TO VAN HORN TO LIVE
> THE CLIMATE IS SO HEALTHY
> WE HAD TO SHOOT A MAN
> TO START OUR GRAVEYARD[15]

Which is much like the yarn that linked Jim Bridger with the famous missionary/pioneer, Dr. Marcus Whitman. He was trying to remove a Blackfoot arrowhead from the mountain man's back cartilage, a three-year-old wound.

> "But weren't you afraid of infection?" the good missionary gasped.
> "Hell, Doc," Jim told him, "up here in the mountains, meat
> don't never spoil!"[16]

A land of marvels, the nineteenth-century West, but also of dangers; perhaps particularly of dangers. And chief among the dangers in popular lore were the Indians. The stories are serious, comic, and farcical. They generally deflate the Indian, making him an enemy that the white man—particularly the Westerner—can deal with; simultaneously, the prowess, skill, courage, and cunning of the white is argued in nearly all these tales. A small number of narratives end up with the joke on the gullible greenhorn.

Among the most popular tales of the West are those of escape from captivity, as they were popular a century earlier among Easterners. And of these, one of the most widely told is that of the escape of trapper John Colter from the Blackfeet. He was captured—the persistence, distribution, and identification with specific places in the region properly allow us to call this story a legend—on the Jefferson fork of the Missouri. Stripped naked, Colter was given a chance to live if he could outrun his captors in a footrace. According to Chittenden's version of the legend,[17] the savages did not want to kill him quickly and simply. But that was all the incentive Colter needed; he outsprinted them all for five miles except for one persistent brave who finally ran him to ground. The two stood face to face for a moment; then the Indian hurled his spear. But Colter caught it in flight, broke off its tip in his hands, and stabbed the Blackfoot with it. The flight resumed. Racing to the Madison River, Colter saw a beaver's house by the bank. Swimming under water, he reached it, climbed inside to an upper story, "and was soon sitting high and dry in a kind of shelter such as probably no man ever sought refuge in before." "Physical endurance," Chittenden concluded, "is a wonderful thing." It is. Jim Beckwourth was once pursued by Indians and according to his own calculations ran ninety-five miles that day.[18]

In the Chittenden redaction, Colter stayed for eleven days and nights chez beaver, although in other versions this length differs. Back in St. Louis they didn't quite take John Colter at his word, and he eventually acquired a reputation, with Jim Bridger and Jim Beckwourth, as one of the great liars of the West. But Chittenden, among others, was not so skeptical, witness the currency of this story and its several variants: in one, Colter first "ran the gauntlet"; in another, he hid not in a beaver house, but rather in some driftwood.

Trapper Thomas Fitzpatrick, one of the Rocky Mt. Fur Co. partners—we will hear from him again shortly—was once separated from his party and his horse taken by Indians; how did that happen to such a skilled trapper? But he effected his escape through a hole in some rocks, which he covered with twigs. At night he put together a raft and started floating away, but his vessel disintegrated in midstream and he lost everything except his butcher knife. He probably would have starved during the next several days had he not found the carcass of a buffalo killed by wolves and scraped out a little meat they had left behind.[19]

Are the Colter and Fitzpatrick stories meant to be taken seriously? That would depend upon their fuller context, the teller's intentions, the attitude of the audience, the whole milieu of transmission. It could be farcical, ironic, or straight, and during the lives of both stories no doubt has been all three. Other stories are less ambiguous in intent, for instance the often-told story of how the famous Indian-fighter, Bigfoot Wallace, defeated a tribe of Comanches by quick thinking and resourcefulness. Tracking down a band of them, trying to recover horses they had stolen, Bigfoot came upon forty-two Comanches. Knowing that he couldn't handle all of them, Wallace tied thongs around the wrists and ankles of his buckskins, and filled his pants and jacket with hickory nuts he found on the ground. It happened to be the right time of year. Then, armed with his trusty muzzle-loader, "Sweet Lips," he joined the battle:

> Every time a bowstring twanged, an arrow hit a hickory nut, split it, and then fell to the ground. Bigfoot said the arrows got stacked up so high in front of him that he stepped up on the pile and stood three inches taller. . . . Finally, all the Indians concentrated on a rear assault. By gravy, he said, those arrows kept jamming the hickory nuts in under his knee joints until he got so tickled he had to bust out laughing. . . . Well, sir, when they saw that their ammunition was all gone and that, though not an arrow had missed, the enormous target was still unharmed, they acted as if a bolt of lightning had struck the ground in front of them. For about a minute they stood with their eyes rolling and their tongues hanging out. Then all at once they stampeded like a herd of longhorn steers jumping off the bedground. They made a beeline for the Rio Grande, seventy miles away.[20]

Another story about Thomas Fitzpatrick's deception of the Indians focuses more on cunning than creative farce. The effect of the story depends upon two alleged aspects of the Indian's knowledge of weaponry. The first is the redman's ignorance of the effect of being shot by a musket; and the second aspect, almost contradictory, asks us to believe that they nevertheless understood that the musket's projectiles fly faster than the eye can follow and strike the body with debilitating impact. In this tale, Fitzpatrick has been separated from his party in the wild country, is surrounded by Indians and, realizing that capture was imminent, removed the ball from his musket. The captors behaved as expected:

> One of the warriors, who it appeared understood how to pull a trigger, then seized the rifle, placed himself in front of the owner of it . . . and fired; but when the Indians looked eagerly through the smoke towards where Fitzpatrick stood they saw he was safe and sound in his place, and he quietly took out of his pocket the bullet he had previously placed there, and tossed it to his enemies who were all amazement. They

declared he had arrested the bullet in its flight, was an invulnerable and wonderful conjurer ... and that some great misfortune would most likely befall the tribe if they did not set him free immediately ... [21]

One Zenas Leonard, while armed only with a knife, was attacked by an Indian, who shot an arrow into his side. Zenas thwarted his attacker by jerking out the arrow and running to safety.[22]

Even in captivity, the white man demonstrates his superiority in his quick thinking and resourcefulness. In the case of Bigfoot Wallace, as one would expect, his face-to-face and hand-to-hand combat with an Indian became an epic struggle, like Buffalo Bill's tussle with Yellow Hand, or Enkidu's with Gilgamesh. In this farcical account, the fallen foe is in the end eulogized, and given a "decent Christian burial," befitting a hero. But since the story is told from the perspective of the victor, Bigfoot, the eulogy and burial at the end of it are demonstrations of his magnanimity and a testimony that it took a mighty big man to kill that mighty Indian. The scene appears to have taken place somewhere west of the Colorado River, when Wallace happened upon a big Indian near his camp. Bigfoot had the advantage in weight, but the adversary was as wiry as a cat and "slick as an eel," greased as he was from head to foot in bear's oil. Bigfoot was a little the stronger—he gauged as the hand-to-hand combat began—but couldn't hold on to his greased opponent. By turns they downed each other, but neither could thrust his cold steel home. At one point, the Indian was on top, knife poised above Bigfoot and about to plunge into his heart,

> Then I thought of my mother, as I remembered her when I was a little boy, the "old home," the apple orchard, and the brook where I used to fish for minnows.... and then I thought of Alice Ann, a blue-eyed partridge-built young woman I had a "leaning to".....

Luckily, blood from a head-wound (suffered when Bigfoot threw him last) partially blinded the Indian so that his thrust missed his victim by inches. Then,

> I threw him off me, and he rolled to the bottom of the cañon, "stone dead." My knife had gone directly to his heart. I looked at him sometime, lying there so still, and stiffening in the cool morning air, and I said to myself, "Well, old fellow, you made a good fight of it anyhow, and if luck hadn't been against you, you would have 'taken my sign in,' too.... And now," said I to myself, "old fellow, I am going to do for you

what I never did for an Indian before. I am going to give you a decent Christian burial."

Wallace solemnly broke the Indian's gun into a dozen pieces, as was their burial custom (!), "so it might be handy for him when he got to the happy hunting grounds ... and then I pulled up some pieces of rock from the sides of the cañon, and piled them around and over him until he was completely covered. ... "[23]

A final type of tale is concerned less with exalting the mountain man over the Indian as it is with greening the horn. Capt. J. Lee Humfreyville relates this story with Jim Bridger as its story-teller within-the-story, though other versions have other tricksters. The narrative situation finds Bridger surrounded by a party of curious Easterners, questioning him tediously about his adventures. Finally, in exasperation, and in response to one request for a hairbreadth escape story, Bridger tells about the time that he was chased by Indians and had shot all but one who trapped him on the edge of a deep gorge.

> I turned my horse suddint an' the Injun wus upon me. We both fired to once, an' both horses wus killed. We now engaged in a han'-to-han' conflict with butcher knives. He wus a powerful Injun—tallest I ever see. It wus a long an' fierce struggle. One moment I hed the best of it, an' the next the odds wus agin me. Finally—Here Bridger paused as if to get breath. "How did it end" at length asked one of the breathless listeners, anxiously. *"The Injun killed me,"* he replied with slow deliberation.[24]

The story was supposed to have been a put-down of the audience, and "freed [Bridger] from further questioning." Put-on it certainly is, but would the response of the audience have been to turn away? After such a fine display of folk wit and narrative skills, one would have expected them to clamor for more. Not as Humfreyville wants to have it, however; it is an example of how Bridger could turn aside persistent lionizers with a witty riposte, not offensive, yet decisive. When Stanley Vestal tells the same joke, the trappers are gathered around a fire and "Old Cotton" is the narrator entertaining some of the boys.

> And someone would narrate the one. ... about the time old Cotton was cornered by the Blackfoot, with no chance of escape. Old Cotton would dwell upon the hopeless situation. Then he would pause, waiting for the

listener to bite. "Well, what happened?" would come the question. Old Cotton would spit deliberately, roll his cud villainously, and would answer, before exploding in a loud guffaw, "Why, dang ye, then the Injun killed me!"[25]

The telling is so similar to Humfreyville's—the narrative-within-a-narrative, the plight of the mountain man, the pause at the dramatic moment, nearly the identical punch line—that one wonders whether Vestal's source was the Bridger version. Vestal himself remarks that "the point of the whopper was always that the narrator himself was the hero."[26] But that does not apply to the "Old Cotton" tale. It has no "hero" except the narrator, and then only because he has tricked his audience. The trapper in the tale—to make a distinction between the man in the story and the man who tells the story; they need not be the same—is barely heroic. And the situation is not plausible in the Vestal "Old Cotton" version. The surprise put-down ending would work with people who had never heard the story before—it is a one-time-only joke. Humfreyville exploits that situation, at least. But how is this joke to be effective among trappers who are retelling the old stories ("And someone would narrate the one about the time. . . . ")? But perhaps I am questioning this material too closely. The story is a good one and lends itself to a variety of narrative situations and a variety of interpretations. It even lends itself to elaboration, as in Gene Caesar's ending when Bridger (again) is out of ammunition—both pistol and rifle—and his knife is lost, and the inevitable query comes, "what happened?" "Old Gabe" replies: "They killed me. Scalped me too."[27]

After Indians, the biggest threat came from wild animals; and of these, bears seem to have been danger of choice. I do not wish to offend the rattlesnake (which will receive due honors later in this book) and the wolf or to belittle the apprehension and fright they caused thousands of men and women in the West, but for the sake of economy this discussion will be limited to the ursine terrors of the region.

In nearly all these stories all the details point to the helplessness of the man in his encounter with a bear. The meeting is accidental, of course, with the man taken by surprise or else in a position where he cannot avoid the confrontation. Who would go out of his way to fight with a bear? Joaquin Miller's *True Bear Stories,* while written for "younger readers," has some interesting observations about meetings with bears all the same. When man meets bear and the bear won't run, and the man has no firearm—and "that is always the time when he finds a bear," Miller observes, "why, he runs himself." One of his yarns describes a hunter who did have a gun when he met his bear, but "of course, he dropped his gun. They always do drop their guns, by some singularly sad combination of accidents, when they start up a tree with two rows of big teeth in the rear ... "[28] With a gentle irony Miller thus comments upon the "real" bear stories he has heard; and while it would be churlish to doubt their reality, we should also be alert to those classic details that are so frequently added to these narratives and the ones that are always retained. Personal experience stories, after all, are dramatized very soon after the actual experience, and become "drama" or "narrative" with surprising speed.

In a few tales, however, there is no fight; the customary posture is flight, occasionally with the bear in panting pursuit. The story will have made its point on most listeners if the beast is only encountered; more is not necessary, unless the narrator is a Davy Crockett or a particularly fearless mountain man.

Common also are descriptions of the assailant's physiognomy, with special emphasis on the fierce fangs and mouth, salivating for human flesh. Scholars, popular novelists, historians, biographers all draw attention to the bear's "snapping" or "gnashing" teeth, to his "chomping and foaming at the mouth like a mad dog."[29] This is how Edward Ellis describes the bear being fought by a fictional mountain man, Relmond: "the blood from his wound trickled down and daubed his mouth; while his red tongue lolled out, his mouth wide open, and his long and white teeth [shining] with terrible ferocity."[30] The blood-ied mouth and the glistening white teeth have become conventional in the description of bears in encounters with men. The bears are made to seem even more ferocious than they are in nature, more dangerous—the mouth-and-teeth descriptions carry the submerged suggestion that the bears are acting with an almost human intention and malice.

The encounter with the rampaging beast is usually the whole point to the story, to show that the narrator is one-up on his listeners because he has endured the experience, or can make light of it. Many bear-encounter stories end anticlimactically for this reason. But in a few instances, the point of the story is the clever way the man escapes or the heroic way he kills the bear, as happens often enough in the Davy Crockett accounts. Either the man backs away, or he outruns the bear (sometimes on horseback), or he swims away, or he climbs a tree, or help comes from an unexpected source, such as the unknown Indian who rescues Edward Ellis's Relmond.[31]

Zip Spooner, a "neighbor" of Crockett's, once fought tooth and claw with a big black bear. He was, at the moment, out of ammunition, as so often happens in these stories, thus his bravery was the greater. This is the one of those bear-encounter stories that does not end whimperingly, but in a triumph. Zip took him on with only his butcher knife, and his good right arm:

> By great exertions he thrust his right arm partly down his throat, and in that manner endeavored to strangle him, but was now hurled headlong down through the bushes. Here, finding the bear gaining on him, he made one desperate effort, and drew the animal's head partly under water, and repeatedly sticking him under the shoulder with his knife, he at last succeeded in drowning him, but he was so chawed up by the bear that he could hardly crawl home.

When the man bested the bear, it was in hand-to-claw combat. Simply shooting the beast had little dramatic appeal, and so Crockett merely states at one point that he killed 105 bears in less than a year, and lets it go at that. The hunting knife or the butcher knife is the close-in weapon of choice, although in one account, a friend of Crockett's who had been hunting (with his knife, of course) was chased by a bear and directed his pursuer past Crockett. Davy distracted the beast while his neighbor smashed it with his axe, dazing the creature. Mrs. Crockett then rammed a hickory pole into its mouth and while it dazedly tried to decide what to do next, Crockett administered the coup de grâce with his own knife. One of the few times in which much is made dramatically of shooting a bear is another Crockett story. A black bear was on top of one of Crockett's neighbors and Davy put a musket ball "through him near the heart." Another neighbor struck the bear with an axe; even so, in its death agony the bear further mauled his victim.[32] Although the Crockett stories may not have shown it as convincingly as some others, the West was a dangerous place.

It was dangerous in the West unless you knew what you were doing. "When in Injun country, do as the Injuns do—and do it better,"[33] was a byword of the mountain men. Cecil Alter wrote that Bridger and others had been chased by Indians but made their escape at night, aided by the light reflected by a huge diamond on the face of a nearby mountain, traveling that way for three nights.[34] The winter of 1830, according to one who knew, "were the wust":

> Half the buffler in the West yarded up just below 'em [Bridger's party] and froze solid. Come spring, Jim had his boys skin 'em out, tumble 'em down and pickle 'em in the Great Salt Lake. Kept themselves and the whole Shoshone Indian tribe fed for more'n ten years—I knowed it for a fact![35]

A less ambitious exploit had "Old Gabe" crossing the Big Salt Desert,

> ... comin' back from California with just two men. Hosses give out'n they left 'em. Then both his men give out. Gabe, he buried 'em t' their necks in sand, set their hats on their faces t'keep the sun off, and went on alone. Walked fifty mile t' find water, walked fifty mile back'n' saved 'em both.[36]

Nobody knew the West better than the mountain men, no whites had been there longer. An Oregon resident, lately come to that territory, is said to have fawned over mountain man and Oregon "founder" Joseph Meek,

> " ... if you have been so long in the country and have witnessed such wonderful transformations, doubtless you may have observed equally great ones in nature; in the rivers and mountains, for instance?"
>
> Meek gave a lightning glance at the speaker, who had so mistaken his respondent.
>
> "I reckon I have," said he slowly.
>
> Then waving his hand gracefully toward the majestic Mt. Hood, towering thousands of feet above the summit of the Cascade range, and white with everlasting snows: "When I came to this country, Mount Hood was *a hole in the ground!*"[37]

Meek may have said it first, but the line, certainly a good one, got around. Vestal put it in the mouth of Jim Bridger: "See yon hill? When I first saw the mountains, that was only a hole in the ground."[38] Gene Caesar has a similar hyperbole told by a friend of Bridger's to a newcomer to the region, and told with evident exuberant relish:

When did Gabe come west?.... You seen Independence Rock comin'
out? Old Gabe heaved a stone 'cross the Sweetwater there his fust year
in the Rockies. You try figurin' out how long that stone's been gro-
win'![39]

   The mountain man knew the country, he knew the ways of the
Indian (and tried to do them better), and he had his trusty long rifle
to protect him. As valuable and life-preserving as these weapons
were, it is no surprise that some of them became legendary in their
own right, like Roland's Durandel and Arthur's Excalibur. And it
also is no surprise that a great many stories arose about the prowess
and the marksmanship of their owners. Wild Bill Hickok shot the
"O's" out of signs and dotted the "I's" at more than fifty paces; Davy
Crockett shot a bear near the heart while it grappled with a friend
(at another time he killed several animals with one shot, but that is
another type of legend); Neill Wilson tells about a long-shot anti-
legend, one of the most effective of its kind:

   "I kin hit," said Old Tex at Sam Tait's place, "a sagehen at a distance
   of a hundr'd yards, but I gotter be loaded."
      Someone "loaded" Old Tex with what his personal muzzle needed,
   and then went out looking for a target. Long before one offered itself,
   the effect of Tex's private charge had worn off, and he demanded more
   internal explosives.
      "I kin hit," he proclaimed, patting his lusty fowling piece, "any
   sagehen with Old Bess here at a hundr'd 'n' twenty-five yards."
      Again the proper charge was rammed home to Old Tex's vitals, and
   his audience waited for a bird. Before one appeared, Tex was really
   ready to assert how Old Bess could shoot.
      "I kin hit," he promised, "any object that runs 'r flies at a distance
   of a hundred 'n' fifty yeards—not an inch less."
      This time a gay-crested roadrunner was spied down the slope at
   just about the distance Old Tex craved. The arrival was busily turning
   over stones and cakes of mud for crickets and millipedes.
      One more charge for Tex, a mighty clicking of Old Bess's hammers,
   and the long weapon was up to its owner's eye and shoulder. For a
   moment he held it there, and all stood waiting. Then he lowered the
   fowling piece. "Shucks," he said, "I kin do it. But I haven't got the heart
   to strain the gun."[40]

One of my students collected a tall tale in Texas from an oilfield
worker who claimed to have shot the eyes out of sagehens at over one
hundred yards; but somehow the story wasn't the same, nor would

any tale of that "Nestor of the Rocky Mountains," Kit Carson, have the same effect.

One very old joke has been told as an anecdote in the life of the famous trapper, Jim Baker, and expresses the rough-hewn ways of the mountain men. For contrast, the setting was one of Denver's more comfortable and genteel hotels, and Baker was in the lobby:

> On one of Baker's visits to Denver, while seated in one of the hotels chewing tobacco, he spat on the carpet. A Negro porter who happened to see him moved the cuspidor to the spot where he had expectorated, where-upon Jim turned his head and spat in the opposite direction. The porter again moved the cuspidor to that place. Jim, not heeding this, spat again on the carpet.
>
> Finally the porter made several attempts to place it within the range of his amber spray, and having been unsuccessful he placed the brass receptacle directly in front of him. Old Jim looked down and replied in his rather droll way, "You know, by G—, if you keep movin' that thing around I'm li'ble to spit in it."

After wearing urban, tailored clothes for a few days, Baker is said to have complained, "I 'speck these store bought cloes make me look kind o' 'spectable, but they hurt and I feel like a durned fool."[41]

Some elements of society may frown upon such crudeness and social ineptitude or be distantly amused by it; in either event, our reactions are not likely to be intense. But the indifference of many mountain men to the death or the pain of others—an attitude that helped them greatly to survive, no doubt, in their environment—elicits a deeper response. The Indian camp in which Jim Baker lived was once attacked by whites. The adjacent stream, Cherry Creek, was high at that time, and those who escaped that way had to swim across. Jim took his infant with him and his horse, and with his squaw following, plunged into the creek. He and his papoose reached the far bank safely, but his wife did not. The man to whom Baker told his personal experience narrative commented that he should have tried to save his squaw. Baker's reply, so revealing of the tenor of life in those days and in that place and among those men, was, "Oh, well, there's lots of squaws."[42]

Others didn't even fare as well as Baker's squaw. Charles "Cannibal Phil" Gardner earned his nickname after he returned from several days in a blizzard, but without the Indian who had gone out with him. Unpacking his mule, he threw a shriveled human leg to the ground, with the exclamation, "There, damn you, I won't have to gnaw on you any more." Later, closer to home, he was once again stranded in a mountain blizzard, this time with his squaw of the moment; he survived by eating her flesh.[43]

But we don't remember the mountain men for their gentleness and their benignity; rather for their survivability and their skills and their contribution to the opening of the West. Few people know, for instance, because it is not consonant with our understanding of mountain men, that Jim Baker once tried to cut off his wife's ears as a punishment for her alleged infidelities. He was drunk at the moment, and the next morning, sober and remorseful, he believed once again in her faithfulness.[44] We would not want to remember such tales, even if known. We would rather remember those great scouts and hunters for their know-how and feel for the land. There is the story of Jim Bridger with an army exploration party: faced with the option of mapping out one of two passes in the Colorado Rockies, Jim recommended one while two engineers thought the other was the lower. Two detachments were sent to measure heights with barometers; Bridger's estimate—made by eye—was the right one.

When he was asked by a baffled army engineer about the height of a particular hill, Old Gabe replied, "cain't say, . . . but I'll tell you how to find out. Dig straight down 'till you hit salt water—then measure it," but he was just funnin'. On a more serious occasion, when he was an army scout, he recommended crossing a river in a bullboat that he would build but was overruled by the officer in charge who insisted on a raft. When that smashed, killing one soldier, Bridger was consulted again. He said that he would arrange a crossing only if Raynolds (the officer) stayed in his tent out of the way. Once safe on the other side, Raynolds thanked God. Bridger responded, huffily, "Damn his holy hide, he never once mentioned Jim Bridger."[45]

How rugged were they? They occasionally did fight against bears with just their knives for the fun of it, and the fights were real —not the ones reported in the *Crockett Almanacks*. And they fought with and against the Indians, and usually more than held their own, taking their share of scalps. They survived the heat of Nevada summers and the bite of Idaho winters. But the stories that would have illustrated these qualities—of endurance and adaptability, mainly— have been told in other connections, as bear-encounter stories, as tales of experiences with Indians, as survival stories. From these narratives, collectively, we know that Easterners knew the rugged, sustaining character of the mountain men, and some of their un-couth, even a few of their savage, traits. For these tales have for the most part been exoteric, the outsider's perspective of the Jim Bridg-ers of the West. And the pictures we have of these men—verbal, in the writing of Ruxton, and visual, in the sketches of Remington—indicate that the popular lore about them, in these respects at least, was in its spirit accurate. One has to shuck away a lot of romanticiz-ing, but at the core of many of the mountain men stories is the kernel of their lives.

Another class of stories presents the same message from the more direct perspective of the inexperienced bumbling or gullible greenhorn. Quite explicitly these narratives exalt the mountain man in comparison with his effete Eastern brothers with no more indirection or subtlety than Aesop's fables. A popular one in Texas has several tenderfeet hitting upon a plan to bag a wildcat, with the scheme breaking down when they can't agree on who will release the animal on the prairie.[46] Bridger apparently liked to tease the inex-perienced, as we have already seen in the "they killed me" tales. He told some newcomers to the region that he had plans to make effi-cient and scientific use of a local lake that was said to have a coal bottom. It continually seeped oil, and its water was so densely alka-line that "you can throw in an egg or a potato, and it won't sink. . . . You dig a ditch t' run that oil in, then tunnel under through the coal, then set your tunnel afire and git the whole lake a-boilin'." The operation, Bridger is said to have assured his listeners, would "make enough soap here in one summer t' last the whole country more'n a hundred years."[47]

Bridger was rich in gag writers, certainly, and he did not lack for agents. It is doubtful, though, that he sought any of this public notoriety, especially those tales that made him appear the illiterate buffoon. His literacy level, like that of his fellow trappers, was low, but he was no fool. To disregard a mountain man's advice in matters pertaining to life in the West was to put one's dignity and occasion-ally one's life in jeopardy, as Raynolds found out to his embarrass-ment. Even the journals of pioneers tell of the sad fate of many of those who would not take the advice of the more experienced. One such account is from *The Emigrant's Guide to Oregon and Califor-nia,* Lansford Hastings's journal of his 1842 migration:

Here we learned that a young man, of the advance of our party, was drowned, in crossing Lewis' River. It appeared that the portion of the party to which he belonged, crossed this river at the usual ford, which is considered entirely safe, by those who are acquainted with it, but this young man deviated from the usual crossing, and disregarding the directions of his friends, was swept away in an instant.[48]

The West really was a place of danger. But the mountain man survived when others couldn't because he was tough, resourceful, skillful, and knew the land and its ways.

Prospectors
and Their Gold

WHEN Jim Marshall's eye was caught by some glittering "color" in the Sutter Mill raceway on the American River that January day in 1848, the greatest internal migration in American history was about to begin. Later that year Monterey and San Francisco had been all but abandoned in the rush for gold, while the population around the mill rose to more than 10,000. Within a few years many gold-seekers had left for other parts of the Mother Lode country, for more lucrative fields to the east, north, and south—the most famous field being Bodie ("home" of the "Bad Man" who was both a folkloric character and the Great Destroyer of Doctorow's *Welcome to Hard Times*)—to places they would name Jackass Gulch, Dead Horse, Whiskey Slide, Hardscrabble, Egg Nog Settlement, and Placerville (neé Hangtown). After that many of the bedraggled argonauts would leave for the Comstock, for Central City (Colorado), Tombstone, Deadwood Gulch, Tonopah, Cripple Creek, Reese River, and after that the Yukon, and after that . . . and so on.

Precious ore was discovered at Cripple Creek in 1891; the population of the area, no more than a handful in 1891, was over 50,000 by 1900. The gold fields were only about six square miles in area; but on that postage stamp roughly five thousand shafts had been dug and eleven distinct towns had been thrown up. In 1906 two fires roared through the towns, turning most of Cripple Creek's civilization to charcoal: left smoldering and smoking were forty-one assay offices, forty-six brokerage houses, eighty-eight doctors' and dentists' offices, seventy saloons, and the coroner's lab.

Gila City, Arizona, had much the same experience. Born in the middle of the eighteen sixties after gold was discovered there, the population rose almost immediately to 1,200, though by 1870 nothing remained but "three chimneys and a coyote." Prentice Mulford, addressing The Associated Pioneers of the Territorial Days of California" in 1878, remembered that at Hawkin's Bar, "once numbering near a thousand voters," he soon after found "one solitary miner still delving away at the same bank he worked in '50," the last of his camp.[1] While the life expectancy of most of the mining boom towns was a little longer than the railroads' "Hell-On-Wheels" settlements, the pace and style of living was no less adventuresome while they lived. Many ended quickly, with a bang or a whimper like California's Panamint City. Others, like Placerville, attracted enough industry and commerce to sustain them when the gold ran out. Still others—Virginia City and Tombstone are notable examples—developed a lively tourist trade.

We usually hear only about the successes, and seldom the failures, though many more miners went bust than boom. The folksong, "A Hit At The Times," expresses the disillusion of life in the gold fields:

> Way out upon the Platte, near Pikes Peak we were told
> There by a little digging, we could get a pile of gold,
> So we bundled up our duds, resolved at least to try
> And tempt old Madam Fortune, root hog, or die.
>
> So we traveled across the country, and we got upon the ground,
> But cold weather was ahead, the first thing we found.
> We built our shanties on the ground, resolved in spring to try,
> To gather up the dust and slugs, root hog, or die.

Succeeding stanzas satirize the "big hotels" on "corner lots" that have been built on speculation, the doctors ("They say their trade it is to cure, I say it is to kill"), the lawyers ("In the public dairy they drink the milk, their clients drink the whey"), and the preachers.

> I have finished now my song or, if you please, my ditty;
> And that it was not shorter, is about the only pity.
> And now, that I have had my say, don't say I've told a lie;
> For the subject I've touched, will make us root hog, or die.[2]

The Gold Rush Song Book contains the satirical lament of another goldless seeker, "The Unhappy Miner":

My happy days are past,
The mines have failed at last,
The canyons and gulches no longer will pay,
There's nothing left for me,
I'll never, never see
My happy, happy home far away.

I mine from break of day,
But cannot make it pay,
Disheartened return to my cabin at night,
Where rattlesnakes crawl round
My bed made on the ground,
And coiling up, lay ready to bite.

My poor old leaky lamp
Is always cold and damp;
My blanket is covered with something that crawls;
My bread will never rise,
My coffee-pot capsize.
I'd rather live inside of prison walls.

My boots are full of holes,
Like merchants have no *soles;*
My hands, once so soft, are harder than stone;
My pants and woolen shirt
Are only rags and dirt;
And must I live and die here alone?

I know how miners feel
When pigs begin to squeal,
Or hens on their roosts to cackle and squall;
It makes my blood run cold
To think it's all for gold,
And I often wish that Gabriel would call!

It's "Starve or pay the dust,"
For merchants will not trust,
And then in the summer the diggins are dry;
Of course then I am broke,
Swelled up by poison oak;
It's even so, I really would not lie.

I've lived on pork and beans,
Through all these trying scenes,
So long I dare not look a hog in the face;
And often do I dream
Of custard pies and cream;
But really it is a *quien sabe* case.

If I were home again,
To see green fields of grain,
And all kinds of fruit hanging ripe on the trees;
I there would live and die,
The gold mines bid good-bye—
Forever free from bed-bugs and fleas.[3]

The complaints are too heavy-handed and unrelenting to be taken entirely seriously, and it is hard to imagine that many miners actually sang this song. How many would actually mouth the words, "Disheartened return to my cabin at night"? It may not be a serious lament, but a self-satirizing ballad. The lyrics, which to some extent do describe real conditions, are believable as satire.

What the unhappy miner's contemporaries wanted to hear— what we want to hear—are success stories. The boom towns existed, to varying degrees, according to the momentary tides of expectation, whim, and rumor. Strikes could not be kept secret. Prospectors developed a kind of psychic radar for new fields—always greener, or golder—than the ones they were working at the moment, and they couldn't keep their information to themselves.

Marshall and Sutter tried, but the others in the area around the mill wondered what they were doing off by themselves for so long. Travelers to the new fields were kept in motion by a steady fueling of tales about the fortunes to be made and the fortunes already taken from the earth. As wagon trains crossed the plains, and criss-crossed, and recrossed, as the emigrants sat around each other's fires at night, the news—heightened and dramatized no doubt—raced across the plains. "The Ballad of Tonopah Bill" captures this aspect of the life of the prospector, again facetiously and realistically, simultaneously admiring the adroitness of Bill and laughing at his self-deception:

Tonopah Bill was a desert rat who had traveled the gold camps through;
He was first to hear of the latest strike wherever the rumors flew.
In the frozen north of the Rio Grande he had looked for elusive pay,
And the tales of his wonderful luck would spread in a most remarkable way.

He talked in an optimistic vein, as fitted the mining game,
And he carried his art to the Other Side when he staked his final claim,

For he started forth in the Milky Way and he rapped on the pearly
gates,
And when St. Peter confronted him he asked for permanent rates.

But the good Saint shook his head and said, "No place in here for you!
We want no more within our door of the lawless mining crew.
They are blasting the golden streets at night to search for the hidden
vein,
With hammer and drill and a double shift they prospect a copper stain.

"They have pitched their tents and staked their claims as far as the
eye can see,
For they cannot forget the lure of the gold in all eternity."
Now Tonopah Bill grinned a knowing grin and spoke in a forceful way,
"Good Saint," quoth he, "there's a trick or two on that gang I would
like to play.

"With a word or two I will send them hence and peace once more will
reign.
They will pass at night through the pearly gates and never return
again."
It sounded remarkably like a bluff but the need of the Saint was sore,
And Bill had a confident way with him, as I have remarked before.

So the gates flew wide and he entered in, and straight to the camp he
drew,
Where he told a marvelous tale to that restless mining crew.
No thought they gave that the tale was wild, no time did they take to
prove,
But straight as the news was flashed around the camp was on the
move.

St. Peter looked in a vast amaze and, "Tell me," he began,
What means you used to start so quick this mining caravan."
"I told them news of a strike," said Bill, "that just was made Below.
A million dollars it ran to the ton, and plenty there to show.

"Free milling rock in a fissure vein, well worth a heavy bet,
And I said if they hurried up a bit some ground was open yet."
The good Saint looked aghast and said, "This story is absurd."
"Perhaps," said Bill with a cheerful grin. " 'Tis a rumor that I heard."

It was not long ere the watchful Saint saw Bill approach again,
His mining tools were on his back and argument was in vain.
"I am mighty sorry to go," said he, "and to say good bye to you,
But I'm off to join the others, for the rumor might be true."[4]

The diction is not that of folksong, and we have no evidence that the song was ever current in oral tradition, despite its inclusion in the Fifes' collection. Nevertheless, it conveys the extent to which miners' lives were controlled by rumor and the hope of a richer strike to be found elsewhere. Placing the scene in heaven gives the miners' susceptibility to rumor an eternal quality, arguing that they were always like that on earth. One way to interpret Bill's behavior is as "the perpetrator falling victim to his own lie"; but it also signi-fies the insubstantial and evanescent quality of the miner's move-ments: so bent is he on striking the gold that has no known site, that he is ready to move at the slightest word, however unreliable, of "color."

Newspapers also carried this "news." In almost every issue, the weekly *Alta California* printed a story about a new discovery of gold or silver. The issue of 15 January 1859 had several items: Yreka, it wrote, was "one of the best-paying leads in the State"; claims in Calaveras County "give evidence of astonishing richness"; and even though not so much as "one dollar" had yet been removed from the first mine, it "exhibits tokens of the most fabulous wealth." The same issue said of another discovery: "the wealth that will flow from these sources alone will make San Andres one of the most wealthy and most permanent mining towns in the States." In February of 1859 the St. Louis *Republican* reported on a field in West Kansas: "it is the general opinion hereabouts ... that the South Park region ... will produce a new El Dorado." In late March of the same year the *Alta California* predicted that "gold ... will, probably, be produced in greater quantities during the spring and the coming summer, than in any previous season." Nearly a month later Colorado miners were insisting, "most positively, that the mines are richer than any they have ever seen in California, as it is dirt from the top to the bed rock." And, the paper noted, "rich strikes, big lumps, and 'good pay', is the general topic of conversation in almost every locality" [of Calaveras County].[5]

Often it was in the local economic interest of newspapers to encourage colonization of the region they served, and many unverified accounts of strikes and subsequent profits were carried as fact. The citizenry should not get up and move on to the next strike; what would become of California if thousands went to Nevada? So, in November of 1859, in response to the Comstock Lode excitement, we find the *Alta California* editorializing: "however, we do not think it

advisable for men in this State [California] to make a stampede for
the new diggings; the gold region may not be as extensive as is now
supposed. . . . Next season will be soon enough to try the Washoe
mines."[6]

So, in addition to the thousands of prospectors on the trail and
in the boom camps, exchanging yarns about gold, writing letters
home about it, journalists added to the flow of information, actual
and fancied, about the discovery and exploitation of mineral wealth
in the West. Many of these tales, (perhaps) recreated anew on the
frontier, nevertheless were analogues to legends found in other
places in the world where mineral wealth had been discovered.
Many were, as Alan Dundes once defined legends of this kind, "rumors of a traditional nature." And nearly all purported to relate
events in the lives of specific people in real, particular places. Of
course, all of them were "true."

While investigating gold-rush lore I collected more than one
hundred narratives told by and about the quest for gold and silver
from 1848 until recently, when the search for the "Lost Dutchman
Mine" was resumed. To reduce this very diffuse amount of material
to a manageable volume, I have here considered only three classes
of gold-mining legends: lost mine legends, lone prospector legends,
and a cycle of stories that seem almost inevitably to arise out of the
life and death of the boom towns. Nearly all the boom-town narratives can be arranged into a cyclical framework—the accounts from
the first moments when minerals were thought to be present, to the
building of the mining camp, to its eventual destruction—and I have
ordered them accordingly, though no single narrative, so far as I
know, presents the "complete" birth, life, and death of a mining
camp utilizing all of these collected legend-motifs. I draw no conclusion from the sequence itself which I, after all, arranged. Narratives
about the Lost Mine or the Lone Prospector are not cyclical, and so
a chronological arrangement is not possible; rather, I have grouped
specimens of each of several types thematically, and have drawn the
conclusions that the resultant synchronic patterning seems to express.

Lost mine stories are among the most common staples of Western lore. They tell of the mine momentarily glimpsed or the nugget
once found in a place that is never located again. Beebe and Clegg,
those inveterate purveyors of folklore in print, write about the Mormon, California-bound during the eighteen fifties, who lost the fore-

sight of his rifle, and replaced it with some soft metal he found nearby. When he arrived in California, he had it assayed and found that it was pure silver. The "mine" became known as the "Lost Gunsight Lode."[7] But the most famous "lost mine" is that of the "Dutchman," who stumbled out of the Superstition Mountains where he and a partner had been prospecting. He insisted to his rescuers that he and his partner had found a cache as rich as an Inca prince's treasure, but that Indians had driven them away, killing his companion. And, of course, before the "Dutchman" could describe the exact location of the mine, he too died.[8] In a closely related variant, the miner sneaks back to his farm (to work up a grubstake?), is kicked by a mule, and dies.[9]

The passage of time accounts for other mine losses. One such story is told about Pegleg Smith, mountain man and trapper in the Southwest during the early nineteenth century. Crossing the Colorado "Desert" in 1829 with a companion, Pegleg is scouting for water when he accidentally kicks up a metallic ball which he takes to be copper. But nothing comes of it, even when he learns, back in town, that the ball is 80% gold. Many years later, when beaver is no longer in fashion, Smith decides to search for the three buttes near which he found his gold ball. But of course the intervening years have taken their toll of his memory, the country has now been transformed by hordes of emigrants, and he cannot find the spot again. Despairing and frustrated, old Pegleg Smith dies a saddened, poor man.[10]

As Wayland Hand has pointed out,[11] many deposits have been discovered (allegedly) because of avalanches, landslides, floods, cave-ins, and so forth, which suddenly revealed nuggets. On the other hand, those same natural phenomena could have concealed or buried rich mines of which only a ledge or a small vein showed on the surface.

Some mines are "guarded" by Indians or wild animals, protecting their contents from the incursions of white men. J. Frank Dobie knew about a mine in the Mt. Franklin region that was guarded by Chief Cheetwah, who had held that little spot of earth for two hundred years.[12] After defeating a Spanish column in 1680, he and his people vanished into the mountains, "there to keep vigil forever that no alien with pick and shovel should prosper from the mineral wealth of the land." Though white men now own the territory, they can never possess the treasure. Similarly, Breyfogle's two friends

were killed by Indians in the Panamint Mountains, though he escaped. While on the run, he found a rich vein, but had to continue
on to Austin, Nevada, where he worked for a while in a quartz mill.
Subsequent attempts to find his lost mine were thwarted by active,
hostile Indians; when finally he did return to what he remembered
as the place, he could not find the mine. In disgust, those who had
followed him into the desert returned to Austin.[13]

Not only Indians but rattlesnakes are said to guard the "Lost
Dutchman Mine." They are also the guardians of treasure in another Southwest "cursed mine" tale which has a young Mexican
shepherd as the discoverer. The pile of gold is in a cave infested with
rattlers. When he returns to his village he agrees to tell his ranch
foreman and two other white men the location of the treasure. But
his mother is deeply upset, and berates him: "Oh, my son . . . do not
show them that place. Is that your gold to give away? Did you put
it there? Don't you understand that the snakes are spirits to guard
it? You will be cursed forever if you tell the secret . . . " The boy goes
to the village priest who gives him essentially the same lecture about
the "rattlesnake cave." But to no avail; the shepherd sets out with
the rapacious whites, but several days later his body is brought back
to town. He has been shot and killed before he could reveal the
location of the treasure-cave. His murderer is never found, and the
motivation for the slaying never determined. [14]

Elsewhere, Dobie retells a local superstition that the ore taken
out of a certain mine will, before even a solitary prospector can reach
civilization, be the cause of his death. [15] But the manner of death is
not specified. He is more precise about the fate awaiting seekers
after the "Lost Nigger Mine," who the initiated expect will be
thwarted by either fire or water or in some other way destined to
meet sudden death.

The theme is so much like Beowulf's last fight with the dragon
that it ought to be mentioned for its historical perspective. Like the
rattlesnakes, the dragon protects a treasure hoard under the earth,
and reaches out in its destructive fury only when the treasure is
threatened. As in the American Southwest, the trouble starts when
a greedy human tries to steal some of the treasure for himself.

In a great many tales of the same type the "curse" on the
treasure is human greed. An old proverb, common among prospectors as well as others, reminds us that "two can keep a secret if one
of them is dead." *The Treasure of the Sierra Madre* is a dramatic

enactment of that proverb, as is Chaucer's *Pardoner's Tale*. In oral tradition the story is so common that Aarne and Thompson included it in the *Types of the Folk-Tale* as "The Treasure-Finders Who Murder One Another."

That lone prospector is an intriguing figure in his own right, someone we should notice when he does appear. Often enough legends about him occur detached from related motifs, and only infrequently does he appear in connection with a lost mine—when he does, it is usually because he has died without leaving a clue as to the mine's location. But several features of the lone prospector himself, as I have just said, are worth examining.

What most people notice about him, probably resent, and are always suspicious of, are his solitary habits. He is a loner, both when he is at work in the hills and when he comes to town for supplies. It is felt that he has a mine "somewhere," but no one is quite certain where, and all efforts to trace him to his mine fail. In some versions even when he is seen toiling on a hillside in the distance, the snoopers cannot locate his diggings after he has left. Like the alchemists of the Middle Ages, his work and his personality conspire to make him a figure of suspicion. Marshall and Cornelius wrote of one old prospector, "Lone Wolf," that he was "stooped, slender," an "unkempt old man." When newcomers Deluche and McCartney ask the proprietor of a roadside stand who the "old fellow" is, they are told, "Oh, he is an old desert rat common to these parts. He's been prospecting around here for a long time." The newcomers want to talk with him but are told, "he's a peculiar old cuss. Like most of those old desert rats he's got bats in his belfrey. He is decidedly unsocial."[16] Frank Robertson tells of another man who was a "peculiar old cuss who lived all by his self and mingled with no one."[17]

When the old veteran leaves town for his mine in the hills (often enough in the badlands), he may be followed, but always to no avail. He will somehow manage to conceal his tracks; or he will double back on his followers and drive them off; or if he is successfully followed, he will be seen working in a place so inaccessible that the observers despair of ever reaching it; if they do reach it later, they can find no trace of the digging. It is as though the forces of nature have conspired to help the old prospector conceal his mine from the eyes of others.

One of the most remarkable traits about the old prospector is his lack of greed; he mines just enough to get by, and never becomes rich from his labors. He does not intend to; it is as though working the mine were the end in itself, that is, the reason for his existence. Perhaps the most famous such miner is the one who supplies the Lone Ranger's silver bullets. The Lone Ranger goes back to the mine periodically to replenish his supply of silver for his bullets and holds brief but congenial conversations with the aged silver-worker (I often wondered why the Ranger would use such a soft metal in his bullets, which would spread rapidly on impact and leave a hideous wound, unnecessarily brutal).

Often the lone prospector suffers (or endures, if you like) some sort of deformity or infirmity that marks him off physically from his fellow men. Marshall and Cornelius's "Clubfoot" is handicapped, as is the equally bluntly named trapper of the San Diego area, Pegleg Smith. Dobie remarks that Old Ben Sublett (no relation to the more famous mountain man), that "crazy prospector," ambled with a noticeable limp.[18] The trait is not universal, but occurs often enough to be significant.

The limping loner is at home in wild areas that frighten others off. As he shuns the company of men, so he seems more at home in those regions where other men cannot fare. Dobie, using a Southwest idiom as colorful as it is descriptive, says of one prospector that he could "live on what a coyote could leave."[19] The loner often heads straight into the hills where Apaches are warring, but always returns. Or he passes through regions thick with dangerous animals or snakes, as does the old veteran who was mining the Rattlesnake Mine, appropriately named for the nest of reptile guardians on the premises.[20] If the prospector cannot traverse the land near his mine alone, his horse or his burro helps him: Clubfoot's animal was so surefooted that snoopers did not even dare to try and follow.[21]

Clubfoot once said, "I ain't looking for gold in loose ground. . . . I want my gold in solid rock where the hole I make won't cave in on me, and I want the vein to be rich."[22] He spoke for most lone prospectors. They do not take their gold from the land's surface, skimming the top, but rather dig into its bowels, into the innards of the earth. This becomes something of an article of religious faith with them. Placer mining is not what they want; they are hard-rock men who get inside the earth they are working.

From these legend-motifs, particularly when they are considered together, a portrait of the real identity of the lone prospector begins to come into focus. He is quite human. His uncanny ability to evade pursuers and to live in very rough country with Indians and wild animals shows that. Often he can go where younger and ostensibly stronger men cannot; and no one can find his mine. He is not quite of this world. But of whose? The deformity may give a clue. In world folklore such impediments usually signify contact with the other world. Jacob walked with a limp after his wrestling match with the angel. Ahab lost his leg in an early struggle with the white whale. Oedipus, who had at least one uncanny power, had a clubfoot. (The Devil is sometimes called "clubfoot"). Stith Thompson records instances of Satan's limp (motifs G 303.45.3 and G 303.5.3).

The prospector's otherworldly associations are also indicated by his exclusive concern for hard rock: the devil is the prince of the underworld, and the lone prospector shuns placer mining—on the surface of the earth. That he can pass safely through nests of rattlers, dens of pumas, and lairs of bears, is only consistent with his otherworldly aspect. The Indian, we may remember from the time of colonial New England, was the child of nature in that he was the denizen of the wild. He is not an animal, obviously, but in this folklore neither is he entirely human; rather, the Indian is an intermediate, on the interface of humankind and those forces of nature closer to the source of cosmic, perhaps demonic energy. The prospector's ability to move among them freely again shows his uncanny nature.

In all of this discussion of the old miner I have been intentionally vague about trying to identify him because I feel that a precise identification is not possible, even in any one specific instance, and that his signification will alter in each legend and probably from teller to teller. It also seems to me unlikely that most transmitters of these legends are fully aware of the kind of material they themselves find interesting enough to retell. Instead, I would rather leave the prospector's identity something of a mystery; enough that he is not quite of this world, that he can move through parts of it where other men fear to tread, and that many of the aspects of nature conspire with him. He is in league with some portion of them. Perhaps he has made a pact with Satan himself, selling his soul for a secret mine; we, who dwell on this side of the badlands, will never know.

One other aspect of the miner's habits need to be pointed out: the subsistence level of his digging. Like the Lone Ranger's devoted menial, he takes out "just enough" to get by. The answer to the puzzle posed by this particular variant appears to have much to do with concepts of whether what is desirable in life is limited or infinite. Research conducted in Latin America close to three decades ago (by George M. Foster) indicates that peasant cultures there feel that what they desire in life, such as money, love, influence, etc., is available only in limited quantity. One can get more of what is desirable only by depriving others. And since that is not acceptable, only luck and fate can bring about a change in one's fortunes. In such cultures, buried treasure stories are very popular because they offer a hope of obtaining great wealth without depriving others of their property.[23]

In America, however, Westerners in particular believed that the desired good is unlimited. Wealth accrues to those who go out and find or manufacture it. The steady-state rights of others are not scrupulously considered. As we will see in those tales about prospectors who "struck it 'rich" but who sold out after taking only a pittance out of the ground, the American attitude is that the wealth of the world is almost limitless. Some stories of the lone prospector, therefore, the man who takes only enough to get by, seem to be involved in some way with subsistence living, what we today would call conservation. Again, a more precise delineation of these legends is not safe, since interpretation would vary depending upon the teller and the situation. But in some way, probably positively and admiringly, the miner who takes only what he needs out of his mine is living conservatively and in tune with nature, and not profiting beyond his needs at the expense of others.

We leave the lone prospector to his work at his solitary diggings, and move along to other mining experiences: the legend cycle that develops around the life history of the boom town. The tales are many and widely varied, but only a dozen or so are of particular interest to me because of their implied messages.

1. The discovery of precious metals is often preceded by a vague feeling, one that persists without any hard evidence, that the area —the mountain, the valley, the flats—is rich in gold or diamonds or platinum. The Rockies were at one time called "The Shining Mountains" and many mountains have been called "The Crystal Mountain" or "The Mountain of Silver," etc. A similar superstition is mentioned in Forsyth's *The Dogs of War,* by no means a folkloric piece of fiction, but one which shows how similar situations will induce both novelist and folk narrator to fabulate similar narra-

tives. Neill Wilson's *Silver Stampede* describes a mountain so rich in veins and ferns of silver that early visitors claimed that at a little distance "the whole peak glistened with it."[24]

2. Often through pure dumb luck a rich strike is made. Pony Expressman Bob Haslam's horse unintentionally kicked a chip of silver from the Reese River field while fleeing from Indians. The chip turned out to be nearly pure silver[25] (he stopped to pick it up while on the run?). William Bodey, digging for a wounded rabbit that had run to ground, discovered the Esmeralda outcroppings of what became the Bodie mines. Or there is the story of the first prospectors to Hamilton, Nevada, (in 1868) who threw up a stone shelter for wind protection, then later discovered it contained about $75,000 worth of silver.[26]

3. The town or the mine is named for some legendary event: the "Vulture Mine" is so-named because its discoverer reached down to retrieve a vulture he had just shot and discovered several nuggets lying around on the surface. "Cheefoo Hill," in the Quinn River valley, Nevada, is said to have gotten its name because the prospector's automobile went "cheefoo, cheefoo, cheefoo" when climbing it for the first time.[27] That was in June of 1907; cars are quieter now. We can only fantasize on the origins of such names as Hungry Hallow, Last Chance, Shirt-Tail Cañon, Mad Mule, Nip and Tuck, and Dirty Bar.

4. The first prospectors sell out cheap after taking only a paltry amount from the earth. Gould is said to have sold his claim on the Comstock for $450; eight million dollars were taken out of his property subsequently by more patient owners.[28] Early in 1859 the weekly *Alta California* reported the story of a miner who "sunk a hole in the ground to the depth of five feet, and in a fit of discouragement, abandoned the work. A month afterwards a man named Webster went into the same hole, digging it to the ledge, and found very rich pay. After he had worked the claim out . . . and abandoned it, another party took possession and discovered still greater quantities of gold in the rejected lava." Several months later the same newspaper ran a brief anecdote about the Virginia mine and its eponymous founder who sounds very much like the ubiquitous Finney: "the Virginia lead was first struck by a drinking character, whose sobriquet gave it a name. He hit upon its decomposed surface while following up a small ravine in the course of ordinary gold washing, and parted with his interest in it for a mere song."[29] The gold had

been nearly depleted in Leadville, Colorado, when the Gallagher brothers struck it rich on silver lying just beneath the gold excavations—according to popular novelist J. H. Beadle.[30]

5. The slick or simply outright belligerently thieving operator either uses guile to get his claim on land where others already have rights, or swindles other miners later. At Panamint, Jack Wilson, late in establishing his claim, armed himself with a Henry repeater, a Murcott hammerless shotgun, and a Winchester 44-40; he jabbed two Smith and Wessons in his belt, and rode up to a Mexican who was setting up camp on his new claim. Wilson insisted that the claim was his, and for evidence pointed to the arsenal on his packmule. He named his mine "Defiance."[31]

But not all the mining camp citizens were as crude as Wilson; foxes roamed the hills as well as bears, as "Shorty," a mine peddler, shows in this *Pony Express Courier* interview:

> I could usually find some way to put a deal over, but sometimes it took real work. There was another time a man went out with me to look a property over. I told him the price was $2,000. I could see that the price was too high because he began to move away like he didn't want to talk about it any more. I needed money pretty badly, and wanted the deal to go through.
> "How much money have you got on you?" I asked.
> "About a hundred and seventy five or eighty dollars," he said.
> "Well, that's my money, and you've got a mine."

When negotiations with another buyer began to bog down, "Shorty" told him,

> I've just got bad news from the east . . . and I've got to get away quick. My father is dying, and my aunt is in the hospital. There is some money to be divided up among the relatives and I must be on the spot when this thing is pulled off. I'll take eleven hundred for that claim right now. [His starting price had been $15,000.]

"Shorty" settled for $1,000, "which was just what I intended to get in the first place; but a man always has to start with a higher figure."[32]

6. Shortly afterwards the camp followers arrive, particularly women—the "soiled doves"—and though they are not well connected, as the saying goes, they will one day prove themselves to

have hearts of gold. The most famous madames of the old West were Mattie Silks, Silverheels, Madame Moustache, and Julia Bulette. The latter was an honorary member of the Virginia City fire engine company, and a club car on the Virginia and Truckee Railroad was named for her. Like so many ladies of her persuasions, she died violently, in bed, at the hands of a jealous lover.

7. A few prospectors do strike it rich, thus generating a variety of stories about their wealth: many of the stories focus on the early-life poverty of overnight millionaires. Laundress Eilley Orrum's stock in various Comstock holdings is said in a short time to have multiplied by fifty.[33] Shares in the Bodie Mine sold for $1 each on June 1 of 1878, but had skyrocketed to $18 by August 7. Those on the ground floor had originally bought the stock for 40 cents.[34] Bill Raymond is reputed to have given his $60 watch as down payment on what became the Raymond and Ely mine in Pioche. The mine eventually produced about $17,000,000 worth of gold and silver—all for a watch, Raymond is alleged to have said, "that always did run a little slow."[35]

8. Some of the ones who strike it rich eventually die penniless. Eilley Orrum and Sandy Bowers are the obvious examples here, but more recently, because of the American opera, "The Ballad of Baby Doe," we should think of H. A. W. Tabor and his Matchless Mine, and his now legendary wife, Baby Doe. The Mormon who took Bill Raymond's watch does not quite fit this category; but the discoverers of the Bodie mine, Brodigan and Brodey, came up with little, and Brodigan operated a spring-water delivery business in Bodie for a time to keep solvent.[36] Miner friends gave Sandy Bowers and Eilley Orrum a bushel basket of worthless stock which—when the Comstock mines came in—was worth well over one million dollars. Drinks for everyone were always "on the house"; they toured Europe and the Court of St. James; and built a half-million-dollar mansion in Nevada of marble and crystal. But Eilley, who outlived Sandy, died penniless.[37]

9. A great many stories describe the high living of the newly rich: many miners are famous primarily because of the extravagant binges they financed after they struck it rich. Bowers and Orrum are, again, probably the most famous figures in such stories as these, but I want to return to them later. So optimistic were many of the miners that they would make their pile, that the motif occurs in folksongs of the day:

And when we each have made our pile,
We'll have a high old time, O,
We'll take it slow and easy, while—
Pop comes the Rhino.

We'll go back to America,
Dressed up so slick and fine, O,
And when there's anything to pay—
Pop comes the Rhino

We'll take the girls to all the shows,
O crack, won't we shine tho'
At balls, where always from the beaux—
Pop comes the Rhino.[38]

10. A few of the more successful boom towns had pretensions to high culture, and hired opera singers and other "celebrities" to entertain its citizens. Lola Montez visited Virginia City; the Washoe Club there could have served her terrapin, foie gras, and tropical fruits.[39]

11. The often rough-hewn quality of law-and-order, such as multiple and full-dress hangings, have inspired another group of narratives. A Wells-Fargo agent is said to have ordered a headstone for a bandit shot down while robbing one of the company's Concords. It read, "Wells Fargo Never Forgets."[40]

12. After the earlier prospectors and miners have either left or settled down to live comfortably off their former discoveries and labors, a later generation of sophisticated developers—not the slickers mentioned before—takes that last of the wealth from the earth. Sometimes these latecomers—always a trifle suspect because they are "hangers-on" and not originals—are corporations. One of the most illustrious of the individual secondary exploiters was San Francisco's Adolph Sutro, whose capital bought the services of engineers who all but cleaned out Nevada's Gold Hill. He went on to become mayor of the city by the bay.

13. Usually through fire or flood—often thought to be divine retribution for the area's sins—the boom town is destroyed, as was Virginia City in 1875, as was Cripple Creek in 1906. Panamint was washed away by a flash flood. It had been called "a suburb of Hell" by a Wells-Fargo manager who refused to run a stage line into the place.

Even this baker's dozen would be too much to manage in a limited space, and I will further restrict my attention to two or three types of legends for the remainder of this chapter, those that describe the first prospectors and their lucky strike, their quick sale to more patient developers, and their extravagant spending. "Pony Bob's" horse's lucky kick in the Reese River country has already been mentioned. The Plumbago Mine at Alleghany (California) was discovered, allegedly, when a rock was scored by a horse's shoe, revealing a rich silver vein. In Placer County a man fired his rifle at a threatening rattler, but the bullet missed the snake and uncovered glistening rock instead. The Morgan Hill mine was discovered when a prospector came upon an exposed outcropping while chasing his mule. George McKnight stumbled over some quartz outcropping while chasing his happily perverse cow in Grass Valley. At both Jackson and Ione, in California, miners had thrown rocks at birds, only to discover that their missiles were in fact rich in gold. The same story is told in Ouray, Colorado, giving the name, the "Camp Bird Mine." And in Utah, the Shoebridge Bonanza Mine was discovered when a disgruntled miner threw away his pick in frustration, and it chanced to dig up surface soil covering a rich silver vein.[41]

"Boob's Luck" tales comprise an entire subgenre by themselves. In tales of this type, the rank newcomer, through no ingenuity or knowlege of his own, stumbles upon a rich vein. Wayland Hand repeats the tale about the Swedish tenderfoot who was told facetiously that he would find his gold under the stump of a nearby live oak. Like a damn fool he went to the tree, dug, and took out about $5,000 worth.[42] Another boob, this one from Massachusetts, was told by waggish locals to dig in a certain area and soon, of course, struck it rich—$80,000 worth in this tale. In other stories the boob throws away some implement in disgust—a pick or a shovel is interchangeable—and it strikes pay dirt. This last version differs from the other, similar, lucky strike story only in the respect of the finder's characterization. The motif has even entered popular video narratives: the canned introduction to the daily episodes of the "Beverly Hillbillies" explains how the Clampetts struck it rich when Grandpa was out hunting rabbit one day, fired wildly, and his bullet sprung an oil geyser.

A motif often related in the action described but usually quite different in intent depicts "last-chance tales." These extol patience. In these narratives, such as the one about miners Cedarburg and Anderson who were down to their last sack of flour when they hit pay dirt, it is perseverance that wins the day.[43] Almost identical

stories about Texas oil strikes have been collected by a former student of mine who was raised near the oilfields in Lubbock, Texas.[44]
There, of course, the "last chance" nets the finder oil and not gold.
Only quitters are losers. As the University of Oklahoma football
slogan has it, "you've only lost when you give up trying." If you stick
it out long enough, these tales seem to be saying, your reward will
come.

A number of the miners, again, according to narratives about
them, were content to skim a little cream off the top and then sell
out to others—often mining corporations from the big city—not caring or not realizing that they were selling the cow that made all the
cream. "Old Pancake" Comstock is said to have sold out his share of
the magnificently fecund Orphir for only $10,000. I have mentioned
Gould getting only $450 (or settling for that amount, and glad of it,
too) for what eventually became a multi-million dollar operation.
The other side of how Bill Raymond got his mine for a down payment
of a sixty-dollar watch centers on the Mormon—nameless because
not the pivotal character in the story—who gave up his claim for so
paltry a thing; and it always did run a little slow. A related tale has
been given to me by Judith Siegel of Seattle, whose grandfather, W.
J. Bell, was a long-time resident and part-time prospector in and
around Winnemucca, Nevada. Having worked the Buckskin mine
for several years, on and off, Bell and his partner, George Ward,
found nothing more interesting than some low-grade float. It wasn't
until Ward died, in 1913, that the mine started producing, some of
the rock yielding as much as $40,000 a ton, though the average was
only about half that.

These tales are based on the authentic experiences of gold prospectors. Many of them are no doubt accurate. The miners themselves
felt that several hundred dollars were equal to the fortune of a year's
wages, or more. They could not drill deeply into hard rock and
possibly had exploited most of what could be taken from the earth
with their limited resources and technology. So, it made good sense
to get what they could from their claim and then to move on in the
hopes of getting in on the ground floor of yet another bonanza where
they might strike it even richer. Prentice Mulford, who knew many
of them, has fairly described the motivation of most prospectors in
the sentence, "They came to get gold, to get all they could, to get it
as quickly as they could, and to get away with it as quickly as
possible."[45] As a former prospector reminisced to a reporter for the

Pony Express Courier, "it was a common belief that the mines were inexhaustible; everything fostered the easy come easy go spirit."[46] The folksong of the "Cherry Creek Emigrants" said it for thousands:

> The gold is there, 'most anywhere
> You can take it out rich with an iron crowbar,
> And where it is thick, with a shovel and pick
> You can pick it out in lumps as big as a brick.
>
> At Cherry Creek if the dirt don't pay,
> We can strike our tents most any day.
> We know we are bound to strike a streak
> Of very rich quartz among the mountain peaks.[47]

So they sold their million dollar claims for hundreds, went on their wild binges in town, and then moved on in search of their next paying claim.

The civic establishment often tried to stabilize the wandering propensities of its transient citizens. In 1862 the *Territorial Enterprise* (of Virginia City, Nevada), editorialized that "not withstanding that the story of the wealth of the mines now appears almost fabulous to persons out of the Territory, they are but taking out thousands where they will extract millions five years hence.... Two years from now people will be found expressing their regret that they did not buy into ground that could have been had at the low price of two or three thousand dollars per foot." Three years earlier, the weekly *Alta California* had responded to the Virginia City/Comstock Lode discoveries with the cautionary, self-serving advice that "next season will be soon enough to try the Washoe mines." At the beginning of 1859 the *California* had declared, " ... our people do not despond, for they know that 'the good time coming' is just at hand, and that shortly we shall again begin to reap the golden harvest of prosperity."[48]

The Comstock's Eilley Orrum and Sandy Bowers were the most fabled of the West's big-time spenders. According to the *Enterprise,* Eilley married when she was fifteen. Her husband Edward Hunter was a Mormon churchman, whose marriage to three other women drove Eilley to sue for divorce ten years later. For a while she worked in a dry goods store, and soon married one of her customers, moving west with him in 1855. Her second husband was also Mormon, however, and when the church ordered him to Utah, Eilley stayed, shedding him too.

The first that is known of her in the Comstock Lode is as the proprietor of a boarding house in Johntown, where she is said to have rented space to the legendary "Old Virginia" Finney. In John-town, she married a part-time prospector and hanger-on named Sandy Bowers, and soon began managing his money. At first that was easy. Fruit baskets full of nearly worthless stock in the Com-stock were given them, again according to legend, by their friends for a wedding gift. But a few years later when the bonanza came in, Sandy and Eilley were in clover, gathering—by one anecdotal esti-mate—$10,000 a month.[49] They built themselves a marble mansion in the desert, and then threw lavish saturnalias in it. Deciding to see the rest of the world, they left for Paris with a quarter of a million dollars, but quickly had to send home for more. Eilley was said to have spent $20,000 in one day in the shops of the Place Vendôme. The end of the story contains no surprise; she and Sandy died penni-less, having spent their money down to the last nickel, as the *Enter-prise* put it. Later in her life Eilley became a fortune-teller, earning only the minutest fraction of her former income, and acquiring the belittling epithet, the "Comstock Seeress." She died in 1903.

The Comstock millionaires had their Eastern counterparts in figures like Pennsylvania's "Coal Oil Johnny," the first of the newly rich to emerge from the Titusville petroleum fields. When his first barrel of money had been accumulated, Johnny went to the big city, Philadelphia, and treated dozens of his friends to a big time. He rented a hotel in the City of Brotherly Love, evicted all the tenants, and partied with his friends until his money ran out. Then he trekked back to the oil fields to work on gathering his second for-tune. Novelist J. H. Beadle (in *Western Wilds, and the Men Who Redeem Them*) summed it up nicely, though in a fictional setting: "men who rarely had an extra dollar in their lives found themselves rich beyond their dreams, and spent money with a lavish hand. . . . Those who make money suddenly, generally spend it carelessly, and life in a thriving mining camp is a continous invitation to prodigal-ity."[50]

What these stories (legends? anecdotes? personal experience narratives?) bespeak is an attitude toward the putative abundance of American mineral wealth. Anyone can strike a gold or silver bonanza and become a millionaire overnight. It doesn't take a great deal of wisdom or technical know-how; even the boob's carelessly thrown shovel can strike pay dirt. The lucky strike doesn't (neces-

sarily) happen to the already rich, the socially powerful or prominent. When the prospector makes a killing, what counts is his
money; not where his parents came from, how long they had been
there, or how they made their money, but the quantity, the volume,
the weight of the miner's bonanza. The lucky strike can happen to
you and me, to the prospector who sticks it out to the very end, and
to the lucky. Lady Luck is egalitarian: it takes luck to find the
mineral wealth at all, it's a matter of luck whether you find a rich
vein or just a few nuggets. As the *Enterprise* said of the old Orrum/-
Bowers mansion, it is "a monument to the wild days when a boardinghouse keeper and her well meaning, but not too intelligent
husband, by stumbling onto ten feet of a mine, could achieve a
fabulous fortune and experiences such as few can ever know."[51] If
it happened to a boardinghouse keeper like Eilley Orrum, why not
us?

"Gold," an old prospector's proverb goes, "is where you find it."
So they found their gold or their silver or their oil, and rather than
wait to develop it fully, to get all that was there out of the ground,
those old prospectors (or wildcat drillers) took out only enough for
a few days of good times, in San Francisco or in the quickly built
saloons, gambling rooms, and bordellos of Virginia City, or in Philadelphia or Houston, and then moved on to greener—or golder—
fields. Many in reality did, as we know. As the old prospector said,
"everything fostered the easy come easy go spirit." And what Dobie
says about two prospectors of his knowledge who left their claims to
try new ones in the Sierra Nevadas, was true of thousands of others:
they felt that the amount of gold in the West was "inexhaustible."[52]
Somewhere over the next hill there was more gold to be found. On
the next hill there was more silver. Under the next hill there was
more petroleum. Why bother hanging around when there were new
regions and new fields to explore, new wells to be drilled, new
streams to be placered?

The lore of the mining camps also indicates that moral character does not depend upon social position or class. It is within the
person, as demonstrated by actions, for instance the whores with
hearts of gold, like the fabled "Silverheels" of the Montana camps
who ministered to the sick during an epidemic. Some narratives
extol the virtues of patient plodding (or placering) while others hold
out the glittering promise that even the most inept and inexperienced can have a stroke of very good luck. And that luck, manifested

in the big bonanza, seems to be beyond man's control. It comes and it goes, sometimes almost capriciously. When Gould sold out his claim for $450, how was he to know that millions more lay beneath the surface rock, out of sight? The continuation of that anecdote is a fable extolling perseverance, demonstrated by the corporation that kept drilling on a claim that appeared to have run out. There are at least two sides to every anecdote; one of them is often a fable.

The idea that the wealth of the American West was inexhaustible drove prospectors back and forth across the plains, and fostered these legends about the life of the gold-hunters: their luck, their bacchanalias, their mobility. The wealth of the land was infinite! The assumption is with us still: in our attitudes about the cars we drive, the way we heat our homes and our businesses, the way we and our government spend our money. There is always more oil to be found (recently, if only we would give the oil companies more incentive to drill for it), there is always more gold to be discovered. It is an idea and an assumption that has become part of the way we view our world and our destiny in it.

This folklore is American, but is it American folklore? I don't know that such legends and such attitudes are peculiar to America, but they do seem to be characteristic of us. These narratives do reflect the way we feel, and while many of the motifs may be found elsewhere—those describing the prospector's luck and his impatience are less common than the others—they have been adapted in a distinctive way and in a distinctive context in the nineteenth-century West that expresses something very deep in the American spirit.

Narratives of the
Overland Trail

WHEN they left Missouri (St. Louis or Independence or St. Joseph) they were greenhorns, but by the time they trudged into Fort Hall (near present-day Pocatello) they were as tough and rugged as the land they had crossed. These were the survivors, those who perservered; the others had long since gone back to the cities and farms of the East—or else were buried in crude graves along the trail. Few of them crossed in those relatively opulent leviathans from the Conestoga Valley of Pennsylvania that the movies and hundreds of paintings have led us to imagine were the staple transportation of the pioneers; most wagons were smaller and lighter than Conestogas and thus more adaptable to soft sands, marshes, and steep hillsides. Yet the casualty rate among wagons was far greater even than that among the wagon-drivers, so rugged and demanding was the journey.

Few of the Easterners who set out on the Oregon/California trails had an adequate idea of the heat and the cold they would endure, the intensity and tenacity of the mosquitoes that would harass them, the numbers of poisonous snakes they would encounter, the fury of the rivers and the electrical storms that would plague them, and the general hard living that the geography and their journey through it would impose on them.

Accounts of the crossings are of two kinds: those written during the voyage—journals and diaries—and those memoirs, books, articles, and biographical papers written years after the fact. The first kind, especially those records scribbled down at the end of each day with no intent to publish for the entertainment of others, are usually sparse and phlegmatic. Few diarists elaborated on the events of the day, which they recorded laconically and simply. The extraordinary topography they encountered—whether mountains, buttes, or prairies—was seldom described. Unusual or beautiful vegetation is seldom mentioned. The interests of the diarists—if the records are to be taken at face value—seem to have been centered on how much ground they had covered that day and would cover the next day. The mileage traveled each day was of great interest and is almost always mentioned. But the quarrels inevitable among people in so stressful a situation, full as it was with danger, discomfort, uncertainty, and privation, are seldom written of.

The experience of the trail seemed to intensify the traveler's awareness of some phenomena at the expense of others. American travel narratives of the western wilderness from the eighteenth century on note many of the same details—buffalo herds, rattlesnakes (some diaries even count the number sighted each day), storm-swollen streams, electrical storms, and the sense of isolation that grows in the middle of nowhere.

Even the diarists were influenced by received ideas of what an overland trail narrative should be. Petty squabbles, thefts among the pilgrims in the same wagon train, how the sun looked at dusk —these were thought to matter little. But an attack of mosquitoes, the difficulties of crossing rivers, the eerie uncertainties of guard-duty at night on the prairie—descriptions of these events were thought appropriate to accounts of the trail. As, of course, they were. What interests us now are the selection process and the taxonomy of events usually included and those usually excluded from the typical trail narrative.

When the writer is reconstructing the story of his adventures long after the fact, whether from memory or from notes (which involves memory to a great extent in that one's telegraphic notes are expanded—from other narratives? conversations with other pioneers? expectations on the part of readers as to the content of such narratives? all of the above?) the accounts are much more detailed: mosquitoes buzz more loudly, streams flow more swiftly, Indians are more threatening, and so forth. But most interesting is the way in which the terrain is described in such lush detail, and emotions are "remembered" with such vividness. Oddly, the plain style of the diarist is often more accurate in descriptions, and seems (to our tastes) more modern.*

Some narratives, however, do not quite fit either category. Artist James F. Wilkins, from England, made copious notes during his journey, describing his fellow travelers and the landscape in rich detail. And the Geiger-Bryarly journal of the Charlestown (Virginia) mining company's odyssey from St. Joseph to California is often detailed, though for a purpose. While it contains entries as short as, "At camp. Remained there over day & branded our mules," which must do for the entire day's events (May 13th, 1849), others are impressively extensive! A portion of the June 3rd entry reported that

> An emigrant party on yesterday killed a fine buffalo & gave chase to a small herd to-day. From several companies we hear of men missing, who have gone hunting & doubtless lost their way. . . . Many murders have & doubtless will yet take place from such a cause.[1]

Yet Geiger was writing for the benefit of others, for in the middle of this passage he moralizes, "emigrants should be careful in relation to this, & ought never to lose sight of their trains." And, a little later on (in the same day's entry), he passes on the popular explanation for the disappearance of emigrants who stray from the trains, an explanation generated by anxiety and uncertainty:

> The Indians hide about in the bluffs & ravines and attack small parties, sometimes killing, and at other times robbing the prisoners of their

*Another important distinction to be made in Overland Trail narratives—almost as significant as that between diary and memoir—is that between narratives written by men and those written by women. When we do read detailed and sensitive descriptions of Western topography, they are likely to have been written by women. Not that females had, particularly, more leisure time than men in which to write their fuller accounts of the trail. Rather, they were, in general, better educated and more inclined as well as better able to depict their experiences in writing. Such also were the observations of Sandra Myers (University of Texas, Arlington) who was at the Huntington Library during the summer of 1979, researching and writing a book on women on the Overland Trail.

Linguist Ann Stewart, examining trail narratives for a forthcoming book on the Western contribution of speech to American English, found the men's narratives much more interesting than the women's. The men's idiosyncratic spelling and folksy syntax give far better clues to the spoken speech of the time; words were spelled the way they sounded to the writer, giving the skilled phonologist a good idea of how the writer spoke. But the women are usually of little help this way; they respect conventions of grammar and spelling.

guns, clothes & c., and inflicting severe lashes, [before they have] turned them loose to find their friends or perish on the wild & desolate plains.[2]

In fact, few diarists had experiences with hostile Indians and few travelers on the Oregon trail fell victim to arrows or tomahawks; far more common were complaints about pilfering among those "red men" invited into the pioneer's camps. James F. Wilkins's convoy once came upon an Indian family—a squaw and three children—who were devouring an ox that Wilkins thought must have been dead for "at least a fortnight." Not at all hostile, the artist found them "the most miserable family of indians [sic] I ever saw. Sunk to the very lowest ebb of misery starvation and poverty. . . . this was the nearest link to the brute creation I had ever seen."[3] Not as the movies would show it.

But Wilkins, as we said, differed from most of the diarists, whose experiences seemed almost predictable.[4] Many seem to have read other personal experience accounts of the trail, or had come to know what their audience, aural or literary, would expect. A great deal of individuality remains, of course, but it is often expressed within a framework that rapidly became characteristic of the genre. Certain kinds of episodes are almost certain to be related: the dangers in fording the Platte, for instance, or the awe induced by lightning on the prairie, encounters with Indians, accidents to wagon train members, or the inevitable story of the pioneer who wandered off too far from the train and was lost—for a few days or forever. So regularly do the same motifs appear in the Overland Trail narratives that a composite account can be assembled which typifies the genre, though it will not exactly recapitulate any one account.

The journals are filled with such entries as, "left the river and went twenty-six miles before we came near it again. Country barren and broken."[5] Narrative in any developed sense is scarce. More significant are those events and observations that the diarist or memoir-writer found interesting or important enough to dwell on, stories that he found interesting enough to note and "tellable" enough to want to repeat in print: these stories are the constituents of this composite.

Every tale has a beginning. Naturally enough, the Overland Trail narratives begin at the point of departure for the travelers, and describe the gathering of provisions, the election of a company captain, the hiring of a scout or guide, local conditions, and the other emigrants also awaiting departure. Ohioan Alpheus Richardson wrote in his diary that "the streets are literally crowded with people and on the wharf there is not room enough for a dray to turn around scarcely for the crowd of people, drays, carriages and wagons bound for California, and provisions which are ready to be shipped."[6] Clarence Bagley was one of those whose remembrances were published many years after the event (in his case 1924). He describes how supplies were gathered, names the others in his company, and then gets to the serious business of crossing a continent:

> At Council Bluffs Thomas Mercer was elected captain. It was a necessary custom to select a captain of each party, who directed the movements of the train about stopping for the night and starting in the morning, about laying over, on Sundays or any other time it was thought best. Otherwise there would have been frequent disputes and disagreements about the movements of the company. The trip was one to bring out all the good qualities and the bad ones, as well, but I do not remember any serious disputes along the whole of the route.[7]

He was lucky; or else the intervening years had softened his recollections.

The first nights out on the plains were often frightening ones for the Easterners, and a variety of dangers—actual and imagined— seemed always to threaten. Guard duty, especially on dark nights, was particularly frightening and lonely. The guard wondered if he was really alone. Luella Dickenson recalled long afterward experiences her husband had on guard duty:

> One night, he was placed upon picket duty some distance from camp. Hearing voices (the moon was shining brightly) he looked down the ravine and saw two Indians between him and the wagons. Creeping towards them unseen, he hesitated whether to shoot or not, thinking if they went in a different direction he would avoid raising the alarm, which happily they did. At another time, he saw something crawling through the grass, that looked like a wild animal, but proved to be an Indian disguised in a wolf skin. . . . [8]

In accounts written years after the fact, the language is more polished, the narrative arranged to be more dramatic (the details are organized to point toward some purposive conclusion), and the outcome known in advance. Few whites on the trail had serious problems with Indians and the narratives complain almost exclusively about their thievery, begging, and exorbitant tolls. The wild Indian with scalping knife poised was an imagined danger far more often than he was a real one.

A far greater danger was disease, from which nearly everyone suffered. Most journal entries merely record that acquaintances were afflicted or had died, but we are fortunate enough to have the diary of a physician (Dr. John Hudson Wayman) who made the journey and who recorded his observations in some detail:

> From the commencement of our journey, the diseases were Diarrhea in two forms, the pale free watery discharges and the Bilious[.] This will be sufficient as a description, until we left Fort Laramie after which Dyesentery [sic] seemed to take the place of Diarrhea—After reaching the South Pass, we encountered some fever of a Bilious Remittent character, not malignant, being easily controlled, when not associated with disease of the Bowels. I have heard of some deaths occuring from this mountain fever, in such cases I think from what I have seen, that it is the result of bad management, and when death does occur, the immediate cause is Peritoneal inflamation. . . . I have seen a number of cases and all seem to weare [sic] this tendency. Though if properly managed there is no danger.[9]

Others, with no medical experience, only record the plight of their friends. Clarence Bagley recalled that "soon after leaving the Pass, father became seriously ill with the 'mountain fever,' then common in that region. . . . we had to remain in camp for several days to let him recover. . . ."[10] James Bennett's diary entry of 9 June 1850 mentions passing a "number of emigrants returning on account of sickness" and notes "many new made graves at different points along the road. In one place we counted three and at another five."[11] In one day's drive of fourteen miles, Elisha Brooks recounted many years later, "we counted thirty-two new-made graves with the inscription on the head-board announcing the death by cholera."[12]

Death could come in several ways on the Oregon Trail, and though the pioneers lived with the possibility from day to day (from hour to hour!), few travelers seem to have gotten hardened to the experience. Joseph Berrien's diary entry of 24 July 1849, notes at some length the revelation that a friend has just died:

> This morning a company of 'Packers' came to our camp and during a conversation which ensued one of them mentioned the loss on the road of one of their companions who died and was buried at the Salt Lake of 'mountain fever' and who to my great grief and surprise I discovered

to have been my old friend Jacob Rapel for whom I was looking every day. This melancholy news joined to the gloomy prospect of the sandy Desert before us, and the weakened state of my team about which I felt great anxiety contributed to depress my spirits to their lowest ebb, and forebodings of the most sorrowfull kind continued to haunt me all day.[13]

More depressing, one would think, would be death seen immediately; but Niles Searls was a hard man, ideal for the rigors of the trail, not one to be debilitated by the death of a friend. In the following passage he describes the death, probably by cholera, of one of the company. His feelings are choked in rhetoric, which finally masks them:

Calm and collected, he spoke of his approaching end without fear or trepidation. His mental faculties were unimpaired up to the latest moment of his life and when no longer able to use his voice, he showed conclusively by signs and gestures that he fully comprehended the remarks addressed to him. Gradually yielding to the embrace of the monster, death, he quietly breathed his last at four o'clock P.M., May 30th, aged 23 years.... Unable to procure other conveniences we wrapped him in his blankets and with sorrowful hearts consigned him to the 'cold earth' there to remain till the last trumpet shall call him forth to meet the reward of his many virtues.[14]

The diary was printed by Searls's grandchildren who did not admit to editing the original. If these are the words that Niles Searls wrote at the time of his friend's death, it is all the more remarkable that he had the presence of mind to record so elaborately this high-intensity event. We are left with as many questions about the diarist as about life on the prairie.

Disease and Indians were only two of the dangers on the trail; accidents also took their toll. Some travelers were victims of their own carelessness with the wagons they drove, others—as reported in James Abbey's journal entry May 2, 1850—died when firearms were mishandled:

We fell in with a mule train, and a Mr. Jamison, a Methodist preacher from Kentucky, traveling to California with his family, who, while under way, was looking down a cracked hound when one of the pistols in his belt fell out on the tongue of the wagon, with the trigger down, and went off, the full charge having passed directly through his under jaw, coming out of his mouth, tearing out several teeth and breaking the jaw in two places. The sight was awful.[15]

Joel Barnett remembered, many years later, how "Mr. Wilson's ten-year-old son fell out of the wagon and the wheels ran over both legs, breaking one of them and bruising the other quite badly."[16] Back home—wherever that was—little Wilson's broken bone would not have been so important or so traumatic. But on the trail, where there were no physicians and no medical facilities, a broken leg was a very serious matter. (This boy was luckier than most: the wagon train was near Fort Kearney; an army doctor came and bound the leg so that the boy could continue the journey to California).

The experience that Niles Searls heard from a friend ended more typically, as his diary entry of 29 June 1849 states:

> A pack horse which had turned his pack and escaped from his owner, ran among their oxen while under headway and stampeded them. They ran with the wagons several miles and ran over three of the company . . . two were so badly injured as to render their recovery hopeless. . . . [17]

Natural phenomena threatened as well. There were violent thunderstorms on the plains, and they often caused flash floods. All the writers exclaimed at the ferocity of Western lightning storms, none so eloquently as Randall Hewitt, whose memoirs were published in 1906. He recalled that on one particularly ominous midnight,

> . . . the approaching storm was heralded by constant and vivid flashes of lightning and rattling peals of thunder, which increased in intensity as the storm came down over the city from the west with a roar which was a little startling. At 12 o'clock the storm burst with all the electric fury it had accumulated; the thunder crashed and rolled with terrible earnestness, while the flashes of chain lightning and the zig-zag kind chased each other with malignant venom. With each succeeding deafening crash of thunder and blinding flash the poor mules would bray out a faint echo, through fear.
>
> Everything that stood upright seemed to be an illuminated pillar of electric flame. . . . [18]

Almost immediately after another storm, James Bennett made the following, more reticent, entry in his diary (for 2 June 1850):

> Last night we had one of the hardest rain storms I ever witnessed. Our large tent was lifted from the ground by the wind and everything contained in it completely drenched with water. In fact everything we had was wet more or less; for the rain came with such force as to beat through the wagon covers.[19]

Joseph Berrien was from Indiana, and so no stranger to tornadoes, but back home they seemed a bit less threatening, less potentially ruinous. From a bluff, on 19 May 1849, he saw one roar across the prairie, awing him as nothing else had before:

A tornado was whirling across the prarie and though there was but little on which to exert its fury still the commotion of the clouds and the immense masses of vapour whirling around with inconceivable rapidity and scattered in fragments while the roaring of the wind could be distinctly heard at 2 miles distance.... After the tornado had passed clouds of Grasshoppers fell from the sky which had been drawn up from the surface of the prairie by the Whirlwind. The cloud presented the appearance of a long funnel the small end downwards as black as ink and at times reaching the ground around which the fragments of clouds where [were] whirled with the speed of light while all the clouds in the vicinity seemed to be attracted to the centre to swell the volume of the tornado.[20]

C. W. Smith's party was bombarded by a hailstorm as they neared Chimney Rock:

This afternoon we had a fine specimen of a hailstorm in this region. A dark mass of clouds were gathering for several hours in the west, till our path was overhung with an impenetrable curtain of black, and at length the wind, which was blowing from the east, turned back, and the storm rushed upon us. It was a real hail storm. When it commenced beating upon our cattle, they became intractable, but we succeeded in unfastening them from the wagons, and having driven them behind the wagons they bore it as well as might have been expected. The hail stones were the largest I ever saw, some of them being as large as hen's eggs, and striking with force sufficient to make a man seek a shelter as soon as convenient.... Two of our men who were in advance to find a stopping-place for the night were less fortunate than ourselves. Where they were, the hailstones were as large as lemons and with force enough to bruise a man severely.... One of our men received a severe bruise on the head, caused by a hail-stone.[21]

Operations which we might take for granted, such as fording a stream, were fraught with danger for the wagon trains. Vehicles, horses, and cattle, as well as humans, were frequently lost in such crossings, particularly in Nebraska; along the Platte, a dozen or more crossings had to be effected in a day. Even if no life was lost or property destroyed, fording was such a noteworthy experience that all the diarists and memoirists remark on it. One of the latter,

Carlisle Abbott, was crossing the Platte with a small herd of horses when he discovered that the current was swifter than he had calculated:

> ... and with the band about twenty feet behind me, we went all right until we reached about the middle of the river. At this point the horses, frightened at some floating object in the water, stampeded, and before I realized the danger, they were practically on top of me, and one of them, reaching over my head and to Pomp's back, forced both Pomp and myself beneath the surface of the murky waters.
>
> Without a leader, the band now stopped and began to 'mill' ... while old Pomp and I were underneath, among their flying feet. I managed to get hold of the mane of one horse, and squeezed my head above the pack, which was now moving rapidly down-stream with the current.... I scrambled onto the back of one horse and then stepped from one to another, as a boy would cross over a lot of logs in a pond, until I reached the one farthest down the stream.[22]

And Abbott was able to save himself and the entire herd, if we are to believe this heroic first-person account, by swimming clear of the horses under water until he could get a look at them, and then scrambling for the bank after seeing that they were all safe.

Nearly all who crossed the continent (and who wrote about it) exclaimed at the wildlife they encountered. The size of the buffalo herds amazed everyone, as did the ferocity of wolves and the number of rattlesnakes. C. W. Smith noted seeing "countless numbers" of buffalo,[23] and Berrien recorded in his journal that

> this day we had the first grand sight of buffalo. I had always discredited the stories I had heard of their great numbers but I do so no longer as I am certain I saw during the day at least 20,000. They covered the vast plain for miles, the surface of the earth being literally black with them.[24]

The good Doctor Wayman took a scientific interest in the animals his company encountered along the way, making the following notes on 31 May 1852:

> One of our party killed a Prairie Dog; being the first one that I saw to handle, it become quite interesting to me (Merely for variety sake) to classify the gentleman. After the examination was over, I refered him together, with the Gopher his next neighbor, to the Rodentia family, and so let it rest. They are very numerous in places, having their Holes

and Observations near to each other, presenting quite a town like appearance. Saw a number of very large grey Woolvs to day, though this common as Cat shit under the stairs, in the states.[25]

Of greater interest than the buffalo—whose stampedes were to be feared but whose meat was desired—was the one creature whose presence was the most threatening. More dangerous than Indians on the warpath or whitewater rapids was the rattlesnake. Surely many of the pioneers had encountered rattlers and other kinds of poisonous snakes east of the Mississippi. Nevertheless, mention of them is commonplace in pioneer journals, diaries, and memoirs. One of the most sinister of pioneer nightmare-fantasies is of being in the midst of a rattlesnake "city," from which there is no escape except across hundreds of their mounds. Of course, rattlers do not live communally, but that is beside the point; the threat was felt to be real. The rattlesnake was the enemy, ever-present, silent, stealthy, repulsive to look at and to touch, merciless, and deadly. One of the central episodes in Willa Cather's *My Antonia* occurs when young Jim Burden first demonstrates his manhood by killing a big old rattler in the cornfield. So detestable were (are?) those creatures that pioneers killed them gratuitously. James Abbey reports that when his convoy stopped for the night he first cooked supper, but also "had to go some two miles for water, killed eight big rattlesnakes, and saw two antelopes." The next day was even more profitable. While stopped for dinner, he set out on the prairie "a-snaking," and killed that day ten more rattlers, one—as he says—with ten rattles on him.[26]

The Indians turned out to be something of a surprise. Many of the emigrants apparently expected to be attacked, or at least ambushed, but in the event their complaints about them were different altogether. Smith's encounter with some Sioux was friendly enough (as he noted on May 22) when they came "to beg or buy provisions, particularly sugar, coffee, and liquor. . . . Their dress is very simple and confined to adults, the children going naked, except a bit of cloth fastened about their loins. This tribe is quite friendly, and the chief signified that anything that we might lay out of our wagons would be perfectly safe. They look quite intelligent for Indians and superior to what I had expected to see."[27]

But few whites were so charitable, however condescending. Hew-itt was typical in his mistrust of Indians, and always assumed the worst of them:

A number of buck Indians came into camp under the usual pretense of
wanting to 'swap' and having 'good hearts for white men' and the rest
of that kind of entertainment. . . . The Indians had with them an assort-
ment of wares they desired to trade with the emigrants. But Indians
are inveterate beggars all the same. This band of Indians belonged to
some tribe a 'heap mile' to the north, from the bad lands, and made it
a practice, together with other wandering bands, of infesting the emigrant trail at the south to trade or pilfer as occasion offered.[28]

No really consistent picture of the Indians emerges from pioneers'
accounts; sometimes they are depicted as pitiless murderers and
sadistic torturers, sometimes merely as primitives. Hewitt, like
many other travelers, thought them contemptible petty thieves,
more pesky than lethal, like vermin "infesting" the emigrant's trail.
James Abbey and his friends felt that a show of force was necessary
to keep the local redmen in their places: "last night we put our
shooting irons in good order for the Indians if they should feel dis-
posed to trouble us. Before retiring to rest, we fired a grand salute,
to show the red skins that we were about in case of necessity." Even
in these two sentences Abbey's bravado reveals his contempt for the
potential enemy. But perhaps fear as well; for the day before—16
July 1850—he had reason to fear the Indians:

Numerous Indians were seen prowling about to-day for the purpose of
stealing. A train of horse and mule teams in advance of us had twelve
horses and ten mules stolen from them in one night. The Indians
caught the man who was on guard, gagged him, stripped him stark
naked, and wounded him in several places with arrows. Another poor
fellow, on a previous night, was shot in the back of the head, and died
in less than twenty-four hours.[29]

The Indians couldn't win. They were the "best light cavalry in the
world" as one army officer praised them, but they had to resort to
stealth and the cover of night for their depredations. Pilfering and
begging was their way of life, if we are to believe the pioneers.
Skillful enough in plains warfare to overcome the horse-and-mule
train guard in silence, they were clumsy enough to be spotted at
night by Luella Dickenson's greenhorn husband on guard duty, who
crept up on two of them without their knowledge. The Indians in the
narratives do seem more like creations of the whites' expectations
and fears than real people; very few of the reported incidents of

Indian thieving, violence, and cruelty were actually witnessed by the writer. Always the atrocities occur in the other wagon train, the train "in advance of us," or in a settlement before the writer's company arrived. Perception of the Indian seems to have been formed east of the Mississippi, and little that happened west of that river changed the minds of many whites, nor was any experience going to be allowed to interfere with formulations already made. Doctor Wayman is one of the few observers who looked at Indians rather than at The Indian: "this afternoon I visited an Indian village," he wrote in his diary entry of 21 July 1852, "and bought a good pair of Moccasins. They had 7 skin tents and as many families, in the whole, presenting all specimens from the most dirty ragged and filthy creatures up to some very fine looking men and squaws. These are the most noble looking that we have yet seen[.] They are sharp traders."[30]

The Mormons were in some ways as exotic as the Indians, certainly in many ways they were as bizarre. We remember the devastating chapters on the Mormons in Mark Twain's *Roughing It,* expressing an attitude prevalent among the Gentiles, though almost none had the wit—however venomous—to make the subject so funny. Pioneer Hewitt later wrote of the Mormons that

a more sinister, brawling, profane gang who would cut a throat or scuttle a ship, it would be difficult to collect together from the slums and cesspools of the universe. Where the particular breed of biped which controlled that cavalcade were spawned no man knoweth. It would be a gross libel on the race to call such creatures human beings, with instincts no higher than the hyena, or credit them with having feelings in common with anything that stood on two feet, clothed in the semblance of man. Fouler, viler and more blasphemous talk never in more continuous volume flowed from the lips of beings possessed of palates than came from those creatures, regardless of even the decencies of life."[31]

Memoirist Elisha Brooks was much less vituperative, though hardly more charitable. He recalled the exorbitant fees demanded by some Mormons to ferry the wagons across the Platte: Brooks's party drew their guns on the Latter Day Saints, ferried themselves across, and then "treating those profane ferrymen to a bath in the Platte to cool them off, we drove on."[32] How much of this rhetoric is for the benefit of the reader we do not know, as we cannot be certain of the authenticity of the incident at the Platte ford. But if the event did not happen exactly as Brooks tells it, the invention is nevertheless revealing.

Harriet Sherrill Ward kept a very extensive diary which she intended from the beginning to show to her children. Many of the harsh discomforts of life on the trail are not mentioned in it, or are quickly glossed over, so it is often difficult to know many of her genuine responses. She seems to have found much to praise in Salt Lake City, even the houses, which were in ways attractive to her, though simply constructed. (None of the houses, she noted, had blinds):

> Still, some of them have neat, pleasant appearances, and could you divest yourself of the idea that they were inhabited by Mormons, would in some instances be truly beautiful, with a fine stream of the purest water from the mountains flowing in front of them. . . . They boast that men are all owed a plurality of wives for the purpose of raising up a perfect race to inhabit this new Jerusalem forever; but not one of them believes a word they preach, and they are a miserable lot of extortioners upon whom the wrath of God will yet be poured out.[33]

However the wagon train emigrants may have felt about the Mormons, Salt Lake City was an oasis in the desert where the weary travelers could pause to rest and replenish the train's supplies. No doubt the Mormons often charged high prices for their goods and services, but the laws of supply and demand were not the devising of Brigham Young. Nevertheless the Mormons, like the Indians who exacted tolls for crossing certain rivers or tracts of land, were hated for profiting from the miserable necessity of the pioneers. The land must have seemed as free and available to all (white Christians) as it was open and unsettled; those who would impose tolls or in other ways charge for passage across that free land, and those who sought to make a profit from the misery of the traveler, hundreds of miles from "civilization," were bound to be resented. That those who were making a profit from the pioneers were Mormons and Indians made them doubly hated.

One characteristically American reaction to the countryside, one rooted deeply in the Protestant psyche, is shared by diarists and memoirists alike. These travelers described the uncultivated landscape—forest, prairie, or swamp—as "desert." Writing well after the fact, Cornelius Cole recalled finding the wild prairie to be in a "comparatively useless condition."[34] To become useful, and in fact to be claimed in ownership, land had to be turned to the plow and become productive. The Indians had utterly failed, in white American eyes, to possess the land because they did not in some wise alter it. For Calvin Clark, the diarist, his sighting of the Rocky Mountains conjured up visions of "rural eases" under the aegis of civilization, "when the poor old Indian shall be closely girted with bands of white brothers who shall teach him by example the nobility of toil and morality. . . . "[35]

The positive aspects of the openness of the geography also had its negative side: isolation. The emigrant had cut himself off from his society in the east, and now traveled through an inhospitable environment, with enemies and dangers on every side. Before the wheels of the wagons had begun to roll, the emigrants had heard innumerable terrifying stories of the dangers ahead. Anxiety and insecurity nurtured rumors and horror stories of the kind circulating around campfires and in the jumping-off towns of St. Joe and St. Louis. Elisha Brooks remembers that "the air was thick at Council Bluffs with tales of Indian massacres, starvation and pestilence. Here we met many people returning with harrowing stories of blood curdling horrors. . . . "[36]

It is always a risk to quote extensively from one source when trying to construct a composite view, but Brooks has written eloquently about the fearful sense of isolation—and desolation—that gripped many an emigrant on the trail:

> You can but dimly realize that from the Missouri to the Sacramento one may encounter not a solitary face of the white man except, now and then, an Indian trader or a trapper as wild as the Aborigines, an Army Post at Fort Laramie, and a Mormon settlement at Salt Lake more hostile than the Indians. It was the home of wild animals in their primeval fierceness, and the hunting ground of the Ishmaelites of the plains.[37]

Time and again with much poetic insight the desert has been compared to the sea. The geography is two-dimensional and the problems of navigation are similar; Conestoga wagons were aptly called "Prairie Schooners." To be lost in the desert (or on the plains or the prairie) was as terrifying as to be lost at sea, though not as certainly fatal. To become separated from the wagon train was a very serious matter, an event that figured in the nightmares of most pioneers and that actually happened to many; stories of such separations were often told as an implicit warning to others. Calvin Clark notes (though rather unemotionally) his finding the grave of a man "frozen to death here last Thursday . . . in a snow storm 1–4 mile behind his teem. At this time thare was several men lost that has never been herd from since."[38]

Not nearly as serious was the misadventure of Harriet Ward, who got lost on the trail for only a few moments, but they were moments filled with terror. Restraining the fright of the situation for the benefit of her family whom she knows will one day read her words, her emotions are nevertheless distinctly projected.

> A part of our train had passed on when the wagon just before Father's met with some little accident in a narrow pass which prevented him from coming on and I found myself entirely alone here. I descried a footpath which I thought from its appearance would save me about half a mile's walk so, without much reflection, I must confess, I commenced the descent, which I found somewhat difficult but at length arrived at the main road. Not a living being could I descry nor the sound of a human voice could I hear. The silence of the grave reigned around me and I began to think an Indian might possibly be peeping, even at that moment from behind the rocks behind me. I turned and retraced my steps with all possible speed, and happy indeed was I to see Father coming towards me. The train which I had lost had turned into a camping ground and had passed entirely from my sight. This will, I think, be my last adventure alone.[39]

In other ways the wagon trains were not quite like lonely ships adrift on a vast ocean. When another ship is sighted, the passengers and crew of each will wave to each other as though they had not seen other humans in months. In that liminal situation, between the "real" settled worlds of embarkation and debarkation, the ship's passenger may welcome other sojourners into the liminal world as sharers in that heady experience in which one's old life is for the moment left behind. On the ocean one is free; or at least one can feel free. Not so with the wagon train members on their way to California. There was competition, not only to get to the gold fields first, but to get to grasslands before the cattle of other trains ate all the forage. Other wagon trains meant more men to fight off an Indian attack, should it come, but it also involved the risk of catching cholera from its members. A wagon train with too many provisions might be willing to sell or barter some of them to a train that was depleted; or hungry men from another company would be tempted to steal from others. A mixed blessing, an uncertain encounter, meeting other trains. Yet diarists and memoirists never seem to fail to mention such encounters. Such episodes are one of the staples of overland trail narratives. Often enough the train encountered has "seen the elephant" and their discouraged return to the East served either to assure the narrator that he and his company are worthier because better able to adapt to prairie life, or to remind the reader that life is hard and demanding in the West and that the writer has conquered its viscissitudes, or both.

There was no more dramatic evidence of the hardships and privations to be met in the West than the litter and debris by the trail's side. These were the signs of the failures of others, demonstrations that where so many came only to wreck, those who pushed their way through safely were all the more heroic—hardy, persistent, resourceful, adaptable, and strong. Characteristically, descriptions of the littered landscape occur near the end of the narrative— not only because such debris was more likely to be seen there (as earlier trains dumped provisions that turned out to be too heavy or cumbersome), but also because it was important to point out that others have given up when the end was in sight, and that they had "seen the elephant" because their endurance had been exhausted.

Noting the carnage near the sink of the Humboldt, Joseph Berrien observed in his diary that

> . . . the loss of their teams and waggons are amongst the smallest hardships the Emigrants behind are bound to suffer. In order to push ahead and lighten their loads they have thrown away every thing (including provisions) which they could possibly spare, and consequently when their teams fail them, in a great many instances, sufferings of the most appalling nature will be sure to occur, and I should not be surprised if thousands lay their bones in that desert valley. The Road across the Desert is even now becoming unpleasant from the stench arising from the carcasses of dead Cattle and Horses and every day adds to the number.[40]

The Humboldt Sink was a popular dumping ground for overland emigrants, but not the only one: Zirkle Robinson wrote of the "Plat" that "it Look Like Destruction here. People Leaving there wagons and packing on poneys and mules and threwing a way meet and flower. Most Every person has to throw a way some thing." On July 23, 1850, James Abbey "counted twenty dead cattle, forty horses, and sixteen mules; also some fifty wagons that had been destroyed or burnt by emigrants intending to pack through." James Wilkins's experience was similar; at the Sink he found wagons and dead cattle strewn about. Within a sixteen-mile stretch he counted 163 dead oxen, mules, and horses; 65 wagons; approximately 70 ox chains, many yokes, harnesses, wardrobe trunks, and axes—and he saw all this wreckage from the trail.[41]

For many of the emigrants—the desert, the endless prairie, heat on the plains and freezing cold in the mountains, Indians and Mormons and rattlers behind them—California or Oregon was the Jerusalem at the end of their pilgrimage. Coming out of the desert (and the last leg of the journey was truly a desert), the western territories became for them the promised land.

Many, like James Abbey, were simply grateful:

> We have been greatly blessed and favored by a kind Providence throughout this long and toilsome journey. Many have fallen by accident and disease, while we have been permitted to progress thus far smoothly and quietly, in fine spirits, and enjoying good health.[42]

Cornelius Cole was more explicit about Paradise:

> ... on reaching [the apex of a hill] the whole of California appeared at once spread out before us, a most inspiring sight. It was to us the promised land. Moses in viewing Canaan from Pisgah's height could hardly have been more delighted. After a tedious, but not uninteresting journey of more than two thousand miles, through one continuous wilderness, lasting nearly three months, we had at last reached the land of gold.[43]

But this moment is recaptured for us many years after the event when Cole has had a chance to develop the dramatic moment of topping the apex of the hill from where he can see "the whole of California." And he has had ample time to compare the experience with Moses on Pisgah. We have no way of knowing whether those comparisons occurred to him during the event. Nevertheless, the metaphor was an obvious one. Elisha Brooks remembered (again, in a memoir) having

> ... washed the dust of the plains, the mountains and the deserts from our travel-stained garments and wayworn bodies, the gladdest pilgrims that you ever saw, for we knew the deserts were all behind us and only the Sierras between us and the Promised Land.[44]

For Luella Dickenson it was a land where the streams were as clear as crystal, stocked with "myriads of fish." Upon the nearby fertile plain gamboled "thousands of elk, deer, antelope, and wild horses." The hyperbole of exuberance, no doubt. Yet not all of the exhilarated rhetoric of the land of plenty is added to the memory later; Abbey's journal records that "for ourselves we had cherries, plums, raspberries, gooseberries, and filberts, which the boys gathered while in camp here" (California).[45] Their trials were over; they had been tested in the arid land and had not been found wanting. Now they would scramble for gold or silver, but that would be another narrative—or narrative cycle. The story of the Overland Trail ended once they got to paradise. That it was for many of the emigrants just the beginning does not matter to the structure of the Overland Trail story. Life had been broken up into aesthetic units with beginning, middle, and end.

Nearly all of the stories, as we have seen throughout, emphasize the tremendous difficulty of crossing the prairie on foot or with wagon trains. And, of course, it was difficult. Analysis of the narratives shows that the difficulty had several aspects, and that several qualities in the pioneers were tested. None will surprise us, though certain aspects, like that of the competition in racing across the continent, is not usually highlighted when we think of the Oregon/-California trail. But the stories of preparations, filled as they are with descriptions of wharves crowded with supplies to be sold to emigrants and the streets of jumping-off cities jammed with people waiting to assemble into convoys, suggests an impatience to be off on the journey. Then, on the trail, many emigrants are explicit about getting ahead or keeping ahead of other trains so as not to run out of grazing grass and not to get to the gold fields too late.

But by far most of the narratives tell of hardship and travail. The West was a lonely, desolate place, as accounts of guard duty at night testify. The inexperienced pioneer was sent out alone on the inhospitable prairie to protect the train from Indians and wolves and to warn of storms. At such moments all the isolation of the pioneer's situation closed in on him, and awareness of life's dangers was all the more acute. More terrifying still was the thought of getting lost, of being separated from his friends or family on the train and finding himself adrift on the endless plain. During the 1850s, so many wagon trains were headed west that getting completely lost was actually a difficult feat, but even if the lost one was picked up by another train going west, the prospect of being separated from one's family for several months or perhaps even permanently was frightening. The sailor lost at sea, the pioneer lost on the plain; terrifying visions.

Hardships abounded: there was disease, particularly cholera, diarrhea, and Rocky Mountain spotted fever; food was seldom plentiful and rarely appetizing; the weather was either too hot or too cold; the mosquitoes were (in Dr. Wayman's colorful observation) "from size of a Gnat up to a Humingbird, with their bills all freshly sharpened, and ravinous appetites";[46] there was little that was entertaining to do, and there were Indians to worry about.

The dangers to be encountered on the trail were even more numerous, and stories of them certainly had as one of their purposes the self-aggrandizement of the teller and of trail life in general. Other purposes existed as well—no tale is ever quite so simple—but this had to be among the major functions of such first-person or repeated narratives. The emigrant was (justly) proud of having endured crossing the continent and emphasized the significance of this accomplishment by seizing upon certain "tellable" events of the crossing and foregrounding them in dramatic form.

Indians may have been bothersome because of their thefts, but they were seldom murderous. Nevertheless, they appear in these writings as at least potentially dangerous. So do buffalo stampedes, packs of wolves, and rattlesnakes. Natural disasters were less frequently encountered (one would imagine) than dangerous animals or reptiles, but they too were repeatedly deemed worthy of inclusion in narratives: electrical storms, flash floods, hailstones as big as lemons, and tornadoes. Accidents were less frequent still, but still a source of possible maiming or death. Bolting horses, misfired guns, children falling under wagon wheels—these and many other accidents also increased the risks of life in a wagon train. And fording was yet another danger to both life and property. Rivers in the West always seem to have been rapid, fords few, and ferries rare. Skill, muscle, and luck (that the river would be low at the moment) were needed if the wagons as well as the young and the infirm were to be gotten across safely. That the operation was dangerous is witnessed by the many stories about fording accidents.

The encounters with Mormons and Indians were exotic experiences. Boredom was one of the commoner hardships of most overland journeys; encounters with members of either group were, at the very least interesting. It is hard to classify pioneer attitudes toward

Indians and Mormons, because they varied considerably. In a very general way it is possible to say that their attitudes were negative, but that does not seem helpful. Their attitudes did change somewhat after encountering members of both groups, but the way in which those changes occurred is also hard to identify. Attitudes toward the Indians seem to be more sophisticated than those toward Mormons and to take into account individual differences: several writers can see beyond the simplified dichotomy of either "noble savages" or "bloodthirsty barbarians." But the Indians do not seem to have been viewed more sympathetically as a result; probably too many cultural differences and too much history prevented that. Contact between Mormons and pioneers seems to have done nothing to raise the pioneers' opinion of the Mormons. The pioneers came west expecting to dislike and condemn the Mormons and wound up doing so. Perhaps because the Mormons were English-speaking Caucasians, the emigrants were disgusted and felt somehow betrayed when they were charged high prices for supplies and services; one expected that of the savages, but one's "own kind" shouldn't profit, so handsomely, from the plight of one's fellows.

But such exotica as Indians (exotic when not at war) and Mormons were not what Overland Trail stories were really about. What emerges is the danger, hardship, loneliness, and boredom of life in a cross-country caravan. The pioneer-narrators were not merely complaining about what they had to endure—hardly that at all. They were proclaiming, and with a justifiable pride, that they had overcome danger and hardship and had mastered loneliness and privation, and had struggled their way through to the end of the road. End-of-trail stories show this quite clearly. The wreckage of wagons, the litter of household goods, the quickly improvised gravestones by the trail's side were not merely curiosities of the journey. They were statements that many had failed—either through death or discouragement—but that the writer had gone ahead and succeeded where those others had had to turn back or be buried. The Overland Trail narrative, one of the few genuinely American genres, celebrates a triumph over nature and adversity. In that way as well it is a genre of the American West.

The Handcart Odyssey

OLUMES full of the lore and history of the Mormons have been collected. The amount, and the amount of analysis, must equal that written about that other intriguing American subculture, the Pennsylvania Dutch. The Mormons have been the victims of innumerable studies by students of comparative religion as well as those by countless anthropologists and sociologists who are interested in the ways that the citizens of Zion relate—and do not relate—to the surrounding Gentile world. And because Mormon culture is somewhat different from that of mainstream American life (yet who is more wholesomely American than Donny and Marie Osmond?) folklorists are interested in what cultural products, transmitted orally, the Mormons generated.

So, in choosing one folkloric form to represent them, one form or item that embodies the Mormon spirit, a great deal of material has to be discarded. The Mormons have themselves done, and have encouraged others to do, a great deal of research on their culture, and the church has not officially decided on such a representative item, or such an event. In one way it is presumptuous for a Gentile to make such a choice, not only for religious reasons but because the Mormon "spirit" will have to be viewed exoterically; the Mormons themselves may feel entirely differently about my evaluation, but since I have chosen the handcart migration, they should not feel slighted; one can hardly imagine a people's finer moment.

The religion officially began on June 6, 1830. Joseph Smith, its prophet, born in Vermont, had divine visions while an adolescent, and when he was eighteen (in 1823) was visited by the angel Nephi who revealed the existence of a set of plates covered with a hieroglyphic writing. Joseph set to work translating them, and though over one hundred pages have been lost, he had finished nearly six hundred others by 1829. In 1830 Smith published his *Book of Mormon* and organized his church, which at first had only six members. From the beginning they were dogged by the hostility of non-Mormon neighbors. They migrated from New York State to Kirtland, Ohio, and were driven further westward by the animosity of neighbors after the Panic of 1837. This time Smith and his followers settled in northwestern Missouri, near the towns of Far West and DeWitt. Here too they were persecuted and Smith led the faithful to Illinois, where he founded a Mormon city, Nauvoo.

By 1843, when Mormon peace was again shattered by the angry and concentrated rioting of their antagonistic neighbors, Nauvoo had become Illinois' largest city, containing 15,000 of the faithful. Around this time the Latter Day Saints became enemies of themselves. Joseph Smith's revelation that some of the Saints could practice polygamy set off a schism within the church, opponents denouncing him as a fallen prophet. In retaliation, Smith ordered the destruction of the presses of the newly-established *Nauvoo Expositor;* his arrest by Gentile authorities followed. Soon afterward, he and his brother were lynched by a mob of anti-Mormons, a lawless act of passion which inflamed the Gentiles throughout Illinois to even further acts of aggression. Leadership of the sect fell to Brigham Young, remarkably talented as an organizer and administrator; he decided that if the faith was to prosper, the people must move still farther west. In the autumn of 1845 Young got Illinois authorities to guarantee the safety of his flock on condition that they vacate Nauvoo the following year. The move was organized with a precision and attention to detail rivalling that of any army of the day. With guidebooks of the West in hand and in his memory, Young led his faithful in stages, through carefully prepared-for way stations, across the American prairie to what later became Salt Lake City. When the Mormons had finally arrived in their Zion, according to Mormon legend, Brigham Young announced, "This is the place."

No history of the American West can ignore the Mormons; the handcart migration was chosen for inclusion here because, whatever special religious significance it may have had for its people, it symbolizes for all of interested mankind the energy, the determination, the perseverance of those religiously inspired people who endured fourteen hundred miles of desert and mountain, heat and snow, disease and hardship. In some ways the lore of the handcart migration resembles that of the overland trail; but the Mormons crossed the plains on foot and, as though to try their faith even more sorely, pushed and pulled their carts as well.

The handcart companies, ranging in size from as few as one hundred emigrants to several hundred, embodied collectively the iron will of all the Mormons who made that crossing to Zion, whether by handcart or in wagons. They embodied that resolution to build a new nation under God—a new Zion—in the wilderness and to worship in their own way without interference from the Gentiles. Crossing the plains on foot, hauling those carts through soft sands and river mud, and over the Rockies, was an appropriate symbolic embodiment of the Mormons' tenacity. Each crossing took three to four months and encapsulated the noblest aspects of religious fervor of the citizens of Zion.

Between 1849 and 1855, approximately 16,000 Europeans took up residence in what became Utah and environs. In the last year of that period alone, 4,225 emigrated across the desert. A great many of these came part of the way by train, a great many more in wagon trains; all had some financial support from the church in Salt Lake. But drought and a plague of grasshoppers suddenly decimated Mormon crops, depleting the church's treasury, making a cheap means of transporting converts across the continent essential. In response, Brigham Young or one of his advisers hit upon the idea of pedestrian traffic from the Mississippi to the Salt Lake, with handcarts to haul supplies and personal belongings. The idea was quickly adopted; the first handcart company was organized in 1856. The Biblical parallel was not lost on the Mormon leaders; it was, in fact, forcefully brought to the fore. Franklin D. Richards, president of the Perpetual Emigration Fund and subsequent scapegoat for the migration losses, editorialized in the *Millennial Star* (1 March 1856):

> When ancient Israel fled from bondage into the wilderness, they had not even the privilege of taking provisions for their journey, but had to trust to the good hand of God for their daily bread. If the Saints in these lands have not seen such times, the future will reveal them. . . . Ancient Israel traveled to the promised land on foot, with their wives and little ones. The Lord calls upon modern Israel to do the same.[1]

These themes—of a new nation of Israel also crossing the desert on foot, trusting only to God—permeated all spheres of Mormon philosophy and Mormon understanding of the world as they knew it, and of the momentous migration that was about to begin. A circular published in early 1856 as a guide for emigrants echoes this Old Testamental theme: "the mode now proposed to the Saints for traveling up to Zion so nearly resembles that of ancient Israel in the wilderness, that it must elicit the peculiar favor and blessing of the Lord upon it."[2]

The first verse of the best-known of the Handcart Songs addresses the Converted Saints of the Old World, encouraging them to make the triumphant crossing:

> Ye Saints that dwell on Europe's shore
> Prepare yourselves with many more
> To leave behind your native land
> For sure God's judgments are at hand.
> Prepare to cross the stormy main
> Before you do the valley gain
> And with the faithful make a start
> To cross the plains with your handcart.[3]

We will never know on a case-by-case basis the reactions of those Europeans who learned that they were to cross "The Great American Desert" on foot, but it is not unreasonable that nearly all of them accepted this as their lot; it would be a portion of what they would have to suffer to dwell in Zion. Granted the ultimate bliss that would be theirs, the crossing may not have seemed prohibitive. Several may have opted out right then; we know that several chose to turn back after the companies had been on the road for a few days and they had had a taste of what the next thousand miles might be like. The first songs and poems written about the handcart idea express a great exuberance for the trek to Zion, and an airy disregard for the luxury of travel in wagons, as Emily Woodmansee tells it:

> Oh, our faith goes with the handcarts,
> And they have our hearts' best love;
> 'Tis a novel mode of traveling,
> *Devised by the God above.*
>
> *Chorus*
> Hurrah for the Camp of Israel!
> Hurrah for the handcart scheme!
> Hurrah! Hurrah! 'tis better far
> Than the wagon and ox-team.

> And *Brigham's their executive,*
> He told us the design;
> And the Saints are proudly marching on,
> Along the handcart line.
>
> Who cares to go with the wagons?
> Not we who are free and strong;
> Our faith and arms, with right good will,
> Shall pull our carts along.[4]

Full of healthy enthusiasm, this song is also full of rhetoric that one does not usually find in folksongs: "mode," "scheme" in this sense, "executive," even "design." The contracted " 'tis," here used twice, is a bit elegant. I do not wish to be misunderstood; the sincerity of these songs is not the question. Their vigorous piety shines through in every line. It is a matter of placing them generically, and the only point of this discussion is to suggest that in the form in which they have come to us, the Mormon handcart songs do not look like the folksongs found elsewhere in America. The significance of that claim, if true, should not be of interest to the defenders of the Mormon faith, but to students of folklore and popular culture.

Elder Philip Margetts' "The Missionary's Handcart Song," written in 1857, touches upon the divine aspect of the journey, sees it as the emergence of the soul from the darkness, and anticipates that the spiritual improvement of the emigrants will give them added strength, rather than diminishing it as the miles stretch out, and that in the future they will see the divine wisdom of the momentary discomfort:

> Then come ye faithful ministers
> With blessings now we'll go
> To gather out the honest hearts
> From darkness and from woe.
> Our strength increasing day by day
> As from this land we part
> We'll bless the day that we were called
> To go with our handcart.[5]

From darkness and from woe into the blessed daylight of Zion . . . Not knowing what that torturous trip would be like, perhaps, or transported by the idea of a modern-day exodus, Lydia Alder wrote her own "Handcart Song":

We climb the hills and far away
Then down where sleeping valleys lay
While still the miles onward roll
Till Zion rises on our sight
We pull our handcarts with our might
Triumphant reach the goal.[6]

It all sounds so easy that we wonder whether Alder had actually made the trip herself and to what extent this is genuinely folklore. The song (poem?) does not seem to have much, if any, oral currency; and while it is no doubt an honest expression of the creator's feelings, the extent to which it expresses the feelings of the handcart migrants is unknown. Its easy optimism, rather, does sound like that of an official church document or at least one that would have church sponsorship. It lacks the texture of traditional folk lyrics; and the idea of gaining strength when the emigrants might well be expected to have weakened, used also by Elder Margetts, is one that would come to mind naturally, given the dynamics of the overland journey. The crossing was going to be exhausting, and the handcart companies were going to need all the strength they could muster. That their energy would increase as they neared Zion, rather than decrease from the labors of their odyssey, would occur, spiritually and polygenetically, to a great many people who thought even superficially about the subject, though the frequent use of this theme suggests that it was current.

The handcarts were usually constructed entirely of wood, even the axles, each of which consisted of a single hickory pole. Hickory was a sturdy wood and cheap; nevertheless, it was not always up to the demands of the journey. Occasionally iron tires banded the wheels, but most of the carts had wheels of wood only. For city streets or smooth country roads they were serviceable, but they were not always up to the conditions the emigrants would encounter on the trail. Most of them appear to have been made for this purpose alone, and for whatever reason were not well-made. Unseasoned wood was often used, which could not stand up to the rigors of the Western climate.

In design the handcarts were basically similar to those used by porters and street sweepers in the East; the design was at least a familiar one to carpenters, though the execution varied. The carts were six or seven feet long, Hafen writes,[7] and four or five feet wide, though the cart in the monument in Temple Square in Salt Lake City appears to be a bit smaller than that. The cargo bed was flat, and boarded on all sides with gunwales about six inches high, although some carts had higher sides. About four to five hundred pounds of supplies and belongings could be carried as a payload, piled high and lashed to the bed (The cart in the monument has a very modest load. I do not draw firm conclusions from this representation since the sculptor had to consider aesthetic proportions in his design more than historical accuracy).

A few of the carts were covered and so had to be sturdier to support the stress of the added weight, but this added durability meant added pounds that had to be manhandled overland. At the front of the cart were two slender poles joined by a bar, sometimes curved, against which the hauler pushed. There were usually two haulers to a cart, one to a covered wagon drawn by horses or oxen. As the songs tell us, and as the Temple Square monument shows, the carts were also pushed from behind. The emigration companies were organized so that approximately every five members had a cart and there were twenty saints to a tent, with each canvas under the supervision of a tent captain. One Mormon poet has eulogized the humble wagon as

> A crude and lifeless thing of wood—
> Two wheels, two shafts, and a box.
> Yet it rolled the road to a Zion home
> With never a mule or ox.
> Propelled by blood of the human heart
> The wood became a walking cart.
> Creeping thirteen hundred miles
> It squeaked and groaned and whined
> Through dust, and rivers of mud and sweat,
> Greased with a bacon rind.
> At night, as silent as the graves
> New-hidden under grassy waves.[8]

Possibly the most interesting line, historically, is one of the poorest poetically, telling us that bacon grease was used as a lubricant. It is not poetry descriptive of the experience (of crossing the plains), but of the spirit of an exodus to Zion. None of the Mormon handcart poems seem to come out of the labor of pushing those crude and lifeless things for more than a thousand miles; they are exclamations of righteous joy and pious pride in the satisfaction of an ideal fulfilled—they do not tell us what it was like bringing it about.

The diaries of Twiss Bermingham and Archer Walters,[9] a carpenter, tell the story of the handcart migration from that other, experiential side. They dutifully record deaths, the mournful chore of fashioning coffins, the heat and the dust of the road, the necessity of having to repair constantly damaged carts. The complaints of these writers sound, naturally enough, like those of travelers on the overland trail to California and Oregon. The pilgrims are "very faint from lack of food," the "storm, thunder and lightning raged fearfully all night, blew up part of our tent and wet all our clothes through."

It will be helpful, I think, to abstract portions of the diary of Archer Walters, a member of the first company, to understand something of what life was like for him that summer of 1856. The first two or three weeks passed uneventfully and the company covered a lot of ground: eighteen miles on July 21st, the same on the 28th, only ten miles on August 6th, but twenty-five on the next day. A storm had arisen on July 22nd about which Walters had little to say; on the 26th he reported that lightning struck and killed one of the travelers, and injured several others. The cart had to be serviced and repaired on August 3rd, and again five days later. That day (August 8th) the company progressed fifteen miles, though on the dimmer side he recorded, "my wife very ill-tempered at times."

One of the older Saints, a Brother Sanderson, got himself separated from the company on that same day, the 8th. As with all others on the trail, as we have read in the accounts of Gentiles California-bound, getting lost was a terrifying experience for the individual involved, and worrisome for the rest of the company. Happily, Brother Sanderson was recovered the next day, a day also spent repairing carts, and one in which the caravan was consequently limited to fifteen miles' progress.

On the 10th Walters recorded that "all or most" of the emigrants are "bad with the diarrhea or purging," the cause being unknown. It might have come from muddy river water which they had eagerly drunk or from bad buffalo meat. The next day, during which they covered seventeen more miles, he reported: "very weak myself. I expect it is the short rations." But on that day the only death was of a cow. On the 17th another of the company died. The same day they forded some creeks, always a major experience for overland travelers, as we know. On the 19th the most significant "news" was the discovery of some buffalo chips to burn. On August 23rd they were sixteen miles closer to Zion at day's end; they shot one of their herd for meat, and Walters remarks that it was "very thankfully received."

On the 24th while the emigrants rested, an event took place which must have happened from time to time but is seldom mentioned by the diarists. One of the Mormon leaders met with the company and chastised them for their transgressions while on the trail: "Brother Ellsworth spoke some time and said we had made great improvement. That last week there had been less quarreling and those that had robbed the handcarts, or wagons, unless they repent their flesh would rot from their bones and go to hell." Occasionally the diaries tell of the quarreling on such trains; when the weather was uncomfortably hot, the rations short, and strangers had been together for several weeks, conflicts almost inevitably arose. Especially on the prairie, with so little in the way of variation of daily routine, and even less opportunity for amusement and diversion, tempers rubbed raw. Thieving from the other carts (or wagons) is something we hear less about, and it surprises us to hear of it because we think of the wagon trains as embodying a great solidarity, the handcart companies even more so because of the religious bond of the members and the compelling purpose of their journey. But they were human, after all.

On August 25th, a day on which Walters saw "many Indians," an axle on one of the carts broke; nothing could be done about it. The company made nineteen miles that day, and the same distance the next when they arrived at Fort Laramie. The diarist traded a dagger for a piece of bacon and some salt and was so hungry that he started eating the bacon raw. On the following day, the 27th, Walters and his family had bacon and meal porridge, the "best supper for many weeks." But by then the company was down to short rations: three-quarters of a pound of flour per person each day.

Though Walters noted for the entry of August 31st that he felt "very poorly, faint and hungry," the company advanced twenty-two miles that day. They had gone the same impressive distance the day before, but on the day after, the 1st of September, they rested, primarily to repair several damaged carts. Walters noted the death of one of the company, unnamed. Twenty-four hours later, Brother Sanderson died. On the 7th the advance was a huge twenty-six miles, but on that day Brother Nipras died. He was simply "left on the road." September 14th was another rest day; only three miles forward, then a halt to mend the carts again, while the women washed clothes in a convenient stream. On that day Sister Mayer died.

September 14th was the last entry in Brother Walter's diary. Of approximately 275 in his company, fewer than a dozen did not complete their journey. Walters managed to make it to the end—to Salt Lake City, but two weeks later he passed away, from what causes we do not know.

One of the oases in the first part of the journey was Florence, Nebraska. When the first companies arrived there on July 17th, 1856, the *Millennial Star* commended their "fine health and spirits, singing as they came along, Elder J. D. T. McAllister's noted handcart song—'Some must push and some must pull,' etc. My heart is gladdened as I write this, for methinks I see their merry countenance and buoyant step, and the strains of the handcart song seem ringing in my ears like sweet music heard at eventide or in a dream."[10] We have already seen the first stanza of that song with its address to "ye Saints that dwell on Europe's shore"; with merry countenance and buoyant step those companies sang

> The land that boasts of liberty
> You ne'er again may wish to see
> While poor men toil to earn their bread
> And rich men are much better fed,
> And people boast of their great light,
> You see they are as dark as night.
> And from them you must make a start
> To cross the plains with our handcarts.

> *CHORUS*
> But some will say it is too bad
> The Saints upon their feet to pad
> And more than that to push a load
> As they go marching upon the road.
> We say this is Jehovah's plan
> To gather out the best of man,
> And women too, for none but they
> Will ever gather in this way.

> As on the way the carts are hurled
> 'Twould very much surprise the world
> To see the old and feeble dame
> Lending her hand to push the same.

The young girls they will dance and sing
The young men happier than a king,
The children they will laugh and play
Their strength increasing day by day.

But ere before the valley gained
We will be met upon the plains
With music sweet and friends so dear
And fresh supplies our hearts to cheer.
Then with the music and the song
How cheerfully we'll march along
So thankfully you make a start
To cross the plains with our handcarts.

When we get there among the rest
Industrious be and we'll be blessed
And in our chambers be shut in
While Judgment cleanse the earth from sin.
For well we know it will be so,
God's servants spoke it long ago,
An tell us it's high time to start
To cross the plains with our handcarts.[11]

We can never know what the *Millennial Star* reporter witnessed when those companies marched into Florence. Perhaps they did sing McAllister's handcart song; one can believe that however tired they may have been, the emigrants would have pulled themselves together for the last mile or so, and driven by a natural enough pride in their purpose and their on-going accomplishment of it, would have sung loudly as they entered Florence. But we are taxed to believe that the words of the song would accurately describe the feelings of those emigrants after several weeks on the plains, or after three months—as they entered Salt Lake City.

Twiss Bermingham was a more loquacious diarist than Archer Walters and longer suffering. He was with the second company, which arrived at the same time as Walters's; Bermingham does not spare us unpleasant details, and we have a better idea of hardship on the trail as a result; in mid-journey, on July 28th, he complains, "rather weak this morning and terribly annoyed by two boils, one on my jaw about as big as a pigeon egg and another on the calf of my leg which torments me very much when drawing the handcart." And the next day: "boils very sore this morning but must draw on the cart still. With such sores at home I would lie upon two chairs and never stir until they were healed."

Two days later Bermingham's discomfort had become more serious still: "I was so exhausted with my sores and the labor of pulling that I was obliged to lie down for a few hours after arriving in camp before I could do anything ... we were obliged to do with a bit of bread and a pint of milk," he complained, "rather little for five persons." He was so ill that he did not cook supper that evening, and just made do. Three days later he had pulled his cart through six miles of heavy sand:

> Some places the wheels were up to the boxes and I was so weak from thirst and hunger and being exhausted with the pain of the boils that I was obliged to lie down several times, and many others had to do the same. Some fell down. I was very much grieved today, so much so that I thought my heart would burst—sick—and poor Kate [his wife] at the same time—crawling on hands and knees, and the children dying with hunger and fatigue. . . . About twelve o'clock a thunder storm came on, and the rain fell in torrents. In our tent we were standing up to our knees in water and every stich we had was the same as if we were dragged through the river. Rain continued until 8 o'clock the following morning.[12]

But life soon got a little better for Twiss and his family, though it would deteriorate again at the end of the month. On August 24th the second company gained only seven or eight miles; Bermingham was so sick he "had to lie on the wet grass all night, and go to bed supperless, there being no firewood to cook." They had had to ford twenty streams that week, he wrote. On the 5th of September he noted, "snow four feet deep on the mountain all around us." But the worst was past; on the 21st of September, he noted with satisfaction that despite the cold, they had traveled about twenty-five miles each day since the 5th, and on two days covered thirty-two miles each. Bermingham's company marched into Salt Lake City on the 26th.

Even with his boils and his meager rations, Bermingham was lucky. He got through before the snows made the trail impassable. John Chislett of the fourth company recalled the horrors inflicted upon his group. Chislett did not keep a diary (or at least none was published); the following descriptions are from his recollections

printed nearly two decades later, after he had renounced his faith
and had left the church. The account is more literary than the
others; it is better organized, more carefully written and more detailed, and the drama of each situation is better prepared for than
in a diary.

> Cold weather, scarcity of food, lassitude and fatigue from over-exertion,
> soon produced their effects. Our old and infirm people began to
> droop.... Life went out as smoothly as a lamp ceases to burn when the
> oil is gone. At first the deaths occurred slowly and irregularly, but in
> a few days at more frequent intervals, until we soon thought it unusual
> to leave a campground without burying one or more persons. Death was
> not long confined in its ravages to the old and infirm, but the young and
> naturally strong were among its victims.... Many a father pulled his
> cart, with his little children on it, until the day preceding his death. I
> have seen some pull their carts in the morning, give out during the day,
> and die before next morning.... When any in my hundred died I had
> to inter them; often helping to dig the grave myself.... We traveled on
> in misery and sorrow day after day.... [13]

And then the snow fell. Once, because of a storm, provisions
couldn't be issued. The emigrants began to slaughter their emaci-
ated cows for meat. When the first rescuers arrived with food, three
days' provisions were consumed almost at once by the starving pilgrims. Dysentery, Chislett adds, killed several in their camp. They
were so weak that on the third day after the rescue wagons had
arrived, nine more died.

Approximately five hundred pilgrims had assembled in Iowa
City that spring. After desertions and drop-outs, four hundred and
twenty people, by Chislett's estimate, began the journey out of Florence (Nebraska). Four hundred of those were assigned to handcarts,
the others to wagons. According to Chislett, sixty-seven (17 percent)
died on the journey, another two or three soon after they arrived.
Many of the Mormons lost toes or fingers, even hands to frostbite;
one woman traveler with Chislett, he says, lost both feet.

Captain Willie, who had responsibility for the Fourth Company,
put the number of dead at sixty-two; the difference between his
count and Chislett's is negligible, it would be pointless to make
anything of so slight a discrepancy, and exactitude is not necessary
to demonstrate the suffering of that emigrant party. The next company, the Fifth—Martin's—had greater losses by far. Between 135
and 150 of the original 622 perished on the trail, twenty-four percent
if the latter casualty figure is used.

When the earlier two companies arrived in Salt Lake City, they were received joyously by their Brothers and Sisters. Counsellor Wilford Woodruff recalled the arrival of one such party:

> . . . my feelings were inexpressible to behold a company of men, women, and children, many of them aged and infirm, enter the city of the Great Salt Lake, drawing 100 handcarts . . . with which they had traveled some 1,400 miles in nine weeks, and to see them dance with joy as they traveled through the streets. . . . We can now say to the poor and honest in heart, come home to Zion, for the way is prepared.[14]

But there would have been no dancing in Willie's or Martin's companies, however else their members would have expressed whatever emotions they were feeling as they entered Salt Lake City. With relief, or out of an exhausted yet brave show of determination, out of frustration and anger, or a cowed thankfulness, or out of joy at being delivered, they might have sung this handcart song as they stumbled or were carried into Zion:

> Obedient to the Gospel call
> We serve our God the all in all
> We hie away to Zion
> We do not wait to ride all day
> But pull our handcarts all the way
> And Israel's God rely on.
>
> CHORUS
> To Zion pull the handcart
> While singing every day
> The glorious songs of Zion
> To haste the time away.
>
> Our prayers arise to greet the sun
> And when his shining course is run
> We gather round the campfire
> To talk of God and all his ways
> His wondrous work of Latterdays
> Until the dancing blaze expires.
>
> We climb the hills and far away
> Then down where sleeping valleys lay
> While still the miles onward roll
> Till Zion rises on our sight
> We pull our handcarts with our might
> Triumphant then reach the goal.

> To those we left beside the way
> To dream where summer breezes play
> Saw in the camp fire's vivid blaze
> Fair Zion with her golden skies
> Grand temples there that stately rise
> And satisfied rest always.[15]

During the four years of the handcart experiment—1856, 1857, 1859, and 1860—2,962 emigrants in ten companies brought six hundred and fifty-three handcarts and about fifty wagons from Iowa City to Salt Lake City, a distance of nearly 1,400 miles. Approximately two hundred and fifty Saints died along the way, most of them in those companies caught by early snowfalls. Because of the possibility of repetitions of those disasters in the cold, and thanks to a better financial situation, the handcart movement was cancelled after 1860. Its success cannot be easily or simply measured; nearly three thousand new Saints were brought to Zion, though at great cost. In the long run, it may be that the determination of the handcart emigrants acted to inspire their fellow Saints both in Salt Lake City and those yet to make the crossing. That the handcart has become a symbol of Mormon tenacity and the strength of their faith is not open to question; the handcart monument in Temple Square shows what the movement has meant to the faithful. And the volume of poetry and song celebrating the events of those five years of Mormon history is further testimony to the great importance of that "crude and lifeless thing of wood."

The handcart folksongs reflect a certain point of view, however. We have seen that they did not arise from the handcart emigrants themselves, that they do not express what it was like to have been in one of the companies; these songs have church approval, and at least one of them, Elder McAllister's, was composed by a churchman. In this sense they are akin to the products of popular culture, that is, those in which the artist's products are mediated in some way before they are released to the public. The mediating agency tells the artist what he may create, and then promotes the creation to an audience. The relationship of artist and audience/consumer is more direct in both folk and elite art.

Are the handcart songs the artifacts of a popular culture rather than authentic folk creations? Probably, but in making that distinction, which is academic and not one that would trouble the Mormons, we would want to decide what is to be gained by this classification. When we think of popular culture, that mediated culture for a mass audience, we usually expect to find both mechanical reproduction and a commercial mediator. Phonograph records made endlessly from a master, reproduced color prints of a Rockwell painting on the cover of the *Saturday Evening Post,* the disposable detective or spy novel published as a (disposable) paperback, McDonald's hamburgers: any one of these items, or any one of a hundred thousand more, can, if properly evaluated, tell us something about the culture that produced and consumed it. The mediating agency is an important element in the artist/audience or producer/consumer chain because it tells us something about artist, audience, producer, and consumer. Studying it will also reveal something about the mediator and about the totality—the society—as a whole.

The handcart songs reveal something about the Mormon church's attitudes during the late eighteen fifties and about its expectations of the Saints. Interpolated, the existence of these songs makes a statement about most Mormons, though unfortunately not as much as we would like about the participating Mormons. How did they feel about that imposing symbol of the faith's persistence, the handcart? We know that at least one of the songs was sung on the road, as "with merry countenance and buoyant step, and the strains of the handcart song . . . ringing in my ears," the company entered Florence. "Merry" and "buoyant" may be optimistic interpretations, but on the basis of this report one would be hard put to argue that the emigrants were not singing MacAllister's song. It may have been given to the pilgrims from "above," but the fact that it did enter oral tradition suggests that even though it may not have been accurately expressive of the suffering most Mormons felt while on the plains, the song did express some ideal to which they adhered. When we speak of "orality," we should consider that composition, transmission, and performance can be oral and that folklore items can embody only one or two of those aspects. Though their composition was as a printed, fixed text, though some of the transmission process (not all) was also in writing, the handcart songs quickly entered into oral currency and assumed a folkloric existence of their own.

Variations of the so-called "fixed" text have now been collected from various informants. I have heard a field recording of MacAllister's song performed by a Mr. Hilton of Utah that varies somewhat from each of the printed versions that have appeared. Hilton's introductory remarks inform us that he *heard* the song when he was a boy and that he has *heard* it sung often. However "pure" the handcart songs may be, then, as folklore, they do express an aspect of the ethos of the Mormon church during the eighteen fifties, an aspect that was interiorized by many of its adherents. Many still do. We should not be too concerned over the folk/popular question in this case, since the materials of both categories reveal evaluations of their host culture; and that is what the folk/popular taxonomy was supposed to have been about in the first place.

"Like Israel of old," Leroy Hafen concludes, "these modern 'children of God' responded to a prophet's voice."[16]

The handcart migration is a modern typological event of a distinctive sort. We commonly think of typology as a certain kind of literary relationship, or of an event in the past related to an anticipatory passage/event in Scripture. The Mormon handcart movement was conceived and executed in the knowledge that the event at hand would be actual, would recapitulate Biblical events, and would also be spiritually symbolic at the same time. We have seen that Mormon commentators on the handcart movement pointed out the parallel with the flight of the children of Israel across the Sinai as the Latter Day Saints pushed and pulled their carts across Nebraska. The migration was, in Dante's terms, moral as well: it represented the movement from sin to grace, a passing also from the darkness and sinfulness of the Gentile world into the light and emerging strength of Zion; the movement was both individual and corporate in that it also brought about the establishment of God's kingdom as a gathering place for all the faithful. Whether the fourth aspect of Dante's scheme, the anagogical, was present, is uncertain, as I have not been able to discover any texts which discuss the migration as a passing of the soul from the corruption of this world to everlasting glory. Perhaps the Mormon concern with this world as well as with the next prevented this final analogy.

If the Mormons remember and revere the handcart movement with pride, that is their understandable and justifiable right. The most eloquent words of memorial come from novelist Wallace Stegner, who understood that the handcart also symbolizes for the outsider an iron determination that transcends sect and region:

But if courage and endurance make a story, if human kindness and helpfulness and brotherly love in the midst of raw horror are worth recording, this half-forgotten episode of the Mormon migration is one of the great tales of the West and of America.[17]

The Mormons remember. The Gentiles should also remember, for the issue is not merely sectarian, it is the universally human qualities of perseverance and determination.

Custer's Last Stand

USTER shares one trait with nearly all the heroes of our civilization: what he is said to have done or not to have done, what he is or is not thought to have been, have little to do with the real man and the real events of his life. He is what we want him—what we project him—to be. Custer was a hero to most people in nineteenth-century America, a goat to most in the twentieth century, yet nothing happened to change the public's opinion of him. He did not rise from his shallow grave on "Custer Ridge" to slay more Indians or to confess to the public that he had made a terrible mistake. No new discovery of battle orders was made, no new witness came forth to insist that Custer be court-martialled for incompetence. Yet our perceptions of him have changed, by almost that proverbial 180 degrees. In this sense Custer is the model example of the assertion that the folk hero is what we make of him.

Custer and his "Last Stand" have been the subject of nearly one thousand paintings and illustrations and more than five hundred essays and books.[1] More than a score of movies have made the Boy General and his last battle the focus of their attention, as has at least one television serial. Custer is the heavy of anti-war sentiment, yet still the hero of a large body of cultists. Seldom given more than a sentence or two in any history of the American West, he is by far the best known of the American military men who fought in the Plains Wars. His defeat was the most decisive Indian victory in the West, yet in the popular imagination Custer is the Indian-fighter par excellence. No survey of the folk and popular lore of the American West can ignore him.

Several legends of considerable antiquity have attached themselves to Custer's name, demonstrating once more the independent life of tradition and its affinity with famous people and dramatic events. I mention briefly here only legends that have to do with his death, rather than any dealing with the battle, because of their implications for Custer as a folk hero.[2] For instance, in a variant of the Pocahontas-John Smith legend, Mo-na-se-tah, a Cheyenne maiden, who allegedly bore Custer's child while she was his captive at Camp Supply (Oklahoma) in 1869, saves the general's body from mutilation by her kinsmen at the Little Bighorn. Her tribesmen are about to maim the "Yellow Hair" when Mo-na-se-tah recognizes her former lover and steps forward to prevent this final humiliation. Pocahontas saved her beloved's life; her Montana counterpart was too late for that, but she was able to protect his corpse.

Another legend, which had nation-wide currency in sensational newspaper articles of the day, was that of "the eaten heart." As the story went, a Sioux brave, Rain-in-the-Face, had sworn vengeance upon Custer for an earlier insult and fulfilled his vow at the Little Bighorn. The program notes to Cassilly Adam's painting "Custer's Last Fight," copied by F. Otto Becker and immortalized by Anheuser-Busch in barrooms around the country, credit Rain-in-the-Face with slaying Custer, but the really striking part of the legend is the detail that Custer's chest had been ripped open and the heart torn from it. Longfellow's poem "The Revenge of Rain-in-the-Face" added the gory detail of the heart impaled on a lance around which Rain-in-the-Face and his friends cavorted.[3]

While this brutal business was taking place, a Presence was making itself felt at a divine service attended by the regiment's officers' wives back in the garrison at Fort Lincoln (near Bismarck, Dakota Territory). The ladies had gathered in Libbie Custer's quarters, and at the very time when the five companies of the Seventh Cavalry and their general were being annihilated, the ladies—without knowing why—were moved to sing "Nearer My God to Thee."

And as was only to be expected after so famous a disaster, particularly one so intriguing, stories of "lone survivors" abounded. Some, like the alleged eye-witness accounts by the Crow scout, Curly, were invented by others, but many survivors were self-proclaimed. These men had their portion of fame ready-made; their bland lives could partake of the glory of having "ridden with Custer." Their stories were as redolent of avoided calamity as are the modern stories of people who at the last minute cancel their reservations on the flight that crashes. Like Ishmael, who alone survived to tell us all, lone survivors have always had their brushes with glory and have "lived" to tell us about it. That they "survived" the Little Bighorn disaster in greater numbers than the known total of men with Custer is a measure of the battle's enduring fame.[4]

Nearly a century after the fact we can speak of the legendary, even epic, quality of the man and his death. In the lives of the heroes of old, people saw more than just a mortal life. For the popular imagination the ardently admired hero comes to embody some transcendental quality that is actually the basis for adoration of him; Ajax is typical, worshipped as a god at Salamis and admired as a great warrior at a Hellespont memorial. In time, many epic heroes —the actual men whose lives are the basis of the narratives we hear and read—acquire many of the same attributes out of a common pool of traditional motifs. They are remembered and revered for some quality that their admirers cherish (Leonidas' civic devotion, Roland's pride and fighting skill, Lazar's piety), and a cult keeps their memory alive, perpetuating and enhancing it. As Jan de Vries says, "priests, cult and myth are inseparable. The heroic legend growing and living in such a milieu cannot but assume the character of a myth. A myth, not of a god, but of a man who raised himself to the level of the gods."[5]

In the century since the event, narratives of Custer and his last battle have assumed a form that lends them to structural analysis. Custer is daring and bold; his second-in-command, Major Marcus Reno, in popular tradition is prudent and cautious. (Reno, with three companies, first attacked the Indian village, but through subsequent retreats he saved the bulk of his command, while Custer and his men perished.) From "prudence" it is no great leap to "overcaution," and from there it is no mighty jump to "cowardice," and many did in fact accuse Reno of that gravest of military offenses. Custer died while Reno survived: the bold and daring and thus the admirable man is destroyed while his shadow, the "ignoble" Reno, lives. This unjust paradox is resolved, as Lévi-Strauss might have it, by bestowing glory and fame upon the deceased: bravery is in this way rewarded, while the bitterness of death is neutralized, even sweetened, by nobility.

Custer has a cult—Associates of the Little Bighorn—and he has several shrines—at the battlefield, at West Point, and at Monroe,

Michigan.[6] Such affection and attention may seem strange to us now, but in the last century Custer was admired with a reverence approaching adoration. Only one year after the battle, James J. Talbot, who was not one of the general's admirers, wrote that he had become "one of the gods of the people."[7] Former Confederate General T. L. Rosser, who had been a West Point classmate of Custer's and his opponent in the Valley Campaign as well, wrote to the *Chicago Tribune* July 8, 1876 (the battle of the Little Bighorn took place on June 25, 1876) that "as a soldier I would sooner to-day lie in the grave of Gen. Custer and his gallant comrades alone in that distant wilderness, that when the last trumpet sounds, I could rise to judgment from my post of duty, than to live in the place of the survivors of the siege on the hills."[8] Such sentiments were offensive to some, of course: When General Sturgis, whose son died with Custer, wrote to the *Tribune* on July 19, 1876, he was dismayed by how far the veneration of Custer had gone in a short time: "What I especially deprecate is the manner in which some papers have sought to make a demigod out of Custer. . . . He was insanely ambitious of glory, and the phrase "Custer's Luck" affords a good clew to his ruling passion."[9]

Nevertheless the apotheosis went on, and the eulogy in the *Chicago Tribune* expressed the sentiments of most of its readers:

> Throughout he was the same dashing cavalryman, whether upon the plains or in the charge down the Shenandoah, the Murat of our service, fearless, reckless of the odds against him, and confident of success against almost any odds by the elan with which he bore down upon an opposing column. . . . Added to his dauntless courage was the loftiest ambition, that made him eager to seize any and every opportunity to distinguish himself in the field. . . . In appearance he was the very beau ideal of the soldier—tall, lithe, and sinewy, with the free, firm carriage of the veteran of many fields, and the dashing grace of the gallant cavalier.[10]

The *New York Herald* began a subscription campaign to erect a memorial to Custer and his men which would "be the people's appreciation of valor and duty, and, as such, we trust it will be taken up by the people in all parts of the country, and be a worthy tribute to the general and his immortal deed."[11] The response was immediate and lavish, but none was more effusive than the letter of a young schoolgirl:

I enclose ten cents, (all I can spare), for a monument to the noble
General Custer. I am a school girl, but can read the newspapers, and
my heart was filled with pity when I read in your paper of the awful
slaughter done by the Indians on General Custer and his army.... I
would give the world to have had one look at the fearless General
Custer; and then he was so young and, as people say, so handsome. I
could cry tears over his sad fate.... Leave it to the school girls and a
monument will soon be raised to the gallant General Custer, for he was
a man.[12]

The popular poetry was, if anything, even more impassioned.
Laura S. Webb wrote two poems about the battle in the same year
it happened. "Custer's Immortality"—the title alone indicates to
which world the author assigns her hero—has it that the Seventh
Cavalry "rode straight into the jaws of Death,/Into the mouth of
Hell" (not even Tennyson was safe!):

> All this the whole world knows, and more,
> For, on the scroll of Fame,
> In letters of Immortal light,
> Shines CUSTER'S deathless name![13]

In "A Wreath of Immortelles," she initiated her hero into Olym-
pus:

> Oh, twine a wreath of immortelles
> Around the storied name
> Of Custer, dashing, daring, gay—
> Who now belongs to Fame.[14]

For Francis Chamberlain Holley, Custer had already arrived in
an American Valhalla:

> Come on, my boys! The fierce battle is won!
> We will stack our arms by the River Fair,
> Here tenting we'll wait, upon Glory's height,
> And drink to the brave from her wine-cup rare.
> And they lay down to sleep—not to dream.
> While radiant forms, from the unseen land,
> Brood softly above them with tender wings.
> It was "Custer's Luck," with his brave command![15]

Ella Wheeler Wilcox accepted the Frederick Whittaker story of
how Custer, given a chance to escape disguised as a Sioux, refused,
choosing rather to die with his men:

Ah! deeds like that the Christ in man reveal
Let Fame descend her throne at Custer's shrine to kneel.[16]

And despite all that we know about Custer, all that we now feel about the treatment of the Indian in America's western expansion, and the change in sentiment generally, we are not free of apotheosis yet. In a book published in 1971 Fred Kaufman describes the awe with which he approached that now hallowed ground above the Little Bighorn: "When we think of the torturous deaths and awful mutilations of these soldiers, we are reminded of another bleak and barren hill in a land far away, and of a Man, who stood there long ago, His garments stripped from Him and His body pierced with a spear. We think of an old saying. 'Take the shoes from off thy feet —you stand on sacred ground.' "[17]

Custer had been raised to the level of the gods, but what manner of god was he? Valhalla has many chambers. A strong case could be made for Custer as a hero of the type described by Lord Raglan, a law-giver to his people, but this is not the Custer most people think of: he is not like Ulysses Grant, who died in a comfortable bed, but rather the reckless paladin who is shot out of a bloody saddle. We would be wrong to classify Custer with Charlemagne; rather, he is a Roland. He is not a latter-day Arthur, but a nineteenth-century Sir Gawain. Not Samuel, but Saul.

Custer as a warrior, rather than as a statesman, dies in harness, surrounded by a small body of men, against an overwhelming force of the enemy: this is the hero Errol Flynn played in "They Died with Their Boots on," a type not classified or indexed by Raglan (or anyone else). And yet there are so many legends of martyred warriors that parallel the popular narrative of Custer's Last Stand that we can speak of a paradigm of such stands, though it is not quite a local legend and it is not quite a hero tale, unless we are willing to accept the American West in the nineteenth century as a "heroic age."[18]

    a) The hero and a small band are
    b) surrounded and overwhelmed by
    c) a much larger force of
    d) racial or national aliens.
    e) Only rash courage or pride has led the hero to fight at all, and
    f) though the battle goes well at first,

g) treason or cowardice among one or more of his men turns the tide.

h) A heroic stand is made in which

i) many of the enemy are killed

j) on or near a mountain from which

k) help has been summoned, though it is too late.

l) The hero spurns a chance to escape, preferring to die with his men.

m) Wielding a sword that has served him well in the past, the hero is

n) among the last to die, if not the last.

o) One man, usually insignificant, survives and carries the news.

p) A eulogy is intoned over the hero's corpse, often by his slayer, and

q) later the victors are punished by the hero's vengeful comrades or countrymen.

When the narrative of the Last Stand is described schematically, it is clear that the scheme describes the last moments of other heroes as well.[19] France's Roland, hero of the eleventh-century *Chanson de Roland*,[20] was the leader of Charlemagne's rear guard as his army labored north through the Pyrenees, and could only count on twenty thousand men to fight against the hundreds of thousands of Saracens ranged against him. Count Roland's pride was as much a part of him as his strong right arm, and throughout the battle he insisted that he would not call for help lest he humiliate his family and that it was better to die than to live in shame. Ganelon's legendary treachery had made the one-sided battle inevitable; nevertheless, the Franks handled themselves well at first, but the relentless surge of the pagan hordes eventually wore away their resistance. In the final moments of his life Roland staggered to the top of a convenient hill, strove to break his sword, Durandal, which had served him well in the past, and among all his twenty thousand was the last to perish. In the Oxford Manuscript of the *Chanson* no Frankish knight survived; but in the *Pseudo-Turpin*, thought to be nearly contemporary with the Oxford Manuscript, Roland's brother Baudouin escaped to bring word of the disaster to Charlemagne. The main army then wheeled and dashed toward the pass at Roncesvalles, where, in a fury of vengeance, they fell upon the fleeing Saracen survivors, hacking them down as they fled across the plains.

The Old Testament's Custer analogue is Saul, the first king of Israel. The story of his death is told by the scribes in the two books of Samuel. Facing the brandished spears of yet another Philistine invasion and fearing that God had deserted him, Saul went to a witch of Ein Dor (Endor), who invoked the spirit of Samuel, who told Saul that he and his men would perish. Nevertheless, Saul went off to battle in God's war. The Benjamites were defeated on Mt. Gilboa, where all of Saul's men and his sons Jonathan, Abinadab, and Malchishua were slain. The Philistines, whom Saul had defeated so decisively in earlier days, relentlessly smashed down the Israelites' resistance and in the final moments of the struggle struck Saul himself with arrows. Though wounded, he continued to fight. Further resistance was useless, yet rather than surrender to his detested enemy, he ordered his armor-bearer to kill him; when that faithful servant could not bring himself to kill God's anointed, Saul fell on his own sword. Later, we are told in the first chapter of 2 Samuel, a nameless Amalekite with torn clothes and dirty countenance stumbled into David's camp to announce the defeat of Saul and to claim that he had slain David's rival.

Sir Gawain is our man in the English Middle Ages, and his story is told in the alliterative *Morte Arthure* (ca. 1360), whose martyred hero is not the once and future king of the title.[21] That splendid and doughty chieftain had recrossed Europe after his conquest of the continent to reclaim his kingdom from the traitor Mordred, and Sir Gawain splashed ashore in the van of a scant seven-score knights to make the first assault. Waiting for them was a superior force of at least sixty thousand, made up of Danes, Lithuanians, Goths, mercenaries, and pagans of every stripe, directed by the arch-traitor himself. With great energy and skill Gawain and his men blew away the Danish contingent facing them and seized their hill. But that good Englishman was a typical hero of the Middle Ages, reckless almost by definition; in a moment of rash impetuosity Gawain charged down from the high ground into the midst of Mordred's ranks. All of the English were quickly surrounded, and Gawain, in a single combat with Mordred, was stabbed to death. The traitor uttered a brief eulogy over the body of his opponent, but soon had to turn his attention toward the pressing matter of Arthur's invasion. When the true king saw Gawain lying dead on the ground, he was nearly overcome with grief and swore upon his sacred oath, by the Messiah and His Mother, to take vengeance.

The moment of glory came for Leonidas when he decided to defend the pass at Thermopylae against the threatening hordes of Xerxes, fresh from victories to the north, who jeopardized all of Greece (read "Western civilization").[22] Leonidas chose his position well: The Callidromus Mountains protected his left flank while the Gulf of Malis anchored his right. Supporting him was a small army of Thespians, Thebans, and his fellow Lacedaemonians, ranged against more than ten times their number. The first two days of their defense were successful, but then a peasant in the region, Ephialtes, showed the barbarians a path through the hills which outflanked the Greek positions. All during the night of the second day and the morning of the third an elite Persian guard of ten thousand picked its way across the mountain top, debouching the next morning well to the rear of the Greek fortifications. At a war council several of the Greek contingents chose to withdraw; Leonidas and his three hundred Spartans made one of the world's noblest decisions—to stay. They were soon hard-pressed by Persians attacking from both east and west, and it was while retreating toward their camp that Leonidas fell. This is a notable variant of the paradigm; in Herodotus it occurs because not only the Spartan king but also his men required praise. Thermopylae is an epic of collective heroism. Even with their king slain Leonidas's men were resolved to stand fast; they are said to have fought with even greater determination to save Leonidas's body from defilement at the hands of the enemy. The last moments of the battle were on a little hillock, the Kolonos, where, when their spears had splintered, they fought with their hands and their teeth to the last man. Several miles to the rear two of their comrades lay blinded by illness; on hearing that the battle was about to enter its last moments, one asked to be led to the thickest part of the fighting (where he was slain) while the other asked to be taken home with the retreating Greeks—where he lived in infamy.

Byrhtnoth, the hero of *The Battle of Maldon* who led a force of Saxons against a party of marauding Vikings in 991, was not the last of his men to die.[23] Nor did he die on a hill. But enough of the important motifs occur to suggest that a "last stand" of sorts is involved. When he refused to pay the tribute demanded by the pirates, they asked his leave to cross the intervening river and fight to settle the issue. Byrhtnoth, whose men had successfully held the ford, agreed to let the raiders cross unopposed; a general combat was joined. The Saxons held their own at first, but when Byrhtnoth was killed the momentum shifted to the enemy. Seeing their leader struck down, the cowards among the Saxons were quick to flee, and despite the determination of several others to stay and fulfill their oaths and their obligations to their lord, the Vikings could not be stayed. It has been rightly said that the purpose of *Maldon* is to separate the sheep from the goats, to vilify those cowards who ran for their lives and to praise those Saxons who remained to die with their chief.[24] For this purpose it is necessary that Byrhtnoth be slain before the end of the battle, for this one event puts the most critical pressure on his retainers; if he died last we would not "see" the dramatic flight of the cravens in violation of their oaths, nor would the men who choose to stay in the face of these defections (and therefore almost certain defeat) seem so noble.

On the plains of Kóssovo the Serbian Tsar Lázar was martyred by the Turks, who, in legend at least, greatly outnumbered Lázar's Christians and threatened again to enslave his country.[25] On the eve of battle an angel came to his tent and offered him either victory in the imminent battle or eternal life in heaven. Lázar chose heaven, of course, but the Serbian ballads have it both ways: he is also said to have been betrayed by his vassal Vuk, who, at a crucial moment in the fighting, when the initiative was swaying precariously in the Serbs' favor, withdrew his men—twelve thousand of them in the legends—allowing the Turks to swarm over the weakened and bewildered survivors. A servant, Milutin, escaped from the carnage and carried the news back to Lázar's household. The Turks decapitated the Serbian leader, as was their practice, but miraculously, his head and body did not decay, and several years later, a young Turkish boy miraculously rejoined them.

At the end of the Middle Ages—the fall of Constantinople in 1453—nothing less than Olympian heroism should be expected, and this is exactly what has been attributed to the Emperor Constantine Paleologus in the defense of his city.[26] His defenders were actually few, and Mehmet's Turks were many, but the disparity has been tremendously exaggerated in Greek oral tradition. The early attacks on the walls had been driven back, and more aid was expected from the West, when the Turkish Janissaries broke through the Saint Romanos gate and stormed the city. Traitors, villains, and cowards abounded: Urban, the Hungarian engineer who built giant siege cannons for the Turks; Mehmet himself, who is said to have broken several pledges and treaties by attacking Constantinople in the first place, and Giustiniani, commander of the Genoese contingent of defenders, who was wounded during the final assault of the gate and who begged to be carried from his position, thus demoralizing all his men.

The Emperor is known to have died at the Saint Romanos Gate, having rushed to the breach in the walls where he sensed, as Runciman thinks, the empire would be lost.[27] I have seen the gate and the land around it, and while it has sometimes been represented as a small hillock, it is level.[28] Constantine probably did perish at that place, though he did not face the thousand Turks of tradition there alone, fighting with his hands and teeth.[29] His body was never found (the Turks cut off his head too), though at least one story relates that the sultan buried this last of the Byzantine Emperors with a munificence befitting his station.

A final illustration of "last stand" narratives shows just how much variation is possible within the parameters of the type. The hero is the sixth-century Danish champion, Bjarki, and he makes his last stand in defense of his king's castle, Lejre.[30] The battle probably was not fought on a hilltop, for a good part of the narrative takes place indoors. We are given no hints about whether Bjarki died last or not, and we can only assume that the king's men were outnumbered by the hostile Goths and Swedes who had been brought to Lejre under the guise of peace by the treacherous Hjarvarth. A guest in the house of the king (Hrolf), the sinister Hjarvarth sought revenge for having been tricked into becoming his host's vassal.

Not rash pride but an appropriate loyalty compelled Bjarki to fight; his pride is evident only in his consenting to fight at all, for from the beginning the situation was hopeless: Hjarvarth's men were also guests of Hrolf, and had been welcomed in his domain. Their surprise attack, therefore, had an immediate success. But before Bjarki rose to repel the enemy, he paused by the fire to warm his hands while his young friend, Hjalti, urged him to immediate action. We have the sense that during this pause Bjarki had a chance to escape, but that he (obviously) made the decision to stay. The decision is crucial to our esteem for the hero, for it distinguishes the man who is merely trapped from one who has chosen to endure adversity: there, and not in victory lies the truest nobility. Roland, too, decides not to summon aid until defeat is inevitable; Leonidas chooses to remain in the outflanked pass at Thermopylae; Lázar decides upon Paradise at Kóssovo, rather than victory; Byrthnoth permits the Vikings to cross over the Pante and dies as a result, rather than choose a safer disengagement.

In the *Bjarkamál,* as in the other heroic legends, heroism is not compatible with rescue and safety. Bjarki rushed into the heaviest fighting and, having received many blows (as he lamented) for each one he dealt out, was finally slaughtered. One man alone escaped the holocaust: Wigg, a rather minor actor in the drama. In revenge, Bjarki's kin returned to Lejre and ended in blood Hjarvarth's short-lived reign as king.

Little will be gained here from summarizing yet other ana-logues, because the reader can easily see how the paradigm applies to James IV of Scotland at Flodden, to the Jews at Masada, to the Israeli "35" in the Negev, to Janos Hunyadi at Varna (not Bel-grade!), to Guillaume d'Orange, to Davy Crockett at the Alamo, to Mynyddawg Mwynvawr at Catraeth.

What these diverse heroic legends share is the shaping of oral tradition, even though most of them are known to us only through manuscripts. We know that though the ambush in the pass at Ron-cevalles took place in 778, the epic account of that battle did not appear for more than two centuries, and then the action had been almost completely transformed. Herodotus visited the area around Thermopylae at least twenty years after the stand there and recorded the "history" as he got it from the local peasants. The last battles of Lázar and Constantine have been transmitted by ballads and other oral traditions; Saul's life (and death) must have been carried orally for nearly five centuries before the scribes of the Old Testament recorded it. Bjarki's fall is known primarily through oral sources eventually recorded in the *Hrolfssaga Kraki* and the *Bjar-kamál,* which no longer exist in any manuscript. Although the death of Gawain appears to be an entirely literary invention (though we should be suspicious of such a pronouncement about medieval narra-tive), nevertheless the story conforms in most particulars to our paradigm.

Tradition has exerted an inexorable influence upon these stories from Scripture, saga, history, heroic lay, epic, and the popular bal-lad, and each of these genres bears the distinctive shaping of oral influence. In the aftermath of the Custer debacle numerous imagined versions of the battle tended toward the same ends. Legend fragments from all over the country began to coalesce—those in personal letters and letters to newspapers, in popular poems, in newspaper articles and editorials, in ballads and in rumors, anecdotes, and legends: the Custer version of the defeated-hero paradigm was being shaped. Frederick Whittaker gathered these various strands, as he tells us, and wove them into a coherent and dramatic narrative in which nearly all the relevant details were given their place. He called it *A Complete Life* and represented it as modern biography, when generically it was much closer to the medieval romance, or to the saint's life.[31] That Whittaker had a medieval or classical model in mind is doubtful, despite his occasional facile analogies between Custer and Leonidas, yet he nevertheless made of his hero's last battle a Thermopylae of the plains, glorifying Custer beyond even Custer's own extravagant intentions.

In folklore we have come to discredit independent creation or polygenesis in the history of complex narratives almost as an automatic reflex, but all of the evidence forces us to insist on this explanation in this legend paradigm. Herodotus had no knowledge of the Old Testament story of Saul when he celebrated Leonidas's stand at Thermopylae. We have no indication that the "author" of *The Battle of Maldon* knew of either account. Given the militant Christian tenor of the *Chanson de Roland,* we must assume Turoldus's intimacy with the Bible, but when Scriptural sources have been hunted, they have been thought to be in the Gospels' account of the death of Jesus. Again, with the *Morte Arthure,* one is inclined to search for sources, but no one has thought of Gawain's death even remotely in terms of either Jesus or Roland.

The most intriguing argument of independent genesis derives from an entirely literary hilltop stand, however, the one dramatized in Flaubert's *La Salammbô.* The hero, Mathô, is the last man alive on the hill to which his army had withdrawn before a horde of enraged Carthaginians. Now we happen to know Flaubert's sources for this, his first novel after *Bovary:* it is the account of the "Inexpiable War" in Polybius.[32] No hills are mentioned in the Greek account of the battle, and Polybius does not bother to identify the last rebel alive on the field, though from what he does say it probably was not Mathô. These epic details were all Flaubert's inventions, and the source for Mathô's grand defeat is not from any oral tradition but

rather from the French realist's imagination. What has happened—
and what I, with apologies, simply do not have the space to defend
at length here—is that Flaubert invoked those episodes and symbols
in those configurations which his culture (and ours) has mandated
as the best way of telling a certain kind of story. We do not render
homage to him as a master of fiction vacuously; but what of those
countless mute and inglorious Flauberts who created much the same
plot for their folk narratives? They too (like Herodotus and Turoldus
and Whittaker) knew how to tell a good tale in the best way; what
the unschooled narrators lacked (naturally enough, since it was not
within the ends of their art) was the academician's sense of the
well-wrought metaphor, the felicitous phrase, which some think
alone will keep a drowsy emperor awake.

Custer has not been so fortunate as Mathô; for the elements of
a great epic were accumulated by the American people, and they are
not to be held responsible because no poet of academically recognized talent used those elements for a "Chanson de Custer." We are
the poorer for that, which is all the more ironic for Custer's status
as a hero. The mystery surrounding Custer's death (the occasional
charges of suicide, which claim he obeyed the "code of the West" by
saving the last bullet for himself; the "question" about the coffin in
which the "right" bones were placed; the claims that Rain-in-the-
Face cut out his heart and the counterclaims that he was untouched
by the victors; the many Indians who have since claimed to have
been his slayer) maintain the notion that he is not really dead, but
that like so many other sleeping warriors (Siegfried, Wotan, Die-
trich, Charlemagne, El Cid, et al.) he is merely slumbering in another world, awaiting the proper moment to return to his people. In
this sense also he is a modern avatar, an analogue to the Son of God
who will return in the last days.

In yet another aspect as legendary hero he is the conquerer of
the pagans—the "fiends incarnate" and the "red devils" in the melo-
dramatic and racist rhetoric of the newspapers—the champion of
white America who planted the seeds of Christianity, Progress, Civilization, and Manifest Destiny in the desert and caused it to bloom.
In several poems (to say nothing of letters to papers and "news"
articles) he is depicted as a major participant in a cosmic battle
against the forces of Satan. And, once more like Christ, he is the
redeemer-hero who escapes from time; as his legend and his won-

drous sword (which appears magically in nearly all the accounts of the battle despite the well-attested fact of its absence at the Little Bighorn) show, he is not only of the year 1876.

That Custer is a projection of some portion of the collective aspirations of nineteenth-century America—perhaps we should say that he was the vessel of an American ethos-projection—should be apparent. Yet this legend may also suggest something to us today other than a sacrifice to the gods of Manifest Destiny. Like Roland's insistence on meeting the enemy on his own terms, like the Spartan who when told that the Persian arrows darkened the sun replied that he preferred anyway to fight in the shade, like Saul who marched cheerfully to battle knowing that he could not win, or like the besieged marines on Wake Island who allegedly sent the message, "Send us more Japs," Custer is the embodiment of our defiance against those people, societal forces and pressures, those institutions, conventions, obligations, and destinal mazes that always seem to envelop and at least partially to enmesh and suffocate those who live in modern society. Custer, surrounded on his hill, brandishing his sword defiantly in the faces of the menacing red enemy who he knows in his heart will soon overcome him, is that part of us which wants to resist capitulation to these forces and that part of us that defies, or struggles to defy, our society, our environment, our situation in life.

The Custer of our dreams is an archetype of Camus's existential man who rises above the inevitability of his life and of his death by bravely fighting his inescapable fate to his last breath. This is the truest heroism. He is Sisyphus, smiling, as the boulder crashes down the slope of the hill once again; he is Tevye ordering the Czar's officer from his land which the Czar has just decreed will be left to him for only three days more; he is Macbeth knowing that he must soon die, yet resolving to die with the dignity befitting a king. This Custer is of course one of America's greatest heroes (as was Leonidas to Greece, Roland to the Franks, Lázar to the Serbs, Constantine to the Byzantines), and, despite recent Indian attacks upon his fame and his memory, he will remain a hero to much of white America.

The Anglo-French chronicler Froissart wrote that because bravery was of all human traits and elements of character the most honorific, he would write a history of the nobles of England and of France that would exemplify bravery. To much of nineteenth-century America Custer exemplified this quality. Like so many other legends of the American West, the Custer legend transcends region and time. Custer is not merely a hero of Montana, or the West, or America, or the nineteenth century; his persistent international fame denies these limitations. Regardless of what he did at the Little Bighorn, regardless of what he was and what he did with his life, he has become for those in the Western world who know of him the exemplar of the brave man. Because there were so many battles in the American West, it seems almost inevitable that all regions of the country should perpetuate his fame. The life in the West was such that bravery would be highly valued; for better or worse, in truth or in imaginative legend, right or wrong, we have chosen Custer to bear that honor.

The Pony Express

MAJOR petroleum company recently advertised to its credit card customers an opportunity to acquire a collection of "historic U.S. Coins," described as "The Old West Heritage Collection," mounted in four frames, each with an appropriate illustration. "The American Indian" was surrounded by ten Indian Head pennies; "The Forty-Niners," which shows several prospectors panning for gold, a traceway in the background, is bordered by Liberty Head nickels; a train passing a herd of buffalo—"a typical scene of the Old West"—is mounted with Buffalo nickels. And the fourth representative scene of the "Old West" shows a Pony Express rider, whose "daring and courage . . . is captured in a dramatic scene of him galloping across the plains." He is surrounded by ten Mercury dimes of "90% pure silver." Of all the many institutions, events, individuals, or groups associated with the Old West, the Pony Express is one of those we invariably think of when the Old West is mentioned.

When Sears wanted to tell the public that its radial tires were rugged and safe even at high speeds, it pointed out that they had been tested over the route of the Pony Express. A map of the United States west of the Mississippi appeared on screen, in sepia tones, and then the outline of a pony rider was superimposed. In slow motion the rider and his pony galloped across the map while viewers were told about the virtues of this radial tire, able take a lot of punishment over the roughest paths and trails and also capable of the light-footed speed of that speediest of couriers, the Pony Express rider, for us as for the mid-nineteenth century, the embodiment of speed.

In St. Joseph, Missouri, one terminus of the Express route, the Pony Express is honored in several ways. A life-size bronze statue of a pony rider and his mount is downtown at Civic Center Park; several blocks away is a monument erected by the DAR in 1912 to commemorate the starting place of the route; and within a short walk of both of those memorials stands the Pony Express Stables Museum, originally the Pike's Peak stables, built in 1858. At the other end of the Express route, in San Francisco, the Wells-Fargo Bank has a "Pony Express Museum" in its main office lobby.

Not bad for a service that lasted about nineteen months before going broke.

Mark Twain has put it best:

The pony-rider was usually a little bit of a man, brim full of spirit and endurance. No matter what time of the day or night his watch came on, and no matter whether it was winter or summer, raining, snowing, hailing, or sleeting, or whether his "beat" was a level straight road or a crazy trail over mountain crags and precipices, or whether it led through peaceful regions or regions that swarmed with hostile Indians, he must be always ready to leap into the saddle and be off like the wind! There was no idling-time for a pony rider on duty. He rode fifty miles without stopping, by daylight, moonlight, starlight, or through the blackness of darkness—just as it happened. He rode a splendid horse . . ., kept him at his utmost speed for ten miles, and then, as he came crashing up to the station where stood two men holding fast a fresh, impatient steed, the transfer of rider and mail-bag was made in the twinkling of an eye, and away flew the eager pair and were out of sight before the spectator could get hardly the ghost of a look.[1]

The idea of an interlocking network of couriers that would regularly carry information and light freight across a vast and desolate plain was not a new one. The Romans had experimented with such a messenger system, as had the Chinese in the thirteenth century. The need for such a network did not materialize until gold was discovered on the American River in 1848 and thousands of immigrants rolled into the area from the Eastern states. In only a few months' time thousands of Easterners had become instant Californians; and they wanted mail and newspapers from home, longed to tell those they had left behind about their new environs. And they needed a safe and regular means of getting gold—if they found any —out of the diggings and to a more secure place.

In 1851, Charpenning and Woodward opened a modest freight route from Salt Lake City to Sacramento. It was neither fast nor safe. The round trip between those cities took around a year, and only two deliveries were made each twelve months. Charpenning was killed on the trail, and Woodward wounded. Later in the decade service was improved considerably when the same firm established a wagon service between Placerville and Salt Lake City to carry mail, the time of the trip reduced (one way) to two weeks. Way-stations were established at roughly twenty-mile intervals where the team could be replaced with fresh animals and the drivers refreshed with food and rest. Government contracts enabled such services to flourish, but in 1860, faced with the expense of a war to fight on the Eastern seaboard, the Government cancelled their obligation to Woodward.

Efficient mail service was a good idea whose time was coming. Alex Todd recognized that one good place for it was the Mother Lode country, and in the summer of 1849 he set up and manned the "Jackass Express," whose name described the nature of his transporation. For the short duration of his business he charged an ounce of gold dust for each letter delivered, eight dollars for each newspaper. He is said to have received $12,500 for delivering a gold shipment—though this may be the kind of "folklore" that gives such items a bad name. He hauled the gold, as he did all the eastbound mail he carried, to San Francisco where it was put on board ship, thence to be sailed East.

The freight-hauling firm of Russell, Majors, and Waddell had extensive experience with their trade west of the Mississippi. Operating principally out of Fort Leavenworth, they tried to exploit the needs of recent immigrants to the West. Some of their operations, like the freight service to and from the Pike's Peak area, failed. But the idea of the Pony Express, a network of swift couriers operating in series across the country from Missouri to California, seemed to fill several of the country's needs. To Russell, Majors, Waddell, and B. F. Ficklin, the line supervisor often credited with the idea, the time of the Pony Express had come. It was near the end of the fifth decade of the century.

Start-up costs were tremendous: over $100,000. The Express had more than 400 carefully selected horses, 119 stations, about 200 tenders ("Wild Bill" Hickok was one for a while), and about 90 carefully chosen riders. The route stretched from St. Joseph through Salt Lake City to San Francisco. Service began on April 3, 1860. But costs were so high—the line was said to have lost approximately $13 for each letter carried—that service was suspended nineteen months later, on October 24, 1861. The telegraph was strung across the prairie during that time and made many of the services of the Express obsolete. Russell, Majors, and Waddell declared bankruptcy just before the first large war-time subsidies were available.

From the beginning it was the speed of the service that most impressed the public; the bravery, resourcefulness, energy, and dedication of the riders would soon be part of the legend. But first—and always—the Pony Express embodied speed. The San Francisco *Evening Bulletin* (21 April 1860) saluted the Pony's swiftness:

> The "Pony" was all the toast last night. . . . The crowd discussed the Pony's time, got out their watches and calculated his rate per mile, argued the effects of his success on the Overland Mail. . . . One asked if the rider's brass buttons were turned black with the fumes of sulpher the little fellow must have kicked up. . . . At every man's dinner table, men, women, and children talked *pony*. There will certainly be a rise in horseflesh.

Another essay in the same issue of the *Evening Bulletin* glorified the Pony in even more effusive terms:

> . . . He was the veritable Hippogriff who shoved a continent behind his hoofs so easily; who snuffed up sandy plains, sent lakes and mountains, prairies and forests, whizzing behind him, like one great river rushing eastward; who left a wake like a clipper's, 'carried a bone in his mouth,' and sent his fame rippling off north and south, as nothing has done before for years; who frightened whole tribes of Indians, that thought it was an arrow whittled into a pony's shape that whizzed by; who made eagles and all swift-winged birds heart-sick, and sent them into convention to devise measures to keep their reputation up; who crossed the railroad track, fifteen miles out of Sacramento, just as the cars had passed, and got into the City of the Plains just as the same cars arrived!

We see how easily exuberant metaphor becomes, if taken literally, the supernatural. No horse in the West was that fast; and every Westerner had seen horses gallop as swiftly as the Express horses at one time or another. Yet the situation demanded the impression of speed; if the mails could now cross the continent overland at a record time, each rider would be made to cover his section of the route in record time as well. The individual was made a microcosm of the entire route.

The anecdotes told about the riders extol their speed. Johnny Frey, one of the most famous pony riders, would rein in his foaming horse in front of the old Troy (Kansas) House and ask, "Is breakfast ready?" It could seldom be whipped up in time, so the eager Frey would be off again, advising, "Well, put something on the fire, and I'll go on to St. Joe and will be back here to eat!" He made the round trip, approximately thirty miles, in "an incredibly short time, returning for his breakfast." It is said that he customarily let fly "a special blast on his horn" when near Cold Springs to alert his lady friends there that he was coming so they could have victuals ready. He would hold up for a second or two for some doughnuts or a piece of pie.[2] Another story has it that the doughnut was developed so that rather than having to slow down to take a bite, he could spear his cake while on the gallop with his finger through its hollowed center.

The Pony Express embodied agile speed, blinding speed, dizzying speed. The St. Joseph *Weekly West* (7 April 1860) was in awe of the flying ponies and their fleet riders:

> . . . and before this paragraph meets the eyes of our readers, the various dispatches in the saddle bags which left here at dark last evening will have reached the town of Marysville on the Big Blue, one hundred and twelve miles distant, an enterprise never before accomplished, even in this proverbially fast portion of a fast country.

Mr. P. L. Gray, local historian of Doniphan County, Kansas, recalled that Johnny Frey's red necktie was the envy of several local ladies, who wanted to use it at a quilting party. (Johnny Frey was the hero of many anecdotes that celebrate the Pony Express rider's speed.) When he rode by one day, in this story, a girl galloped up alongside him and asked him for his tie. But, dedicated to his mission as he was, Johnny replied by spurring his horse to even greater speed. The frustrated girl grabbed for his tie anyway but came up with only a tatter of his shirt-tail. And that inglorious fabric was sewn into the quilt.[3]

Mark Twain recalls for us how it was:

> We had a consuming desire, from the beginning, to see a pony-rider, but somehow or other all that passed us and all that met us managed to

streak by in the night, and so we heard only a whiz and a hail, and the
swift phantom of the desert was gone before we could get our heads out
of the windows. But now we were expecting one along every moment,
and we would see him in broad daylight. Presently the driver exclaims:
"HERE HE COMES!"

Every neck is stretched further, and every eye strained wider.
Away across the endless dead level of the prairie a black speck appears
against the sky, and it is plain that it moves. Well, I should think so!
In a second or two it becomes horse and rider, rising and falling,·rising
and falling—sweeping towards us nearer and nearer—growing more
and more distinct, more and more sharply defined—nearer and still
nearer, and the flutter of the hooves comes faintly to our ear—another
instant a whoop and a hurrah from our upper deck, a wave of the rider's
hand, but no reply, and man and horse burst past our excited faces, and
go winging away like a belated fragment of a storm!

So sudden is it all, and so like a flash of unreal fancy, that but for
the flake of white foam left quivering and perishing on a mail-sack after
the vision had flashed by and disappeared, we might have doubted
whether we had seen any actual horse and man at all, maybe.[4]

In this passage, one of the most vividly effective descriptions of the
pony rider, Twain's metaphors and similes cross over the boundary
into the realm of the spectral. The rider, "so like a flash of unreal
fancy," is a vision flashing by and disappearing, silently and hardly
actual, is not quite earthbound. Only a flake of white foam provides
any evidence of his corporeal existence; it is a hyperbolic metaphor
we can accept, for even Twain doubts the reality, or the unreality,
of what he has just experienced: "maybe."

Daring riders on wild horses. The company officers are said to
have chosen the mounts with care, but as the embodiments of speed
they could hardly be gentle or tame. So we learn that it was "common" for a rider to find that he had a bucking horse under him when
he rode out of a station: "that was one reason why we gave them the
spurs right from the start and kept them going," another rider, Gus
Cliff, later recalled. "A good many of the horses we had were half
broke—some of the best of them, in fact. A few days on the trail
cured most of them of bucking, but some never quit, especially right
after they had been saddled."[5]

Riders who rode like the wind were bound to make and then to
break records. So important was their speed to the public that it was
constantly being quantified—by the public at large, even by the
riders themselves. "Records" were probably rhetorical matters

rather than the formal, "official," documented affairs certified by a disinterested agency. Nevertheless, nearly every rider's repertoire of personal experience narratives included at least one about his fastest ride. Henry Avis was one of a string of riders who carried Lincoln's inaugural address, covering the entire route in three days less than scheduled. When he had to ride through a region swarming with warring Indians, he volunteered to ride on to the next station because the regularly scheduled rider refused. This act of commitment is said to have earned him a bonus of $300. When rider Don C. Rising was only sixteen—few of the riders were very much older —he made what was to him "his famous ride," from Big Sandy to Rock Creek, averaging twenty miles an hour. As he recalled with pride, he "had important government dispatches to carry and was told to make time."[6] Dispatches from several governments provided the Pony Express with a large portion of its gross income. For those European nations with embassies on the Eastern seaboard, it was a great advantage in communicating with Asia to have such rapid postal service across the continent rather than waiting for sea-borne mail to take its slow way around Cape Horn.

The San Francisco *Evening Bulletin* once reflected that "the swiftest riding we have heard of on the route, was Mr. Bedford's, from Martinez to Oakland, which 24 miles he accomplished in one hour and 45 minutes; yet the Pony did not shed his shoes, his rider did not break his neck, nor was there any appreciable smell of fire upon his garments when he came in."[7] That recollection was in an editorial, showing just how pervasive were stories of the speed of the Pony. We expect such anecdotes and personal experience stories when former riders reflect upon their days of glory: for nearly all of the riders, life was decidedly downhill after they left the Pony Express.

But when in the saddle . . . Jack Keetley, to settle a wager, rode from Rock Creek to St. Joe and back, and then on to Seneca, a total of 340 miles, having spent thirty-one consecutive hours in the saddle. Joseph Barney Wintle was one of those who helped carry the news of Lincoln's election; on that day he rode 110 miles in just five hours, making ten horse changes along the route. Wintle remembered that ride so clearly and so proudly that it became one of his favorites, his son, John Wesley Wintle, reminisced in 1937.

A number of these tales, like those just related, begin to highlight not only the rider's speed but his endurance. Jack Keetley's ride illustrates this; is the important statistic the time he spent in

the saddle or the distance traveled? That depends upon the situation, of course; when we now read accounts of great feats of pony
riding we should be alert to the implications of distance as well as
of speed. William E. "Pony Ned" Van Blaricon used to tell of his
most famous ride, which also involved news about Lincoln, this time
the news of the assassination. The date indicates that Van Blaricon
made his ride while part of another organization, since the Pony
Express of Russell, Majors, and Waddell had gone out of business
several years before. In any event, "Pony Ned" had just finished
riding 110 miles to Silver City and back when the news of Lincoln
came over the telegraph. But his relay was indisposed. Often enough
in these reminiscences "indisposed" means afraid of Indians or outlaws or storms. Van Blaricon's relay was drunk, and Ned was ordered—happily for the stories he would one day tell his children—
to take the drunk's place and ride on to Boise, 65 miles up the road.
When he had finished that trek and totaled his stats for the day, they
came to 175 miles in 18 hours, 22 minutes. He had used only four
horses in the last 65 miles.[8]

How close many of these stories are to those which extol endurance! Buffalo Bill, at the time only 16, is said to have once ridden
over 320 miles without rest, arriving at his destination on time.[9] In
retrospect, Buffalo Bill could hardly do anything in less than superlatives; he wouldn't have been Buffalo Bill if he did. Some of the
same aura hung about the best-known rider of his day, "Pony Bob"
Haslam. In a newspaper article entitled, "Pony Bob Makes Record
Time," the details and statistics of one of his great feats of horseman-
ship are highlighted. The title praises speed, the article adulates
endurance. One day, after completing his own route, Haslam was
asked to continue on over his successor's, $50 being offered as induce-
ment. He set off at once for Smith's Creek; when he returned—from
a round-trip of 190 miles—he was informed that the attendant at
Cold Springs had been killed by hostile Indians. So Haslam climbed
into the saddle once more, this time to ride to Friday's Station to
warn attendants along the way that there might be trouble with
Indians. His bravery saved the life of the man at Smith's Creek, who
was able to leave the area before war parties arrived. When it was
all over, we are told by the *Pony Express Courier* article, he was only
three-and-a-half hours behind schedule.[10]

Speed was the message of many Pony Express stories—to much
of the public it was central to the meaning of the institution. Closely
related, often inextricably, were tales of endurance; these were often

anecdotes in which the rider rode rapidly over an extended route.
The lead-line of the article admiring Bob Haslam, just cited, summarized his accomplishment thus: he rode 380 miles in 36 hours
through hostile country. All three elements recur frequently in personal experience tales and anecdotes of the Pony Express. The extended narrative, of speed, endurance, and bravery, is an obvious
one to incorporate all of these elements. The rider sets out at great
speed, for reasons beyond his control he is obliged (or volunteers) to
extend his route far beyond what is required of him, and this takes
him through country made dangerous by Indians, outlaws, wild animals, or hazardous weather. The following odyssey is told of Bob
Haslam by the popular historian of the Pony Express, Fred Reinfeld.
The rider's ordeal began routinely enough. After having ridden sev-
enty-five miles to the Reese River Station, where he expected to
change horses, he was told that all of the available horses had been
requisitioned for a recent campaign against the warring Paiutes.

> Though his mount was exhausted, Pony Bob had no choice. He got back
> on the weary animal and set out for Buckland's, fifteen miles away. But
> when he arrived, he found that the rider who was scheduled to replace
> him refused to do so. . . .
>   No one else was available to carry the mail, so Pony Bob, bone-
> weary as he was, had to start out on a new run. . . . Before he was
> through he had passed three more stations—an additional hundred
> miles, or 190 in all, of almost continuous riding!

But his odyssey was not at an end. At the end of this first "lap,"
instead of turning his *mochila* over to the next rider, he was told
that his relay man had been badly hurt in a fall. This motif—of the
indisposed relay rider—is, as already indicated, a common one. Its
function may be in some cases to emphasize the dangers of the
profession, but far more important, it enables the pivotal character
to ride on, demonstrating his speed and endurance.

> . . . after an hour and a half of deep sleep, Pony Bob was roused to make
> the return trip. . . . At Cold Springs Station, which he had left a few
> hours earlier, he found that all five men of the crew had been murdered
> by the Indians, and all the horses had been stolen.

Back at Buckland's, finally, he waited for nightfall to facilitate his
evasion of the Indians, and the delay enabled him to get a bit more
sleep.

Then Pony Bob continued on his weary way to the next station, though he was in constant danger of being trapped by Indians. Once a party of Indians sighted him, but he was too quick for them and escaped to safety. Finally, after 380 miles he was back at his starting point. And despite all his hardships, he had lost less than four hours of the scheduled time.

For this remarkable feat the company presented him with a special hundred-dollar prize.[11]

The specific mileage, 380, is the same as that in the *Pony Express Courier* story cited above. We may have here two accounts of the same exploit, though it is hard to be sure. Neither writer cites his source. One of the stations is mentioned in both accounts—Cold Springs—but Buckland's and Smith's Creek are not shared. Details differ: in the article from the *Pony Express Courier,* Haslam is offered $50 to ride farther, but in the Reinfeld version, he is rewarded $100 for a job superbly completed. In one version he saves an attendant's life with his warning; no mention is made of this by Reinfeld, who does include the detail of the five-man crew found dead at Cold Springs. If this is the same story, some tradition—oral or written cannot be determined—had been at work, a tradition in which attention to accuracy and precision of transmission is not a serious matter. It is a tradition in which the active bearers have felt at liberty to modify their source in whatever way they found useful to enhance the dramatic artistry of their narrative. If these stories do not derive from the same source, either written or experienced, they have obviously both borrowed from several of the same sources, possibly oral, and they have both benefited from that pool of narrative material which had gathered around the Pony Express, and had been aroused by its wake. An index of narrative motifs that might be compiled to describe the tales of the Pony Express would be a short one, owing to the limited nature of the activities possible in such an occupation.[12] From this narrow and shallow pool many tellers and writers borrowed the materials for their tales, and given the limited variety of motifs available, it is really not surprising that so much repetition of episodes should occur.

Several of these motifs occur in the following account of the odyssey by another rider, Henry Avis. He and his colleagues were not soldiers and could not be given medals, which gesture could concretize one's feelings of admiration for honorific deeds. Instead, they were awarded cash bonuses, perhaps the civilian counterpart.

Certainly it is the symbolic counterpart: the presentation of a material signifier by a grateful superior (individual or institutional) to a deserving performer. For his act of heroism, Avis was given a "special bonus" of $300:

> On one of his trips Henry finished his run at Horseshoe Station, the western end of his route. The rider who was to replace him for the westward trip to Deer Creek Station refused to do it when it was reported that a party of Sioux was on the warpath in the area.
>
> Arriving at Deer Creek safely, Henry found that the station had been burned and all the horses stolen. Now it was the eastward-bound rider who refused to take the mail. So Henry fastened the *mochila* on again and turned back to Horseshoe station. Again he made the trip safely, after completing 220 miles of hard riding.[13]

While on the trail—besides deserted or burned way-stations and drunk/disabled/fearful fellow riders—the Pony courier of fiction had to contend with those dangers he might possibly have encountered in the event: Indians, outlaws, endangering weather, and ferocious animals.

In his newspaper column, "Pony Express Riders I Have Met," George J. Remsburg once quoted ex-rider "Charlie" Cliff on the realities of life in the Express, which was for him not very exciting: "during the service, none of the St. Joe riders met with any adventure worth mentioning."[14] Despite that modest disclaimer, the rest of the interview does include a tale of the time that Cliff was obliged to do double duty, on one occasion riding 80 or 85 miles (riders were often enough asked to double their routes), and escaping from an Indian attack at Scott's Bluff. It is hard to know what Remsburg considered routine and uneventful, since he relates that at Scott's Bluff Cliff he received "three balls in his body and twenty-seven in his clothes." The reader will have to judge for himself the likelihood of this anecdote. Despite the prevalence of such tales of close encounters, during the eighteen months it was in business the Pony Express lost only one mail and only one rider was killed in service.

Nevertheless, encounters with Indians seem to have been the rider's anecdotal stock-in-trade. Chapman relates that an "R. E. Egan," when chased by Indians, suddenly wheeled and ran directly at them, yelling as loudly as he could and brandishing his pistol. The Indians fled.[15] Reinfeld tells a similar story about another (?) Egan:[16]

Howard Ransom Egan also had a remarkable adventure when he replaced a sick comrade. Riding through Egan Canyon in the dark, he caught the gleam of a camp fire. On approaching it cautiously, he discovered an Indian war party.

His first impulse was to gallop off. But he reasoned that another war party was at the other end of the canyon waiting to trap him. Thereupon, he came to a bold decision. Spurring on his horse, he galloped into the camp with deafening shouts and fired his revolver into the air. The startled Indians, fearing an attack by a large group of white men, scuttled off without a second look. He then took a short cut and arrived safely. The next day he learned that just as he had suspected, another Indian war party had been waiting to ambush him.

Writer Maurice L. Howe interviewed former rider Joseph Wintle who had several encounters with the hostiles during his tour of duty. He was at one time hotly chased by Indians but managed to keep ahead of them until he could reach his relay station; but his horse barely made it, and when it reached the station, it fell over dead from the bullet and arrow wounds it had received. On another occasion Wintle rode by mistake too close an Indian camp to get away unnoticed; like rider Egan, he chose boldness and rode straight through the enemy camp—it was a dark night—and "soon he went his way without molestation." A third incident showed even more daring. Coming over the top of a hill on his route, he found himself nearly at the edge of a village whose dwellers he knew to be on the warpath. (How well did he know the terrain he plied almost daily? And if he knew Indians in the area were warring, how did he let himself stumble into their village, not an easy assemblage to hide on the plains? And why did the Indians set up their villages on a Pony Express trail?). However it happened, Wintle was there; he was immediately seen, and he knew that the only way out was by bluff. He galloped to a nearby lodge, dismounted, and tightened his saddle girth. Then when he was satisfied as to its tension, he rode off before any of the braves could recover.[17]

The encounters begin to border on episodes taken from Dime novels. Pony Bob Haslam is said to have galloped into an ambush of thirty Paiute warriors. "Calmly, he drew out his revolver as he approached them. At the last moment the leader let him pass unharmed, perhaps out of admiration for his daring."[18] Others sound as though they were written—in the following example I do not know how far removed the printed version is from an oral source, if there was one—with early Western movies in mind.

... At the Egan Canyon Station, Henry Wilson and Albert Armstrong were quietly eating their breakfast one morning, when they suddenly found themselves surrounded by a war party of Indians. Quickly snatching up their rifles, Wilson and Armstrong killed or wounded several of the attackers before they were overcome by sheer force of numbers.

Their captors tied them up and piled brush and firewood around them, intending to burn them alive in their cabin. But fortunately, the Indians had not had their breakfast. They ate all the food in sight and went rummaging for more.

Suddenly, the welcome sound of hoofbeats was heard. The captives cried desperately for help. They were lucky. A band of soldiers from a nearby post was on patrol. They opened fire on the Indians, eighteen of whom were killed. The rest ran for their ponies and quickly made off.[19]

It was, we assume, a very large cabin. And eighteen Indians killed would have made it a major engagement in the Plains Wars. The rider/heroes of Dime novels were frequently as lucky, or as daring. As a young boy, Buffalo Bill ("Billy" then) was once ambushed, but like Wintle and Haslam, he decided quickly that his best chance was to ride straight at the Indians. Stunned, they could not recover their composure until he had ridden past them. Then they gave vehement chase, two braves in particular closing in rapidly. Glancing over his shoulder, Billy realized that if he could get the horse of one of them he could outdistance the rest easily: reining his own horse back on its haunches, "he suddenly wheeled in his saddle and fired." Quickly (!) he changed saddles with the man he had just killed as his other pursuer put a bullet through his cap. In a brief skirmish Billy killed him just as the main band arrived, and they renewed the chase. But with his stronger mount, Billy was able to outrace them to the closest way-station, only to find the tender dead and scalped. Without a moment's hesitation, Billy set out again.[20] But that is the beginning of another story.

Anecdotes of encounters with outlaws are much less common and, in general, less interesting. Those I have collected are so undramatic they sound authentic; nevertheless, the following are from a boy's novel about Buffalo Bill and the Overland Trail. In his first encounter with bandits, Billy outsmarts them by handing over a dummy express package. He avoids a Sioux war party by outracing his assailants for twenty-four miles, but is held up by another bandit. This time it is character, not merely cleverness, that wins the hour; the robber is so impressed by the young rider's cool courage that he lets him pass. Another young rider, named Davy, handles his bandit by spurring his horse into him, knocking him down, and escaping through the ensuing hail of bullets.[21]

That outlaws or bandits should present the danger to the rider and not Indians appears to be a phenomenon of popular culture rather than folklore. In the era with which I am dealing such a distinction is not so decisively made as it might be today, largely because no live informants survive, but also because factual and historical reporting is barely distinguishable from creations of pure imagination, and because writers generally took such liberties with their sources that often they are not to be trusted even when they are ostensibly merely interviewing participants/informants. So bombastic, so hyperbolic was much of the rhetoric of the times that it is hard to find comments on or evaluations of events that accurately reflect the actualities of the situation, even from newspapers. Or perhaps that should be, "especially from newspapers." Journalistic interviews with former riders, the media's coverage of the Little Bighorn, and its descriptions of life and prospects in the Mother and Comstock Lode country, are all cases in point.

Less dramatic, but more likely, were the problems encountered during periods of bad weather, particularly of snow. Chapman relates the following narrative about pony rider Upson's winter ordeal in Nevada. It is a tale of endurance and persistence rather than speed, and because of the nature of the test, begins to have the length of an odyssey; but it is not, being a focussed anecdote in which there is only one danger to overcome:

> From Sportsman's Hall to Strawberry the trail grew worse at every step. Heavy snow was beating down from the range. Wagon tracks were covered and the rider had to break his own trail. In some places Upson had to dismount and lead his own pony. He was familiar with the road, but the snow had blotted out landmarks. There was a danger of going over the trailside into a canyon. The pass seemed to act as a funnel, through which the cold wind roared. Loose snow on the mountainside was swept up and added to the stinging particles which were coming down from the low-hanging clouds.
>
> At Hope Valley there was a change of horses. Then more battling with the storm on a hazardous trail. Twenty-one miles of fighting, and Upson arrived at Woodbridge. From there to the old Mormon settlement at Genoa it was easy going—twenty miles, with the snowbanks gone and the pony hitting a faster pace. From Genoa to Carson City it was fourteen miles, and Upson clicked it off in fast time.

Late at night he struggled into his home station, Carson City, the end of an eighty-five mile obstacle course.[22]

Occasionally the weather posed other problems. Early in the life of the Express one rider had to cope with flood waters in Nebraska:

> The waters of the Platte were high at the crossing which had trapped many a California-bound emigrant. The rider, whose name is not known, spurred his horse into the stream. The animal was swept off its feet, and horse and rider drifted downstream into some quicksands. Seizing the *mochila,* with the mail, the rider swam and crawled to safety. Leaving his horse to be rescued by the onlookers who had gathered to speed the mail, the rider commandeered a mount and rode to the relay station, where the *mochila* was passed on to the next courier.[23]

Even less occasionally was the rider endangered by animals. Many years after the event, one rider remembered encountering a huge herd in Nebraska:

> The greatest danger I faced on the trail was buffaloes. They were along the trail in Western Nebraska by thousands. If a rider ever ran into a herd, he was gone. Wolves were numerous—big fellows. One winter night I saw some fifteen or twenty of them around a crippled horse which they had killed. They followed me for fifteen miles to the next station. The next day I went back and doctored up the carcass of that horse with strychnine. Twelve dead wolves were lying around the bait, the next time I went back.[24]

Undaunted by wolves, snow storms, bandits, and warring Indians, often riding double duty, almost always on time, the Pony Express rider emerges from these tales a hero with an unflagging commitment to his duty. The anecdote that best illustrates this quality is that of the rider who had been attacked and wounded by Indians and who staggered into Dry Creek station where he died a few hours later, his *mochila* stained with his blood.[25] The mail must go through. The story is often told about rider Nick Wilson and his scrape with death. Arriving at Spring Valley, Nick headed toward the stables to get a fresh horse when he saw several Indians stealing them.

> Instead of thinking of his own safety, Nick pulled out his Colt and started firing at the Indians. . . . Impulsively he ran after them, following them into a cedar grove. Suddenly another Indian jumped out from

behind a tree, drawing his bow at Nick. . . . The stone-tipped arrow hit the boy above the left eye and more than half of the arrowhead penetrated the skull. He lay among the cedars, unconscious.

Then, by happy chance, two men who were walking out of the desert found him. They carried Wilson into a shady area, did what they could for him, and went to the nearest relay station for medical aid. They next morning two Expressmen went out to the place where Wilson lay, expecting to find him dead. But he was alive; tying him across a saddle, they headed back to their station, doubting that he could survive the trip. He did survive, and eventually recovered to ride again for the Express.[26]

Speed, endurance, commitment: these are the themes of nearly all the tales of the Pony Express examined here. And given the seemingly limited nature of the rider's activities—as seen from outside—we are not surprised at the limited possibilities for narrative. The rider departs from his initial station and rides to his destination. On the way he encounters a very limited variety of obstacles, all determined by the kind of hazards the public thought he might encounter. If he and his cargo are not threatened, he may have some experience—eating on the gallop or trying to dodge young women who want part of his clothing for a souvenir—that will further heighten his concern with speed. The same pattern can be extended somewhat if, on arrival at his original destination, he is obliged to ride on, taking over his relay rider's route as well. Such options are exercised when the point of the story is the rider's endurance or commitment; stories of speed, and many of danger, are usually brief, and end at the intended terminus. We can easily construct a narrative flow chart of Pony Express tales:

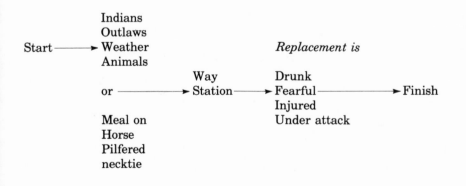

Though the range of these stories is narrow, and the variants few, they are expressive of the public's conception of the Pony Express. Speed, endurance, commitment. Tales of the Pony Express are dramatizations of what newspapers were writing explicitly in 1860:[27]

> The loud peals of thunder, and the fierce flashes of lightning, or even the falling of the drenching rain, detains him not. . . . Whether sun-dried or soaked, snow-covered or frozen, by day or by night, in starlight or darkness, be he lonely or merry, forward he hastens, until the thrice-welcome station is just there, in sight, when he leaps from his saddle, and with full heart rejoices that his task for the present is fully accomplished. . . . He rides all alone, over prairies and mountains, whether up hill or down, on rough ground or smooth, among true friends or foes, he hies swiftly on, until in the shadowy distance the relay is seen, and his duty's performed.

The folk and popular narratives of the riders of the Pony Express said pretty much the same thing, often as eloquently and as vehemently, but in their own mode. The mail must go through.

Custer, the dashing cavalier, was to his countrymen over a century ago the embodiment of the brave soldier, as Brady's portrait expresses. *U. S. Signal Corps*

More than hearts were buried at Wounded Knee; subsequent mass burials render this scene more sinister and poignant.

Markers for the dead at the site of the Last Stand; the marker for Custer, more illustrious in defeat than in life, is in the middle of the group of three at the center.

Making the West even more exciting: Remington's Indians attack "The Emigrants" when they are most vulnerable, fording a river. *Hogg Brothers Collection, The Museum of Fine Arts, Houston*

The swiftness of the Pony Express is captured in this Remington oil of the spent horse still saddled while the fresh one leaps toward its next station. *Thomas Gilcrease Institute of American History and Art, Tulsa*

An original recruiting poster shows an unhurried and sedate rider.

Two gingerbread leviathans sprint for the finish line in a contest the Currier and Ives artist made a close one. *Missouri Historical Society, St. Louis*

Red women were perceived as forbidden, darkly passion-
ate, and unquestioningly faithful to their white lovers.

Remington's sketch of the craggy, quietly dignified mountain man looks very little like Jim Bridger—who it's supposed to be—but a little like many early trappers as
Easterners imagined them.

The Race of the *Natchez* and the *Robert E. Lee*

IFE on the Mississippi has always been thought to be rough, rowdy, and robust. Mike Fink, exemplar of river boatmen during the last century, is fabled for his hard drinking, his harder fighting, and various displays of great physical strength. Davy Crockett, angered once by the wake of a steamboat, uprooted a tree, mounted an alligator, and paddled upstream after the offending vessel. He overtook it. New Orleans, queen city of the river, was the haunt of pirates and outlaws, a vigorous and exuberant town, where virtually no man was a stranger to physical violence. Jim Bowie and his legendary knife were at home there; and the mountain men, in need of diversion and amusement after a year in the wilds and the back-breaking trip down the river, drank and caroused in New Orleans before starting back up river for the next year's work.

Before the days of the steamers much of the cargo on the river was carried on small boats, whose only power was provided by the crew: bullboats, flatboats, keelboats. On the smallest, the pirogues, that crew was one man. Canoes specially built to float several hundred pounds of skins (or other merchandise) were common. So strong is the current that few trappers even bothered to try and get their small craft back upstream; in New Orleans they sold them, often for scrap, and then made their way north, along the Natchez Trace. The larger bullboats and the famous keelboats were too costly to destroy after just one voyage and had to be manhandled back up the river. The means of propulsion varied, but all were muscle-stretching.

Some boats were poled upstream: crewmen thrust their poles into the mud while standing on the foredeck, then levered the boat forward as they moved toward the stern where they removed their poles from the water and scampered back to the bow to repeat the process. Other boats were cordelled—the crew walked along the bank hauling the boat on towropes. Whatever the method, the work was rupturing, back-breaking, blood-vessel-bursting; it demanded of the Atlases who labored on the Father of waters more than most ordinary men could give. An informant who had sailed (steamed?) on the river for fifty years remarked to me that in the old days it was common on entering the captain's pilothouse to see his hernia truss lying on a workshelf, but in recent years what one more often saw was a large bottle of Valium.

When we relive the famous race of the *Lee* and the *Natchez* we need to keep in mind the physical strength life on the Mississippi demanded. A race, on such a "course" and with such an audience, is hardly the sprint of two greyhounds; for four days during the summer of 1870 the two boats pounded and beat and hissed their way upstream from New Orleans to St. Louis. The event, and the two boats, have become a part of the American consciousness to an extent that is not at all justified by the historical significance of the race. In fact it had no historical significance whatever; yet it is remembered by thousands as one of the great sporting events of the century. Accounts of the contest usually mention with pride the fact that the *Lee's* time on that stretch of river, heading in that direction, has never been equalled. Though the race would never get into conventional history books, the great enthusiasm it generated at the time and its perpetuation in the American memory mark it as a "folkloric event."

One of the songs made famous by Al Jolson includes several lines describing life in Alabama: "way down on the levee/in old Alabamy.... " They know that "it's the good ship *Robert E. Lee* that's come to carry the cotton away." The song is "Waiting for the *Robert E. Lee*"; in fact the *Lee* plied the Mississippi, and Alabama does not front on that river. But in any romantic setting in nineteenth-century America, what other river steamer would we want to wait for?

During the Civil War commercial traffic on the river virtually ceased, ruining many ship owners, among them Captain Thomas P. Leathers. When river life began to recover after the war, he began operating charter ships, and in 1869, when he had saved enough capital, he contracted for his own vessel again. It was to be called the *Natchez*, actually the sixth steamer to carry that name. When she was commissioned shortly after, the *Natchez* quickly built a reputation for speed, her most spectacular feat being a record-breaking voyage from New Orleans to St. Louis in 3 days, 21 hours, and 58 minutes. The fastest time until that date had been set 26 years earlier by the steamer *J. M. White.*[1]

In 1866 Captain John W. Cannon had the steamer *Robert E. Lee* built, under contract, to ply the New Orleans and Vicksburg cotton trade. But Cannon, known as a shrewd businessman, soon expanded the *Lee's* routes to include Louisville, Kentucky; during those early years after the war, the *Lee* also quickly established her own reputation, for her impressive good looks, her luxurious appointments for passengers, and her swiftness in the water.

The Mississippi steamboats had come to embody something characteristically American, however common they may have been elsewhere in the world. So "American" are they that two "steamers" are the central attraction of "Frontierland" in California's Disneyland. And much about them was luxurious and bespoke wealth. Passengers' cabins and accommodations rooms were often lavishly panelled, and the food, though prepared with the plainness of the day in the United States, was the best available. (The Nittany Lion Inn of State College, Pennsylvania, still calls its leanest, richest slices of roast beef the "steamboat cut.") And the exterior woodwork was elaborately carpentered—the steamboats looked like floating gingerbread-and-icing palaces.

Though powered by steam, these riverboats represented an older, more gracious way of living than their hissing boilers and sooty stacks suggested; to much of the South, they were a constant reminder of a comfortable, decorous recent past. The Civil War's ravages were still very much a part of the defeated region's daily life in 1870, the War hardly forgotten or forgiven, when the *Lee* and the *Natchez* jockeyed for positions in New Orleans.

A great deal of the public enthusiasm over the race was the exuberance of breaking out of the confinement of the war's restraints. Much of the war had been fought in the South, and much of that on and near the river. As in nearly every war, necessities were often hard to get; luxuries, nearly impossible. People were restricted in their life-routines, suppressed in their desires and abilities to earn a secure living, hampered in their ability to travel, and toward the end of the War, in the South, deprived of their optimism for a satisfactory conclusion to hostilities. For several years after the War the South was a defeated nation; despite the enlightened plans of Lincoln to reintegrate the region quickly and amicably, Federal garrisons were a constant reminder of defeat, the area seemed to have been overrun by rapacious carpetbaggers, and much of the area was in ruin, physically and financially. There was little to cheer about or for. When the *Lee* and the *Natchez* went to their starting posts, then, the South (as well as those who lived on the northern river areas) had an excuse for long-suppressed enthusiasm. The race, redolent of so many symbols of a former, better life, was an ideal vessel of the public's enthusiasm, making up for nearly a decade of somber perseverance and deprivation.

Captain Cannon is said to have named his boat the *Robert E. Lee* in order to capitalize on strong sectional sentiment in the region he serviced. Perhaps—but however cynical was the motivation for the naming of his vessel, it seems to have had the desired effect. One Indiana newspaper expressed a prevalent Northern feeling when it editorialized that:

> The people hereabouts who are interested in the race are friendly to the Natchez for many reasons. A steamer named for any accursed rebel General should scarcely be allowed to float, much less have the honor of making the best time, especially one that is notorious as a rendez-vous for thieves. Nearly every one of our boatmen who have returned on her on different occasions have been robbed. . . . we say, 'Success to the Natchez.'[2]

Cannon and Leathers were not only bitter business rivals, but personal enemies as well. Roy L. Barkhau's pamphlet on the race remarks that "at one time, in a personal encounter, it is said they actually came to blows."[3] That story is also in oral circulation, though none of my informants were certain that this fight actually took place: "It is said that. . . . " Captain Fred W. Way, who spent nearly fifty years on the river, told me in an interview in 1975 that the two men had radically different personalities; their boats were much alike. Captain Way was born thirty years after the race and knows only the folklore of others who were alive then and who have passed along such descriptions and narratives. But according to him, John Cannon was heavy, physically imposing, and courtly; Thomas

Leathers, lean, hard, and brusque. Cannon was engagingly jovial; Leathers, all business and no frivolity.

The contestants—the boats—are personified by their captains, much as "Custer's Last Stand" became a contest between the "Boy General" and Sitting Bull. Recently, a toy manufacturer of a board game pitting armies of "tanks" against each other, pictured in a television ad "Field Marshal Rommel" sitting down to play this game against "Montgomery." The North African campaign comes down to this: Rommel vs. Monty. And the great race of the *Natchez* and the *Lee* became Cannon vs. Leathers. Further, these two historic Captains came to be polarized by their personalities, heightening the conflict between them, placing them in conventional dramatic frameworks that will be familiar to nearly all readers and listeners. Even if they were not bitter business rivals, the stories repeated about them would make that a "fact," for that rivalry adds further drama to their race against each other. This race was in some sense a serious business, as contemporary comment on the name of one of the steamers shows, and it would not do to have the captains of the rival boats on the best of terms. That might make the race appear to be more an exhibition than a true contest. But as we have seen again and again, we make a drama of our realities, we retell our experiences with the devices and techniques of the writers of fiction, so that at one point it may be impossible, without recourse to very careful "historical" investigation, to distinguish between accurate accounts of events and fanciful recapitulations of them. (I pass over the impossibility of ever capturing the reality of an event as a philosophical and epistemological problem beyond the scope of these pages.)

In late June of 1870 both boats were headed, as though by unstated agreement, toward New Orleans. The *Natchez* was cruising south after her recent record-making trip to St. Louis; Captain Cannon was guiding the *Lee* down the Ohio. According to legend, because the men were not on speaking terms, no formal challenge to race was issued. Yet each captain seemed to know what was going to happen, and by the time both boats were in New Orleans so too did half of the American public. The New Orleans *Times-Picayune* commented on June 30th that "the great event of the day will be the departure of the two finest and fastest boats on the river, Robert E. Lee and Natchez. . . . No doubt the levee, as far up as Carrollton, will be crowded to see these two fast ones pitted against each other."[4]

Public interest ran high, as all contemporary accounts remark; the morning after the race began, the *Times-Picayune* commented that "never before in New Orleans has there been such excitement regarding a steamboat race ... than between these two splendid river palaces."[5] According to the reporter, many heavy bets were being made. In sporting circles the race was the only topic of conversation, and the levee front was crowded with people from all walks of life. As the steamers paddled into midstream, the *Times-Picayune* man estimated their speed at eighteen miles an hour or more. The first boat to reach St. Louis would thereafter be entitled to the epithet "Champion of the Mississippi River." Two of the newspaper's seven front-page columns were devoted to the race and related news.

Contemporary news stories observed that both boats were being stripped for greater speed. In the case of these river leviathans, that meant removing any elaborately carved lattice-work that might catch the wind. Most of the *Lee's* after-guards were removed, as were portions of the wheelhouse. Captain Leathers only removed some gingerbread from the *Natchez*. The *Natchez* took aboard about ninety cabin passengers, the *Lee* about sixty; those on the *Lee* were bound for Ohio River ports only—they would have to be discharged when the *Lee* reached the Ohio, before St. Louis. A number of passengers on the *Natchez* had booked passage to the city of that name and would have to be dropped off in mid-race. Accepting such passengers was in keeping with the refusal of either captain to acknowledge publicly that a race was about to begin.

There had been steamboat racing on the Mississippi for many years. It was a dangerous sport. The Mississippi is difficult enough to navigate under normal conditions, when deliberate care can be taken, as we know from reading Mark Twain. Hundreds of riverboats had run aground on shifting sand bars in midstream or been pierced by snags and tree trunks lurking just beneath the surface of the river's notoriously muddy waters. And hundreds more had burned up when their boilers exploded. Racing, which put great pressures on a ship's boilers, increased the dangers of fire and explosion. For several years before the race of the *Natchez* and the *Lee* racing had been discouraged by a concerned public. The St. Louis *Missouri Republican* editorialized:

> We thought in this age men would not indulge in so reprehensible, if not criminal, a practice. And should an accident occur during such a race, how could the officers of these boats expect to meet the friends of

the lost? Would they not be regarded justly or unjustly as murderers? We are told that it is not dangerous! Neither are loaded bombs, if they do not explode, yet they are by no means pleasant playthings. We hope the rivalry among steamboatmen will not lead them into the indiscretion of jeopardizing the lives of passengers.[6]

Captain Frederick Way has told me that his passengers always clamored for him to run faster than other boats heading in the same direction and that he often had to refuse to do so.[7] But Captain Way raced with steel boilers, not iron ones, and his *Betsy Ann* of the nineteen twenties and thirties was much safer than ships with iron boilers.

Scenarios for races, whether of machines, animals, or humans, are likely to be one of four types. In the first, one contestant gets an early lead and simply maintains it to the end. This is probably the least interesting of contests. In a second type, one racer overcomes the other's initial lead, usually after a long struggle, and often near the finish-line. In a bid of the challenger. And in a last type, the contestants continually alternate as front-runner, with the see-saw contest not decided until the last instant. If contests of whatever sort do not follow one of these patterns, they are nevertheless likely to be retold that way. These scenarios exploit the inherent potentials for drama within the event itself.

The race metaphor is easily shifted to other arenas; the electoral process is often a lengthy one, from a candidate's declaration of intention to "run," to the finish line, the actual vote. Frequent polling and sampling of public opinion and attitudes—and the publication of these results, often with careful statistical breakdowns— gives political campaigns the semblance of a race. "Dark horse," "front-runner," and "challenger" are common terms for candidates and derive from the individual's relative position vis-β-vis his opponent at various media-determined stages, almost corresponding to the turns and loops of a racetrack.

And the same four race scenarios can also be shifted, with only slight modification, to athletic contests. One team gets an early lead and holds it; the other team plays successful "catch-up" ball and overcomes its opponent, most dramatically in the ninth inning or in the last few seconds; or one team successfully holds off the challenger; or one or the other finally wins after a struggle in which the lead changes hands several times. Each scenario also has subordinate details that seem to emerge as the "ploy" of the event unfolds or is analyzed after the fact. And very often, many of our minor, incidental perceptions of events—boat races, political campaigns, baseball games—are influenced by our overall perceptions of the nature of the flow of action—the scenario of the plot.

Actually, the race of the *Lee* and the *Natchez* adhered pretty closely to the first scenario (one contestant gets an early lead and maintains it), with only minor modifications. At five in the afternoon the *Lee* pulled away from her wharf, forcing the *Natchez* to wait until the *Lee* had cleared before she too could enter the main flow of the river. By the time the *Natchez* fired her signal gun—at two minutes past five—the *Lee* was already a mile under way. It was a lead she never relinquished. The crowds down by the river sent up a cheer; the boats steamed past several excursion craft positioned upstream to watch the event, and lumbered away into the night. At the one-hundred-mile point the *Lee* was six minutes ahead.

One of the *Lee's* pumps went out about thirty miles above New Orleans and steam pressure was lost, but the problem was resolved in a short time, and Cannon's boat resumed her lead. At Grand Gulf the *Natchez* played out her role of business-as-usual on this trip, putting in to shore to discharge passengers and take on others. The *Natchez* began to gain on her rival, ever so slowly, but at Buckhorn Landing her cold-water pump died. The boat had to be landed, and the ensuing repairs took thirty-three minutes. That half-hour was crucial, for the *Lee* passed out of sight.

On Saturday the one controversy of the race was spawned, as the *Lee* was refueled by another steamer, the *Frank Pargoud.* Captain Cannon had earlier arranged with the skipper of the *Frank Pargoud* that a hundred tons of pine knots be delivered to the *Lee* in mid-river while both boats were under full steam. Fans of the *Natchez* later claimed that the speed of the *Pargoud* added to that of the *Lee*, giving her an unfair advantage; while supporters of Captain Cannon's maneuver argued that the *Pargoud,* being a slower vessel, actually slowed the *Lee* down. The *Natchez* landed to pick up fuel, thus losing more time to the leader. At the head of Island 82 the Mississippi is so twisted back upon itself that both boats were in sight of each other, though the *Lee* was a good twelve miles ahead. Her lead was never challenged in this disappointingly one-sided race, and that was the only time during the race when both steamers were in sight of each other.

The famous Currier and Ives print shows them side-by-side in midstream under a full moon. But this is for dramatic effect only; the real *Natchez* never got that close. And, pictorially important as a full moon might be, in fact both boats were hampered by fog at night, particularly above Cairo. The *Lee* ran aground several times but backed off successfully each time, and with the *Natchez* an hour behind, ran the third night at slow bell. The fog lifted for the *Lee* much sooner than for her rival, and she was able to steam full speed ahead toward St. Louis several hours before Captain Leathers felt it was safe for him to do so. The *Natchez* is said to have lost several hours because of the fog. The *Lee* steamed into St. Louis to the cheers of a swollen Fourth-of-July crowd after 3 days, 18 hours, and 14 minutes, a record that stands yet.

Though the first scenario—the "Lee" takes an early lead and maintains it throughout—accurately describes the race, the retellings that I have heard and read place considerable emphasis on the disabled pump, the midstream refueling by the *Pargoud,* and the fog. The attempt, naturally enough, is to make the story an interesting one by making the reader/listener think that the outcome was in doubt until the last hour, that there was suspense in a race that was really by and large suspense-free.

At the time, there was a great deal of interest: the comments of contemporary observers range from exuberant to superlative. The steamers *Wm. S. Pike, Henry Tete,* and *Mayflower* waited several miles upstream for the racers to pass, those excursion boats' decks crowded with enthusiastically cheering fans. As daylight waned, the first of what was to become an unbroken succession of levee-side bonfires was lit, outlining the river all the way to St. Louis. The *Times-Picayune's* comment that "never before in New Orleans has there been such excitement regarding a steamboat race...." has already been cited; and it was pretty much the same in every town along the route of the race. Cincinnati, a river town, though several hundred miles away from the Mississippi, nevertheless shared the fever: "the race ... has created more of a sensation here today than anything of the kind that ever occurred."[8] The excitement, said a story datelined Memphis, though also carried in the *New York Times,* was as intense as it had ever been anywhere. Betting was heavy, one of the surest signs of spectator interest; in New Orleans one confident fan of the *Lee* was said to be willing to bet $10,000 to $500 on "his" boat. A miller from the same city was said to be looking for someone willing to take up his $10,000 bet—even odds—on the *Natchez.* From Cincinnati it was reported that more than $200,000 had been wagered on the contest.[9] At each major point of the river, the time of arrival was telegraphed elsewhere around the country, and the elapsed time since departure instantly calculated.[10] Above Vicksburg, owing to the controversy of the *Pargoud* refueling, many bets were called off. Still, it would be the sporting event of the decade.

The character of the boats is significant to any understanding of their place in the public's mind. Although both the *Lee* and the *Natchez* are praised for their great speed, and the latter particularly for the way she so easily slipped through the water, neither vessel —nor any other of their type—could properly be called graceful. Certainly the Mississippi River steamboat had none of the lithe, svelte appearance and movement of the Clipper ship, none of the grace of any ship under sail. Both boats were as long as a football field; the pudgier *Lee* was 48 feet wide, her slimmer rival slightly over 42 feet in the beam. They seemed to lumber rather than sprint, yet both boats were capable of good speed: eighteen miles an hour, and that upstream. That speed would give either boat an edge over any Clipper then afloat, a fleetness that was realized because of the great strength of the steam-driven side paddles. Beating the water with awesome force, the steamer's paddles pushed the boats forward amidst a noisy splashing that exuded an overbearingly great sense of strength. The black smoke and sparks that gushed from their stacks reinforced this aesthetic.

Their speed, therefore, was not that of the cheetah, but rather more like that of a rhinoceros. Fleetness, in this case, is inseparable from power, a quality of the steamers we should always remember in any description of those boats. For the American public they connoted the steam-driven might of the young nation, the dynamo that was both an object of worship (as Henry Adams thought) and a villain when it beat John Henry down. The steamboat, conjuring up the names of American inventors Fitch, Stevens, Evans, Rumsey, and Fulton, has long been thought an American development; it quickly came to characterize much that was American, in ideals, in attitude, in ethos.

Though the race between the *Lee* and the *Natchez* was unsuspenseful from the point of view of racing aesthetics, in the folklore about the race every effort was made to make it exciting. The captains as well as their boats are pitted against each other in terms we would expect to find in fiction. John Cannon, that epitome of the chivalric Southern gentleman, locks horns with blunt, acerbic Thomas Leathers, known on the river as the most skillful of swearers. Yet it was Cannon who was accused of cynically naming his boat the *Robert E. Lee* because of its sentimental appeal to his Mississippi River clients; it was Cannon who stripped his boat for faster steaming, who refused passengers for destinations that would force him to stop en route; and it was Cannon who arranged the questionable refueling transfer with the *Pargoud.* Narrative conventions rule our perceptions of this, and all events, even though they "really happened."

The Ten-Mile Day

 GREAT deal of folklore has been collected about the railroads, though o nly a small portion of it involves the building of the transcontinental railroad. Yet that "most marvelous work of human hand"—as the St. Louis *Missouri Democrat*
of 10 May 1869 exuberantly exaggerated it—was one of the major
factors in the development of the American West. It encouraged the
colonization of the land west of the Mississippi by making it possible
for emigrants to travel hundreds of miles quickly, painlessly, and
safely, and it enabled them to ship back to Eastern markets the
produce they grew in the West; it established the long-sought direct
route to the Pacific and ultimately to Asia; it made possible the
shipment of livestock from cattle towns (which were "created" for
this purpose) and brought about the advent of that characteristically
American figure, the cowboy; and, in the words of the Department
of the Interior plaque at the site of the Golden Spike ceremony, "it
achieved the great political objective of binding together by iron
bonds the extremities of continental United States, a rail link from
ocean to ocean."

At first I wondered what folkloric or popular event might symbolize "the railroad," or "the Western Railroad." Of railroads in
general, the lore is voluminous and varied. By a kind of engaging
perversity, the train has made folk heroes of several of its most
successful antagonists: from the Reno brothers, who pulled off the
first train robbery at Seymour, Indiana, in 1866, to our most famous
train robbers, the Jameses and the Youngers. Sam Bass, memorial-

ized in folksong, also turned his hand to plundering the iron horse at one time, as did Butch Cassidy. And the abuses and authoritarian policies of the California roads turned Chris Evans and John Sontag into outlaws who were folk heroes to many of California's small farmers.

Other "heroes" worked for the railroads. A number of anecdotes retell incidents in the lives of those who owned and controlled them, such as the story of Andrew Carnegie's assiduous attention to duty or Vanderbilt's retreat to a baggage car to smoke his favorite cigar. Others became legendized through their deeds: risking their lives to warn an oncoming engineer that the bridge had washed away; fighting off bandits or Indians against seemingly impossible odds, and thus saving some valuable freight or gold shipment; oiling a faulty "hotbox" by leaning over the side of a fast-moving train; performing errands of mercy like the heroic efforts of the engineer and crew of the train that went into Hinckley, Minnesota, to take out citizens entrapped by a great forest fire.

An appropriate amount of folklore commemorates those whose deeds were involved with one of the obvious qualities of the Iron Horse, speed: "Death Valley Scotty" raced against the clock when he chartered a train from California to Chicago, for the publicity and the promotional gain and—one hopes—to see if it could be done. Union officer John Andrews rendezvoused with several other Union spies in Marietta, Georgia, stole a locomotive, and raced against their Confederate pursuers toward the Union lines in Tennessee, though most of them wound up in Andersonville. At least two movies have been made about that race: one a Walt Disney production, which takes the matter pretty seriously and dramatically, and "The General," with Buster Keaton, which does not take the idea very seriously, though the film is at least as memorable as the Disney film.

The railroads gave us Casey Jones, the epitome of the hero in the machine age, who died for his commitment to his duty and who was the exemplar, par excellence, of the man-at-one-with-his-machine. He is said to have loved his Number 638 engine as much as he loved his wife. And the railroads have also given us the epitome of the victim-hero of the machine age, John Henry, that steel-drivin' man, who died working on the railroad, symbolized in its turn by the hard-driving locomotive whose steel and fire will overcome and easily destroy any flesh-and-blood that gets in its way.

The train had other dramatic possibilities for use in folk and popular culture. It seems to have been for some observers in the nineteenth century in many ways like the passenger airliner is for us today. The train is the vehicle of liminality; once aboard, passengers pass through geography that seems to have little relevance to their immediate condition. One leaves a portion of one's life behind and moves on to another. But between, one lives, for the moment, on the train—or plane. Few novels of the period, and no folklore that I know of, have exploited the dramatic possibilities of the situation —passengers removed from their home environment and society and cast into a terrestrial limbo. The train becomes, for the length of the journey, the world for its passengers. The train wreck is apocalyptic, as has often been the plot line of doomed airliner stories. And the runaway train has its updated counterpart in the airplane whose pilot is incapacitated in some way or dead. Both are, in these respects, analogues of the ship at sea, whose relationship to the airplane is evident in the job titles of flight crews—pilot, captain, first officer, navigator, steward(ess), and so on—and in terms used in describing parts of the aircraft—rudder, bulkhead, stabilizer, cabin, port and starboard—and in terms describing action relating to the process of flight, such as debarking and embarking. In recent years, as the airlines have surpassed the surface carriers to become the predominant means of transportation, new terms appropriate to the industry, its equipment, and its personnel have begun to re-place the older, sea-related terminology. Aircraft now have flight engineers, stewardesses are air hostesses or flight attendants, pas-sengers de-plane at their destinations.

However, not very much of the folklore of railroads concerns the West. Casey Jones met his death in Tennessee; Vanderbilt and Carnegie were Easterners; and John Henry is identified with no particular place. Hinckley, Minnesota, may have been "the West" in 1894, but it is not the "West" that non-Minnesotans think of today. Certainly, little of that heroic rescue suggests "the winning of the West," or "the conquest of the plains," or "Manifest Destiny." Yet because of the major role the railroads played in that settlement process called by those (and other) terms the Hinckley rescue cannot be ignored. Building the transcontinental railroads was not "an event," but a very complicated conglomerate of them. One factor that characterized the construction of the American rails across the country was the deliberate attempt to do it as rapidly as possible, often to the detriment of other considerations. We may think of the fascination with speed, or the compulsion to get the job done in a hurry, or to have our accomplishments immediately recognized as being characteristically, if not essentially, American. The haste with which the Union Pacific and the Central Pacific put down tracks has in it something that is importantly American.

The one "event" that most people seem to remember in this several-year construction project is the golden spike ceremony at Promontory Point, Utah, on May 10, 1869. Though he did not live to see it, it was the culmination of more than a decade's work and hopes for Theodore Judah, whose unrelenting intensity on behalf of the idea of a transcontinental railroad earned him the sobriquet "Crazy"—"Crazy Ted" or "Crazy Judah." First he tried to interest Congress in his scheme, and when that failed he returned to California to raise the necessary money through private capital. When silver was discovered at the Comstock Lode, several wealthy merchants in the West became interested in putting rail lines through at least as far as the Washoe mining regions. Four men, whose last names have since become the most prominent names in California —Leland Stanford, Collis Huntington, Charles Crocker, and Mark Hopkins—incorporated the Central Pacific Railroad of California during the summer of 1861. In the fall, when they had approved chief engineer Judah's land survey, they sent him to Washington to try again for government aid.

The first shovelful of earth was turned in Sacramento on January 3, 1862, as the Central Pacific officially began its eastward march. The Union Pacific was much later in starting work (December 2, 1863) and from the first was hampered by shortages of manpower and iron caused by the war, which barely impinged upon the consciousness of the Californians. Ground-breaking was for the Union Pacific a gesture only. During 1864 hardly any progress was made, and it was not until July of 1865 that track-laying began, and then it was at the pace of about one mile each week.[1]

Grenville Dodge was given the job of chief engineer on the Union Pacific in the spring of 1866; a former Union general who had been impressive on Sherman's "March to the Sea," he and supervisors Jack and Dan Casemate organized the construction process in a precise, "military" regimen. The metaphor of the military operation runs throughout descriptions of the Union Pacific's construction work and later spills over into descriptions of the work of its West coast rival. William Bailey described it that way:

> The men who go ahead are the advance guard, and following them is the second line cutting through the gorges, grading the road and building the bridges. Then comes the main body of the army, placing the ties, laying the track, spiking down the rails, perfecting the alignment, ballasting and dressing up and completing the road for immediate use. Along the line of the completed road are construction trains pushing 'to the front' with supplies. . . .[2]

At first, each track-layer was given a pound of tobacco if the crew laid its mile of track before sunset; then the incentive was a fifty percent increase in the day's wages (from $2 to $3) if they could put down a mile and a half; and that was raised to four dollars each day that the layers put down two miles.[3]

Still, the progress of both roads moving slowly toward the intermountain basin was not a competition, and speed did not become an issue until Congress removed the restriction prohibiting the Central Pacific from construction farther east than a point 150 miles east of the California-Nevada border; that meant that the railroads would be united at a place decided by the speed of their progress across the country. One other factor contributed to the desire for speed, though that was by 1866 not an important one: Congress had set a time-limit on the construction, decreeing that subsidies would cease by July 1, 1876, the nation's centennial. But even by the fall of 1867, it was clear that meeting that deadline would be no problem.

In *Hear That Lonesome Whistle Blow* by Dee Brown, the chapter describing the years 1867–69 is aptly titled "The Great Race." It must have seemed as though everyone in America wanted the railway finished in a hurry: the owners and stockholders in the railroads, of course, because each mile of track laid earned the companies at least $16,000 and 12,800 acres of right-of-way land—and mineral rights. Through the Sierras the Central Pacific got up to triple the dollar subsidy. Those who did not stand to gain financially, but who longed for the colonization of the land west of the Mississippi, wanted the railroad through. The railroad provided work for thousands of unemployed soldiers at the end of the Civil War. The Easterner "in the street" wanted it, as a matter of national pride. The Westerner wanted it because it would greatly improve communication with his "home" back East. The Mormons wanted the railroad built through to the West because it provided their men with work and their contractors with a lucrative market; and it would also bring contact with the East, and perhaps an understanding of their ways.

Although they had originally wanted to preserve "Zion" for themselves, by 1869 the Mormons saw the virtues in the inevitable, as the words of "The Railroad Cars, They're Coming" reveal:[4]

The great Pacific Railway,
For California hail!
Bring on the locomotive,
Lay down the iron rail,
Across the rolling prairie
'Mid mountain peaks so grand,
The railroad cars are steaming, gleaming, through Mormon's land
The railroad cars are speeding, fleeting, through Mormon's land.

"A sense of urgency prevailed," wrote Robert Athern, "that seemed to call for speed, without regard to cost."[5]

The New York *Commercial Advertiser* thought that the railroads were the greatest undertaking of Western civilization; the *World* expected that this "grand highway of all nations" would shift the world's financial center from London to New York.[6] And a Dr. Henry Parry at Fort Sedgwick in the Colorado Territory wrote of the iron horse, that "every cloud of its white smoke seemed to bring with it peace and civilization over the plains of the Far West."[7]

More loquaciously smug was an article in the New York *Herald,* datelined from the heart of California:

From where I am now writing, in the heart of the city of Sacramento within two blocks of the centre of business, a gentleman informs me that only nineteen years ago he could, with a Minie rifle, have killed wild deer. Now what do I see and hear? Steamboats that are fit to be side by side with those of the North and East rivers; the bell of the locomotive that is here to-day and tomorrow hundreds of miles away on its track across the Continent; and I am surrounded by blocks of buildings wherein a prosperous trade is carried on, and dwellings that vie in beauty and size with any in the country.[8]

"A sense of urgency prevailed." Dee Brown notes that despite considerable difficulty, ethical as well as financial, the railroad owners, "with the assistance of the national press, . . . kept up a drumfire of propaganda upon the populace that was designed to inspire sweating laborers to 'win' at all costs."[9] Durant of the Union Pacific stressed the need for speed rather than good and careful workmanship and attention to detail. He once telegraphed to a subordinate: "What is the matter that you can't lay track faster."[10] The tracks were often hastily laid, sometimes in "S" curves that as well as avoiding obstacles such as hills or ravines also added millions in subsidy profits per mile. Later, millions of dollars more would have to be spent to straighten "crooked" track laid in haste. Some ties were placed on ice and were suspended when it thawed. Bridges sometimes seemed the flimsiest of structures, swaying vertiginously in high winds.[11]

Tie cutters on the Union Pacific were offered a bonus of 29 cents for each piece over fifteen they cut each day; as a result, much of Nebraska was deforested.[12] Once in Laramie, and within a couple of hundred of miles of the meeting point with the Central Pacific, Jack Casement motivated his men to even greater speed with extra pay for work on moonlit nights and Sundays. During the winter of 1868–69 the Union Pacific workers were not put in winter quarters —the usual procedure in those days—but were kept on the job throughout the bitter cold. Informed by Casement that the Union Pacific workers were nearing the breaking point, Durant offered to double their wages if they would continue construction.[13]

As spring came to the Great Basin, the Union and Central Pacific companies rounded the far turn. An editorial writer for the Sacramento *Bee* observed:

> The contest is between two great corporations as to which shall construct and forever own most of the national highway. . . . They are coming together on the home stretch and each is using the whip and spur to hasten forward everything connected with construction.[14]

"An air of excitement developed across America" as it became obvious that the transcontinental railroad would be finished, and seven years ahead of time.[15]

In this context we must place the event of April 28, 1869. The meeting point of the two roads had been arbitrated at Promontory Point, Utah, thus ending the race as far as incentives for mileage subsidies were concerned.[16] It was all over but the shouting. But one more event was yet to be staged. And that event would encapsulate, in one working day, the message of speed, determination, pride, and back-wrenching labor that went into the building of the railroad across the country. According to legend, Charles Crocker of the Central Pacific and Thomas Durant of the Union Pacific had once gotten into a friendly boasting match about the prowess of each other's work crews, and a bet was made for $10,000—a huge sum in those days—that the Central Pacific could lay more than ten miles of track in one day, an extraordinary feat.

The event most people have read about and associate with the building of the Pacific railway is the Golden Spike Ceremony at Promontory Point, Utah, two weeks after Ten-Mile Day. That marked the official completion of the road, consummated when Leland Stanford of the Central Pacific was to drive in a golden spike on the "last rail," and Durant drove in one of silver. The day has not escaped without its humorous asides: both men are said, in some waggish versions of the ceremony, to have missed the spike entirely, and that nearby workers had to be enlisted to do the job. Other versions have it that the spike holes had been bored so large that the spikes slipped into them easily and without pounding. The Andrew J. Russell photographs of the occasion clearly show two men cavorting on the front of each of the locomotives involved, "Jupiter" and "119" of the Union Pacific, waving champagne bottles, but all depictions of alcoholic beverages are missing from Thomas Hill's *Driving The Last Spike,* based on the Russell photo. Justly famous as is the Golden Spike Ceremony, there is nothing about it to suggest those qualities of human endeavor and aspiration that went into the building of the Pacific railroad.

April 28 was Ten-Mile Day. The press of the nation congregated at Promontory Point for the grand finale, but for the railroad workmen, as Dee Brown says, "this event was of greater importance than was the final joining of the rails,"[17] and everyone except the participants was given the day off. The race of two corporations, lasting several years, would be symbolically condensed in the race of a single day, of a Central Pacific work crew against time and the limits of their own endurance.

Ten-Mile Day was a stunt in at least one respect: Crocker and his field superintendent, James Strobridge, had the land graded in advance and ties strung out along the right-of-way. The job was made somewhat easier, so the "event" was not a typical working day nor a typical working schedule, procedure, or pace. But, then, the Golden Spike Ceremony was also a staged event, its official formalities choreographed for the press and a number of dignitaries. Neither was spontaneous, neither emerged uncorruptedly from the minds and hearts of the participants; but on April 28, 1869, the workers of the Central Pacific entered into their task wholeheartedly and the eight rail carriers, carefully chosen iron men, became the "sporting heroes of the day."[18]

Several years of track-laying experience lay behind the Crocker-Strobridge planning for that day. Rails, fishplates, spikes, and bolts were hauled to the end-of-track periodically; once empty the rail cars were manhandled off the track to make way for a loaded one, then manhandled back and drawn in its return to the supply depot. Then this procedure was repeated, the replenished cars being drawn forward to the new end-of-track position as the crews pushed further out into the desert. Then the freshly emptied car would be manhandled off the tracks, and the process repeated. Still, the procedure required the transfer of supplies from rail car to horsedrawn wagons, and from the wagons the railcarriers would haul the rails into place. In 1868 and 1869 the crews of both roads could lay—under normal conditions—four rails each minute, positioning each spike with three strokes. There were ten spikes for each rail and four hundred rails in each mile of track.[19]

Edwin Sabin described April 28:

With nippers the eight selected rail-carriers—four in a squad—seized a pair of rails from the rail-truck and running them forward plumped them down. They were adjusted instantly, the spikes had been dropped, the fishplate fastenings and bolts followed, there was one man told off for each spike, one for the fishplate and one for each bolt; pursuing them closely marched a solid column of Chinamen, the outside files with picks, the middle file, between the rails, with shovels, to ballast the roadbed. Bending their backs another squad of the Chinamen shoved the rail-truck onward over the newly-laid rails, keeping pace with the advance.

The moment that the supply was down to a few lengths, these were thrown off, the emptied truck was tipped to one side, another truck, loaded high, galloped forward, up the cleared way, and the work proceeded without a hitch.... Union Pacific watches timed the march at 144 feet a minute—five pairs of rails, or a pair every twelve seconds. End o' track was moving forward as fast as a horse might walk.

When the panting truck-crews slowed through exhaustion, another crew of the pig-tailed host sprang to relieve them. The rail gang was dripping with sweat, but worked with automatic precision.[20]

Crocker called time for lunch past one o'clock on ground later called "Camp Victory"; six miles of track were already on the ground, and his bet was safe. He offered to relieve any man who wanted out, but they all chose to finish the job. It was to be a great day in railroad history, it was to be a day in which they would show the Union Pacific men which was the better outfit, and everyone who was part of it wanted to remain in it; why would they quit before they had won? Work resumed after the hour's break, and by seven that night the laurels were theirs. They had even exceeded the boast of Charles Crocker; by 1800 feet wrote Sabin, citing a letter to him from Strobridge,[21] but contemporary news accounts, perhaps less inclined to stretch that distance, put the overage at "fifty or sixty" feet.

No matter; anything past ten miles would be gilding; it was, at "only" ten miles, a day for the record books. Those eight iron men —Sullivan, Dailey, Kennedy, Joyce, Shay, Killeen, McNamara, and Eliot (Brown's roster; Sabin lists a "George Wyatt" instead of "Eliot")—established for themselves one of those records, which like most popular events, will never be "officially" recorded. On April 28 they hauled about 1,970,000 pounds of rail in all, approximately 246,000 pounds for each man;[22] 3,520 rails were secured to 25,800 ties. Fifty-two thousand pounds of spikes had been dropped into place during those twelve hours, 14,000 bolts were fastened by 28,-000 nuts. All told, on that warm Utah day, the Central Pacific crews had carried and put into place more than two million pounds of iron.

Ever the practical man, with his eye only on Promontory, Grenville Dodge wrote to his wife of the event several days later:

> Our road is in excellent condition to Wasatch. I have seen some of the Central Pacific track. I saw them lay their special ten miles on that wager, but they were weeks preparing for it, and bedded all their ties beforehand.[23]

Most newspapers, not having their own reporters on hand, simply printed the austere wire services dispatch, a kind of filler while they too awaited the more important event at Promontory; "the track-layers are compelled to desist on account of unfinished grading. The iron was laid out at the rate of a mile an hour."[24]

But San Francisco's *Alta California* had its own man on the spot, and being caught up in the excitement of the day, he wired a lengthy story back to his paper that ran on the front page and was headlined, "Greatest Tracklaying Feat of the Age—Ten Miles of Rail Laid by the Central Pacific—Their Competitors Give it Up." The great feat was detailed in the story with an exuberance and pride of accomplishment that suggests a regional bias as well as admiration for a remarkable deed:

> The great feat of laying ten miles of track on the Central Pacific Railroad was successfully done to-day. The organization was perfect; the men were aroused to the highest pitch of enthusiasm and everything went off with perfect smoothness and success.
>
> This is the greatest feat in laying track that has ever been accomplished. . . . It must be understood that all the paraphernalia of the camp for over five thousand men was transferred over this ten-mile stretch in a single day. Two or three miles of the track had been hauled out beforehand; but all the massive rail, fishplates, spikes, etc., were teamed out today, and a good deal of it had to be brought up from the rear before it was pushed out in front. . . . The camp equipage, workshops, boarding houses, offices, and in fact, a big settlement, literally took up its bed and walked. . . . And all this work [the track-laying] was done on a heavy up-hill grade, with innumerable curves, some of them so abrupt that rails actually were bent before being spiked down. . . . And such was the enthusiasm of the men that they were willing to work for hours longer. . . . The material only exceeded fifty or sixty feet of the promised ten miles. . . .[25]

The Sacramento *Daily Union* noted the day with two items, one pointing out, with obvious sectional chest-thumping, that the previous day's high had been the Union Pacific's mere seven and one-half miles. A second item called it "the greatest work in tracklaying ever accomplished or conceived by railroad men." The article was concerned with yet another statistical set, this one reporting the number and weight of ties used in the record day. We recognize today our interest in the statistics of sporting events, both daily and compositely. The same interest was present in 1869; was this the natural means of a young nation to compare itself with older peoples? America could never claim that any important historical figure earlier than the sixteenth century had "slept here," or that any of its cities had originally been a Roman fort or a medieval castle. But Americans could claim an advantage in quantity. History was bunk, or was soon to be, but not statistics. Englishmen may have invented the locomotive, but Americans would build more of them, and they would be more powerful, and would travel over greater distances, hauling more freight and passengers, over tracks laid in record time. The *Daily Union* reporter, on April 28th, counted and weighed ties:

> The ties for over seven miles had to be hauled by two-horse teams from five miles where they were first laid to over twelve miles where they were last laid, and this over a rapidly rising grade and mountain road. As there are about 2,400 ties to a mile, and they are from eighty to ninety pounds weight, it makes 1,244,000 pounds, without the 16,000 ties teamed and laid.[26]

When it was all over, the Westerners had shown the rest of the country that it could be done; they could also beat upon their sectionalist drums in other respects as well:

> The feat of laying down ten miles of rail in one day, last week, astonished the Union Pacific managers. It is also a fact that the laborers on this end have been much better behaved and disciplined than on the other end of the road. We do not now recall to mind a single death by wanton violence on the line of the Central Pacific during the past year, while hardly a day has passed on the other end of the road without some sort of murder or other atrocity. We think a great deal of this good order and absence of violence is fairly attributable to the natural docility of the Chinese race, who have composed a great part of the force on the Central Pacific. . . . The Chinese have honestly won a compliment for good order, sobriety, and good work, which ought to shame those white ruffians who are in the habit of traducing their morals at the same time they are murdering each other.[27]

As with so many public events, even the laying of ten miles of track became an occasion for moralizing. We have seen the same, on an even grander scale, following the Custer defeat in 1876. According to the Sacramento *Daily Union,* there was an "other" end of the track, where "white ruffians" toiled away—though not so effectively or so peacefully—while they occasionally murdered each other. The *Union* is able to argue that Westerners, even the Chinese in Western employ, are qualitatively as well as quantitatively superior. They lay more track than anyone else and they do it with tranquility.

The moral issues of the construction of the transcontinental railway are with us still. Dee Brown's recent *Hear That Lonesome Whistle Blow* revives an earlier generation of muckrakers' attacks on the corruption that was at the heart of railroad financing: the rapacity of the Central Pacific's "Big Four" and various owners, directors, and financiers of the Union Pacific and Credit Mobilier, the corruptibility of congressmen and senators, the few who became very wealthy at public expense, the often shoddy construction practices perpetrated in haste, and so forth. Many of these facts were known, even in 1869, and criticized in the press, though to little avail. Frank Leslie's weekly *Illustrated Newspaper* berated railroad corruption in the same issue (May 29, 1869) that lauded the road's completion at Promontory:

> This is one of the grand events, not alone of this decade, but of the age itself, and is worthy to be celebrated by pen and pencil, and its anniversary to become a national holiday.[28]

But Ten-Mile Day has a kind of purity all its own. Though it was "arranged" to settle a $10,000 bet, Sullivan, Daily, Kennedy, and friends were not in it for the money. They were volunteers because of the challenge and because it would be a chance to show what they could do. Pride in their accomplishments, in their determination, skill, strength, and tenacity motivated them to lay more than six miles during the first shift and then, during lunch, to refuse to quit: in the afternoon they would finish the job they started, because "it was there;" because it had never been done before (it has not been equalled since):[29] because despite the moral maelstrom at the top, those eight men and the spikers, bolt-droppers, and others, could still put in a simple, untainted ten-mile day.

Their feat is hardly remembered now except by railroad buffs. Most academicians who know something about the Pacific Railroad think of Promontory as its most important event—as it was. Ten-Mile Day is thought of as a bit of railroad trivia; few non-academics have heard of it at all. It is in danger of becoming, now, almost a folkloric non-event, sustained in oral tradition mainly by those people who have read about it and have researched it in the diaries and memoirs—the printed sources—of those who often were not even participants.

The Outlaw

USTER was the embodiment of dashing courage to most of white America in 1876, and Americans made of the defeat on the Little Bighorn an epic that was, in essence, a dramatic enactment of the abstraction of bravery. Each element in this epic—the early success, the impact upon the battle of cowards and traitors, the heroic last few minutes, the spurned chance to escape, and the leader's death at the battle's end—was invented by people who wished to show that Custer's death was truly heroic. Some of the events may actually have happened as imagined. The cavalrymen with him may actually have been initially successful, but there is no convincing evidence for this one way or another, and what is important is that in the absence of facts the battle was imaginatively reconstructed in such a way. Every element in the popular legend of the Last Stand reinforces the idea of bravery; each one of those details is a variation on the central theme. Even the invention of the sword for Custer to carry and to wield so effectively during his last moments is another motif, another aspect of the hero's bravery. Custer did not carry a sword into the battle; but it is the weapon most white American civilians associated with dashing horsemen, with the glamour of warfare, with battlefield panache. And so it was necessary to create a sword for Custer to use at the Little Bighorn; and this detail is only one of a score that demonstrate that events are recreated according to our interpretative perceptions of them and that they—and the characters in them—become what we wish them to be. The narratives about such people as Custer, be they legend, anecdote, or personal-experience story, and be they contained in history, novel, exemplum, or epic, are in large portion didactic.[1]

The Custer paradigm has nearly twenty segments, or motifs, within it. Yet the likelihood is that the creation of this paradigm was polygenetic; that is, each society, each author or storyteller who put his imaginative talents to retelling this tale, had to fabulate it anew. The Custer cluster includes Saul, Leonidas, Roland, Sir Gawain, and the garrison of the Alamo; we have no evidence that Herodotus (whose version of Thermopylae is the most important) copied or even knew of the Old Testament account of Saul's death; that Turoldus or whoever was the writer of the *Roland* knew of Herodotus or made Saul his model; or that the alliterative *Morte Arthure* is based on any of these; or that the Alamo legends arose in imitation of those other heroic stands.

Most accounts of gunfighters are simpler. The most commonly imagined tableau is the two-man shoot-out, and it was *Harper's New Monthly Magazine*[2] that first realized the potential of this dramatic form:

> Just then Tutt, who war alone, started from the courthouse and walked out into the squar, and Bill moved away from the crowd toward the west side of the squar. Bout fifteen paces brought them opposite to each other, and bout fifty yards apart. Tutt then showed his pistol. Bill had kept a sharp eye on him, and before Tutt could pint it Bill had his'n out.
>
> At that moment you could have heard a pin drop in that squar. Both Tutt and Bill fired, but one discharge followed the other so quick that it's hard to say which went off first. Tutt was a famous shot, but he missed this time; the ball from his pistol went over Bill's head. The instant Bill fired, without waitin ter see ef he had hit Tutt, he wheeled on his heels and pointed his pistol at Tutt's friends, who had already drawn their weepons.
>
> "Aren't yer satisfied, gentlemen?" cried Bill, as cool as an alligator. "Put up your shootin-irons, or there'll be more dead men here." And they put 'em up, and said it war a far fight.

Adding characters seldom complicates the plot, only the landscape of this single motif. Several gunmen on either side may be killed or wounded without changing the basic nature of the gunfight. If one of the combatants is the hero's Quaker wife, as in the movie *High Noon,* the battle motif is only slightly more complicated, though it is the conclusion of the several quite complicated actions and developments beforehand.

The gunfighter's quick-draw ability is also legendary, and usually imaginary. What seems to have counted is his ability to fire at another human being at close range without hesitating to squeeze the trigger; quick-draw experts are rare, and the most famous of those chosen few become small-arms experts for the FBI or the NRA (rather than gunfighters), while "fanning" in actual combat is largely the contribution of Hollywood. Will Hale, self-proclaimed cowboy and traveler in the West during the eighteen seventies and eighties, and a writer of sorts,[3] described a gunfight involving Billy the Kid that Hale claims to have observed:

> After the kid and his men had spent most of their money, they came back to New Mexico, to continue their outlaw work. After getting back to Fort Sumner he had to kill a man, to give anyone an idea how rapid he was with a revolver.
> I will tell about this killing. After the kid and his men came back from Tascosa, they spent their idle time around Sumner. They had a great many enemies at this place, caused by the [Lincoln County range] war, and, as I was going to say, the kid was leaning against the wall of the house, when a man said to another, 'I will bet you drinks I can kill a man before you can.' The other fellow said, 'I will take the bet.' The first man out with his revolver and snapped it twice at the kid. The kid out with his revolver and shot him six times before he touched the floor. He began to fall at the first shot.
> After the kid killed his man he out with a couple of revolvers and said, 'All you fist and bantams walk up, and have something to drink, or I will shoot some more.'

Single combats have been with us for centuries; like Last Stands they are not uniquely Western. But they do seem to be characteristic of the West in the nineteenth century as depicted in movies and popular fiction. The world seems to think that such events commonly occurred on the American prairie; whatever the reason for such a belief and whether it is true or not, it is prevalent. Custer's Last Stand had a cast of thousands, making an intricate orchestration necessary. Few gunfights in Westerns are so lavish; they are murders for the chamber and not the full symphony hall. But what they lose thereby in magnitude, gunfights gain in focusing the viewer's/auditor's concentration and projective tendencies.

By *gunfighter* I mean people from a wide variety of occupational roles who are only occasionally called upon or compelled to fire their weapons in anger. Gunfighters are cowboys or ranch hands (like

Billy the Kid) or lawmen (like Bill Hickok or Gary Cooper in *High Noon*) or ex-gunmen who just happen to be around when their skills are needed (like Shane). Their adversaries are as varied in their primary occupations. But at the moment of the gunfight occupational roles are secondary, often irrelevant. The important identifications are of Good and Bad—overstated and overused as white hats and black—and of the audience with the actor.

In his correspondence with Einstein, Freud argued that each of us derives a very basic and profound gratification from slaying an enemy, however imaginary the act, and from viewing him prostrate at our feet. In movies, in Western literary fiction, we are the gunfighter and we ritually slay our adversaries again and again. We are our projected selves who destroy, with an imagined bullet, our frustrations, our obstacles, our guilt, and we slay them with anger, hostility, and relief. The scenario is a simple one, one against one. We can confront the enemy, can meet him face-to-face, and can destroy him in front of us. No long-range shots are necessary. The enemy is slain in front of our eyes, we see the bullet entering his body (or imagine we do) we see the body suddenly and violently hurled backward with the impact of the bullet's blow, and then we see it crumple to the ground before us. When our frustrations are thus eliminated, we are relieved, our anxieties alleviated, however temporarily.

One of the most appealing parts of this murder is that it is painlessly and simply done. It is a victimless killing. There is no blood and no pain, and yet we derive that great satisfaction of experiencing the obliteration of feelings in ourselves that call for destruction. The experience is cathartic, renewing.

The lone gunfighter does not have to have a specific identity for us to relate to him. He does not have to be Bill Hickok or Wyatt Earp or Bat Masterson (to name three actual persons since made famous by the media); his name could be entirely fictitious, like Shane's, or it may not matter at all, be entirely forgettable, like the name of the sheriff played by Gary Cooper in *High Noon*. Who remembers the name of the character portrayed by John Wayne in *Stagecoach?* We identify with him as a symbol, as an embodiment of certain of our desires, and not with the counterfeit of real people. Because he is isolated, usually, facing his enemy alone, he concentrates our attention upon him; there are no distractions, no one else to vitiate the intensity of our identification with him. Everything rests with him;

he alone will kill or be killed, and us with him. It is a fight with little
ambiguity about its outcome; one participant is going to win, the
other lose—probably his "life." If the hero or one of his party, if that
narrative option is exercised, is wounded, the injury will be slight.
Its purpose will be to show the danger involved, and not to indicate
a failing or a defeat.

As a single motif, the gunfight is not capable of sustaining the
entire weight of a narrative. By its nature, violent and purgative, it
is ideally placed at a drama's climax, to be followed by a denoue-
ment. It can be used flexibly, of course, also appearing in the middle
of a sustained narrative. But when so used, it will be most effective
as a climax all the same, though perhaps as the conclusion to some
subordinate dramatic peak.

The cinema gunfights in *Gunfight at the OK Corral* and *My
Darling Clementine* develop the emotional climax of the narrative.
The fame of this gunfight is largely the creation of the media, especially these two films. In life, neither was the climax for the participants, except for those of the Clantons who fell before the Earps' fire.
Morgan and Virgil lived through the fight, meeting violent ends
later, and the fight was by no means the climax of Wyatt's career,
though subsequent writers would try to make it appear that way.
But the real Wyatt Earp continued to go about his business in Tombstone for several months; then he left town under suspicious circumstances. He eventually went to Alaska after gold was discovered
there, finally returning to Southern California where he died.[4] For
the purposes of drama, however, it is important to have his life "end"
after the OK Corral fight—not literally, but dramatically, because
we are not really interested in Wyatt Earp after that event. How
many people, aside from Western buffs, know what really happened
to Wyatt after that Wednesday afternoon, October 26, 1881? When
the fight with the Clanton gang ended, most of our interest in Earp
ended. He survived the fight and thus gained immortality in the
popular imagination. He lived happily ever after because the one
event that is of interest to us was over.

That stories fitting the Custer paradigm can be found in scripture (1 and 2 Samuel), classical history (Herodotus), and epic poetry
(the *Song of Roland*), as well as the popular material that developed
in the United States after the defeat at the Little Bighorn, should
be revealing—about the distinctions we usually make between art
products in folk and "high" art spheres and about those elements of

narrative most important in the making of a "good" story. In the story of Billy the Kid's struggles with Pat Garrett we can see a few of those features of very serious, learned drama emerge in folkloric and popular productions. Many people have seen in their confrontation an analogue to that of Jesus and Judas, a Passion on the plains, created by people who may well have had the Biblical parallel in mind.

The two men become locked in a struggle that seems to exclude the external world and any possibility of intrusions from that world. To a great extent, of course, the dramatis personae have been determined by history, but we have on all social levels of narrative creation not been content to let the cast alone. The pivotal figure is William Bonney (sp?); and whatever he does, however we interpret him, we necessarily interpret Garrett accordingly. Their confrontations are enclosed within a hermetic circle that they cannot leave and that no influence can enter. It is all Bonney and Garrett, and the other characters are aides or obstacles or doubles of the main contenders.

Kent Ladd Steckmesser has already documented the split in our apprehension of the Kid:[5] he is either saintly or satanic. When he was in his late teens—or more likely his early twenties—he was a ranch hand employed by John Tunstall in Lincoln County, New Mexico. His employer and an Alex McSween were the business rivals of three other principals in the region, Murphy, Dolan, and Riley. The rivalry escalated into a range war, one of the first casualties being Tunstall himself. The Kid escaped; meanwhile arrest warrants were served on the killers, two of whom were "shot while escaping." McSween's men retaliated and after killing two of the opposition in a gunfight, they invaded Lincoln and became engaged in a fire fight during which they were driven to some buildings owned by Tunstall and McSween where the latter was killed. Billy and the others with him managed to escape, and for a while lived out in the bush, rustling and stealing to stay alive and comfortable. The Kid was soon captured by Pat Garrett at Stinking Springs in December of 1880, but escaped from the Lincoln County Courthouse on April 28, 1881. Garrett began tracking him down again. Garrett caught up with him outside of Fort Sumner on July 11, and taking him by surprise at the home of his friend, Pete Maxwell, shot him.

Most folklore and popular legends pay scant attention to the Tunstall/McSween-Murphy/Dolan/Riley conflict or other aspects of the Lincoln County War and focus instead on the Bonney-Garrett confrontation. One view has it that the Kid was little short of a homicidal maniac, at twenty-one (his real age is not known) having killed a man for each year of his life. The Lomaxes published (in *American Ballads and Folk Songs*[6]) a song about Billy with these apposite lines:

> When Billy the Kid was a very young lad,
> In old Silver City he went to the bad;
> Way out in the West with a gun in his hand
> At the age of twelve years he first killed his man.
>
> Fair Mexican maidens play guitars and sing
> A song about Billy, their boy bandit king,
> How ere his young manhood had reached its sad end
> Had a notch on his pistol for twenty-one men.

The actual number of people he killed cannot be known. The gunfights he is known to have joined had several men on each side, and probably even the participants could not always be sure whose bullet killed whom. If we are going to think of the Kid as a mad killer, then the rest of the actors, and their place within the drama, are determined. Tunstall is justly fighting the combine of Murphy/ Dolan/Riley, trying to free the area from their economic stranglehold and return it to the rightful owners, the small farmers. Tunstall's opponents were actually backed by the "Santa Fe Ring"; but Steckmesser has argued persuasively that rather than being a champion of justice for the little man in New Mexico, Billy's employer sought to establish a monopoly of his own.[7]

The foil in this scenario is Pat Garrett. A demonic Kid requires a nobly dedicated sheriff who tirelessly hunts him down. Garrett should be brave, committed to law and order and the protection of the citizens of the borderlands even at the risk of his own life, and in several ways the embodiment of frontier justice, if he is to be the Kid's slayer. And that slaying must be pictured as a righteous act of justice; there must be nothing cowardly or suspect about it. Garrett shoots the Kid in a fair fight and triumphs because he is good. The Kid may be inherently devilish or he may have been forced into a life of crime by the evils of society; in either event, once we establish that he is bad, it becomes the moral obligation of Pat Garrett to hunt him down and to dispose of him so that he will never again terrorize the people of New Mexico.

When Garrett is hardly present at all, different narrative rules apply. That is the situation in two ballads collected by the Lomaxes which so closely focus on Billy's life that there is neither time nor space to develop Garrett's character; he is simply Billy's killer, "a whole lot badder" (a better gunman?) or a man who "once was his friend"—which could be a comment on either man. In the song "Billy the Kid" the Mexican point of view is not that of the narrator (consider "Greasers"), but neither is it that of the "other side" (also consider "He kept folks in hot water," etc.); the Lomaxes do not cite the author or the place where they collected this ballad, but it has the tone of one that is removed from the locale described. This ballad has become abstracted from the immediacy of Lincoln County and its problems, and has turned to the transcendent matter of a troublesome bad man and his death.

> Billy was a bad man
> And carried a big gun;
> He was always after Greasers
> And kept 'em on the run.
>
> He shot one every morning
> For to make his morning meal.
> And let a white man sass him,
> He was shore to feel his steel.
>
> He kept folks in hot water,
> And he stole from many a stage;
> And when he was full of liquor
> He was always in a rage.[8]

Enter Pat Garrett, "a whole lot badder," who took care of Billy and now "we ain't none the sadder." Nevertheless, Garrett does not emerge as especially heroic in this ballad account; he is hardly an opponent at all, rather the instrument by which Billy is brought to justice. The concentration is entirely on Billy; the ballad simply expresses relief that "now he's dead." The same point is made in the second ballad about the Kid collected by the Lomaxes; Garrett is hardly a participant, and the song's emotional core is a lament for a young man gone wrong:

> 'Twas on the same night when poor Billy died
> He said to his friends: "I am not satisfied;
> There are twenty-one men I have put bullets through
> And Sheriff Pat Garrett must make twenty-two."
>
> Now this is how Billy the Kid met his fate:
> The bright moon was shining, the hour was late,

Shot down by Pat Garrett, who once was his friend,
The young outlaw's life had now come to its end.

There's many a man with a face fine and fair
Who starts out in life with a chance to be square,
But just like poor Billy he wanders astray
And loses his life in the very same way.[9]

The point of view is ambiguous about both men. The Kid is "poor Billy," even though an earlier stanza says that in Silver City "he went to the bad." Garrett is neither praised nor blamed: we are told only that he once was Billy's friend. Neither song seems to have a clear conception of the morality of either combatant, and the latter draws its conventional moral from an imaginative construction put on the fact of a young man's violent death.

The perception of Billy as "one of the kindest and best boys I ever knew" has been expressed by Miguel Otero's *The Real Billy the Kid;* the opinion is held by many, though not always expressed in such superlatives. He was "a perfect gentleman and a man with a noble heart" who was "forced" to kill others in defense of his own life. "Loyal to his friends" and loving his mother "devotedly," Billy was a "victim of circumstances." Following consistently from this premise, Pat Garrett "was a cow thief himself, as everybody at Fort Sumner knew," according to Higinio Salazar.[10] Garrett was in it for the money and the prospect of office; he is, by a rough-hewn analogy, Judas, selling out the saintly Billy for a pocketful of silver.

Since so little is really known about the real Billy, he and the situation of his last months, and his death, are ideal vehicles of projection. Those writers who claim to have known him "when," wrote their memoirs and biographies well into this century. Nevertheless, he was a real hero to a great many people in New Mexico: the names of his most ardent supporters—Otero, Salazar, Chavez— may provide a clue. Of course it is no longer possible to determine how people in the Lincoln County area in 1880 felt about Billy, but it does appear that Billy's admirers were the Mexican farmers in the area (and now their descendants), and that those who were associated with or identified themselves with the Murphy/Dolan/Riley combine, the "Big Business" interests in New Mexico, have condemned Bonney. Mrs. Sophie Poe, whose husband rode with Garrett and who knew the territory, observed that Billy was "good to Mexicans. He was like Robin Hood; he'd steal from white people and give it to the Mexicans, so they thought he was all right."[11] This is not to say that the dime novelists were in collusion; they found in the combine's version a good way to tell a story in which they could use the pivotal character's (putative) age and (alleged) good looks and possibly his poor circumstances to dramatize a moral tale.

Billy became, illogically yet understandably enough, the champion of New Mexico's poor farmers, slain by the monied interests who were able to buy the services of relentless hired guns. His employment by Tunstall helped; his escape into the countryside where he probably rustled cattle to keep alive reinforced his position; and his death at the hands of "the law" would have solidified his martyr's role. As an outlaw he was almost automatically a hero of those peoples who were socially and economically oppressed.[12] Just as automatically would his death come about through treachery.

Willy Sutton was once asked why he robbed banks; and he replied, somewhat astonished at the question's naivete, "Because that's where the money is." What is the profit in robbing the poor? In the recent movie *Dick and Jane*, an out-of-work aerospace engineer (George Segal)and his wife (Jane Fonda) take to armed robbery to support their upper-middle-class lifestyle. One of their jobs takes them to the local service office of a telephone company. When customers waiting on line realize what is happening—the phone company is being robbed—they give the withdrawing bandits an enthusiastic ovation.

Billy the Kid is said to have been good to Mexicans; the James gang robbed banks and railroads, both wealthy institutions. Poor people, "ordinary" people can hardly respond to such crimes with deep indignation; if they are resentful about their own economic situation, they may well applaud taking from the rich. And if these robberies occur in a context in which the public feels that the law is corrupt, the violator of that law will have an added bonus to his popularity.

If the outlaw is a hero with a following, several episodes of his life will share narrative events with the legendary lives of more conventional heroes. In the death of Billy the Kid—as told by those who idolized him—it is almost mandatory that treachery be the cause.[13] As with Custer, Roland, Arthur, Siegfried, Lincoln, John F. Kennedy, even Bonnie and Clyde (in the movie version), the deaths of Billy or Jesse James or Sam Bass or a dozen others are analogous. The scope of the scenario may be reduced, but at the heart of the story there is still that most salient feature, treachery. In the ballad

"Sam Bass" the hero's end is also in this tradition, and the ballad is one of the most explicit statements of its kind.

"Sam Bass" was written soon after the death of the hero of the title. Early collectors give credit to John Denton, of Gainesville, around 1879;[14] within a very years it had become a staple of campfires and dancehalls. Its melody is borrowed from an older frontier song, "The Range of the Buffalo." The stanzas that are of interest here describe, in detail—the death of Sam in an ambush, arranged by the traitor Jim Murphy, a Texas Ranger plant. Several versions have been collected, but one of the most stable stanza sequences describes Sam's last stand:

> Jim Murphy was arrested, and then released on bail;
> He jumped his bond at Tyler and then took the train for Terrill;
> But Mayo Jones had posted Jim, and that was all a stall,
> 'Twas only a plan to capture Sam before the coming fall.
>
> Sam met his fate at Round Rock, July the twenty-third,
> They pierced poor Sam with rifle balls and emptied out his purse.
> Poor Sam he is a corpse and six feet under clay,
> And Jackson's in the bushes trying to get away.
>
> Jim had borrowed Sam's good gold and didn't want to pay,
> The only shot he saw was to give poor Sam away.
> He sold out Sam and Barnes and left their friends to mourn—
> Oh, what a scorching Jim will get when Gabriel blows his horn!
>
> And so he sold out Sam and Barnes and left their friends to mourn,
> Oh, what a scorching Jim will get when Gabriel blows his horn!
> Perhaps he's got to heaven, there's none of us can tell,
> But if I'm right in my surmise he gone right straight to hell.[15]

One variant stanza included by Fife might well serve as the epitaph of all Western heroes:

> In an unmarked shallow grave
> They laid him down to rest
> His saddle for a pillow
> And his gun across his breast.[16]

It is an ending and a eulogy befitting that most famous Robin Hood of the American West, Jesse James. The version presented here, the "standard," was anthologized by the Lomaxes; only Jesse's death and glorification are given here:

It was on a Saturday night, Jesse was at home,
Talking with his family brave;
Robert Ford came along like a thief in the night
And laid poor Jesse in his grave.

The people held their breath when they heard of Jesse's death,
And wondered how he ever came to die;
It was one of the gang called little Robert Ford,
He shot poor Jesse on the sly.

Jesse went to rest with his hand upon his breast;
The devil will be upon his knee.
He was born one day in the county of Clay
And came from a solitary race.

Jesse went down to the City of Hell,
Thinking for to do as he pleased;
But when Jesse come down to the City of Hell,
The Devil quickly had him on his knees.

This song was made by Billy Gashade,
As soon as the news did arrive;
He said there was no man with the law in his hand,
Who could take Jesse James when alive.[17]

The traitor—whose presence will be foregrounded if he exists, and invented if he does not—serves at least two purposes. First, he is a foil created to further heighten the noble or at least invincible character of the hero: only a treacherous shot in the back or a deceitfully planned ambush could defeat James/Bonney/Bass. Open and fair fights always end in the hero's triumph. And then, his character is further glorified by this contrast with the deceitful adversary. The hero gains stature when he defeats enemies of stature; and he is also raised in our esteem when only "dirty little cowards" can gun him down from behind.

The betrayer is as inevitable as the hero's (usually folkloric) generosity and kindness. Taking from the rich will usually be grounds enough to plant the idea of generosity; the other half of that equation, usually interpolated, is "giving to the poor." This law of contrast seems to operate almost universally, and in areas well beyond the topography and communities actually visited by the bandit/hero. In the region traveled by the James/Bass/Bonney figures, local legends are likely to arise, specifying individuals and locations. Elsewhere, hundreds and even thousands of miles away, the legend will probably lose much of its specificity but retain some message in outline. For instance, in the Northeast or the far West, Jesse James may be thought of by some as one who was chivalrous, sentimental, respectful of the elderly, and imbued with a sense of justice, as well as being generous to the poor.

In July, 1975, Stephen Poyser, one of my students at Indiana University, collected a story from Mrs. Lula Andrews of Scottsville, Tennessee, that illustrates the above traits. "Strangers" ride up to a farm and ask to be served breakfast. The women of the farmhouse, who are alone and fearful, prepare a meal, which the strangers eat in silence. When the strangers depart, the women discover a five-dollar gold piece left under each plate on the table, and later, when they hear that the James gang is in the area, they deduce the identity of their guests.

A related tale, but with the added feature of the hero's depriving the greedy rich of their heartlessly gained money, is again told about James. Other variants make the hero Sam Bass, Butch Cassidy, or even Robin Hood. Jesse and his pals stopped on one of their long rides to have the widow at a farmhouse prepare them a meal. While the boys were sitting around the humble cabin, they noticed that the woman was crying. A little questioning revealed that the (rapacious) landlord was going to foreclose on her mortgage that day. Without telling the poor woman his intentions, Jesse extracted from her the amount of the payment, a description of the man, his expected time of arrival, and the road he usually took when riding to the cabin. Suddenly, Jesse rose and persuaded the woman to take a "loan" for the amount of money due which she could repay at some indefinite time in the future. Later that afternoon, when the mortgage collector was riding home, his wallet brimming, Jesse and the boys relieved him of his greedy gains.[16]

In the Bass version, Sam is put up for the night at a modest farm. He learns that a moneylender is to foreclose on the property the next day. Bass pays off the mortgage when the Scrooge arrives, then robs him on his way home.[17]

A Robin Hood romance of the fifteenth century tells essentially the same tale. The story has the imprimatur of the Child canon, being number 117.[18] Robin and his men invite a "gentyll knight" to their woodsy retreat, and when he comments that he has not seen such a meal as they offer in three weeks, the Sherwood Foresters learn of his poverty, and that the rich abbot of Saint Mary's Abbey is going to foreclose on his estate. The church as secular agency is the villain, more particularly one of its fallen prelates; the knight, ranking low in the aristocratic hierarchy and thus closest in station to commoners, is suitably a subject of sympathy. Robin loans the payment money to the knight—it would be inappropriate to give it to him and incongruous in a medieval story for a knight to accept such a gift from commoners—and then when "two blacke monkes,/-Eche on a good palferay" come riding along an expected trail, the outlaws stop and then rob them. When the knight later returns to the forest to repay his debt, Robin releases him from his obligation, saying (vaguely) that he has been repaid by Our Lady.

It hardly seems likely that this old story was known directly by those people in the West (or in Tennessee or Missouri), though it is possible that the tale had become so much a part of the American's heritage of romantic narrative that it was distantly remembered, and then given a new life around the flesh and bones of Jesse James. I think it more likely, however, that given the basic narrative elements—poor and deserving tenant, rich and greedy landlord—that the composition of the basic tale as we have it would not be a difficult matter to recompose "originally" each time. The wielder of justice has only to appear at the strategic moment to learn of the impending foreclosure for him to steal from one and give to the other to make everything morally or at least sentimentally right. The Robin Hood story had been reprinted by Joseph Ritson in the eighteenth century and again in the nineteenth (1887), still a few years before the first of the Jesse James analogues have been recorded. But evidence of direct transmission is lacking; and it does seem improbable that such an uncomplicated tale could not have been reinvented. The narrative elements are simple enough, the plot brief, and the characters few. Folklorists prefer not to consider seriously such polygenetic explanations; however, such "laws" were formulated to apply to the complex folktale. "Jesse and the Poor Widow" seems to be simple enough to escape from this law.

In two of the most popular roles—as gunfighter and defender of the poor—the Westerner with the gun, both as lawman and as outlaw, as popular culture and folklore have defined him, is an ideal vessel of projection. As gunfighter he is our persona who destroys what is hateful in life. Popular novelist Robert Fish has one of his *Pursuit*[19] characters exclaim,

Do you expect me to deny it? I liked being at the front and seeing a man die under my bullet. All men like killing. If they didn't, there would be no wars. Why do men hunt? Because they enjoy killing; in fact they call it a sport, a blood sport.

Perhaps not all men, and not at the front where they might see real bullets shot and real men die. But on some level of abstraction there is a great deal of truth in the assertion of Fish's character. Of course, it is "just" a novel, and Fish is not the Shakespeare of our time, let alone the Freud, but the words are no less true for that. The Western gunman, alone, is us alone, facing down the enemy, and making him/it pay.

Literature, and even more cogently the movies, can embody those abstraction-fantasies as the objects and people of everyday life. To see a body crumple under the impact of a bullet, to see bodies dismembered on the screen is satisfying, if executed properly. And the body has its surrogates: explosives shattering concrete or splintering wood; the cowboy's wild shot that raises a small geyser from a watering trough; machine-gun bullets fragmenting pottery in Peckinpah's *The Wild Bunch;* a car going off the road, rolling down a hillside, and bursting into flame. All of these dramatic scenes— overly dramatic, actually, since they are more vivid, more destructive than the reality—are used as mini-climaxes within the larger framework of the entire narrative. Violence, thus employed aesthetically, is cathartic. The explosion, whether of flesh or machine, is artistic climax.

Hence we can easily ignore any scruples we may have about violence or killing because the event is in literature, and thus not quite real, and because the gunman, as a projection of ourselves, is "killing" whatever it is we hold to be hateful: frustrations, obstacles, hostilities.

The gunman's other acclaimed role, as outlaw/Robin Hood, also makes him a readily accessible vessel of other projections. In his actual existence as well as in his fictional representation, the outlaw is no threat to the humble—not only do they have nothing to be stolen but they project on him their hostilities toward the wealthy and can watch him act out their desires to take from the wealthy. In this role, the Western gunfighter becomes the (projected) instrument of social and economic equality.

A great deal of sentimentality has been invested in the legends of the Robin Hood/gunman figures, and it is of the sort we would expect if the gunman is ourselves and embodies our values. Much is made of Jesse James's family, his "talking with his family brave" when Robert Ford came along, "Like a thief in the night." Like Billy the Kid, he is said never to have killed unnecessarily (unless in self-defense), he never took from "preachers, widows, or orphans," never drank hard liquor and was always "polite, deferential, and accommodating."[20] In the story presented above, the mortgage-holder is a "skinflint," the "victim" a poor widow moved to tears by the sight of men around the house again, reminding her of her late husband. She is hard-working, honest, thrifty, and generous to strangers, but still can't manage to hold her farm together financially. A list of the qualities of those people helped by the outlaw, when added to his, would fairly well summarize those attributes the informants held dear; those of the mortgage-holders, bankers, and carpet-bagging Yankees who James and Bonney victimize embody much of what Middle America held in contempt nearly a century ago. There is a lot of us in the gunfighter/outlaw as we have created and popularized him; but given the tremendous popularity of Western movies abroad, we can reasonably assume that his significance, as in several other instances examined in this book, transcends in time and scope merely the American West.

That James, Bonney, Hickok, Earp, Bass, and others have come to mean more than sectional signifiers is apparent in their national, even international, reputations. One of the reasons often given for the outlaw's initiation into a criminal life is the alleged injustice of the law in his area. Jesse James returns from the Civil War to Missouri to find it being plundered by carpetbaggers and various vindictive Unionists; and so he turns to outlawry to fight for justice as opposed to the law. Steckmesser has argued effectively against such a case being made, for James and Bonney at least,[21] but he does not point out that if local injustice were all, how are we then to explain the extent of James's—and the Kid's—fame? What these men embody, clearly, is not only a regional personification; it is a universal.

The Moslem Princess
of the Prairies

THE Pocahontas/John Smith story, so touching in its naive sentimentality, signifies much more than appears on its ingratiating surface. The Indian maiden may be earth mother or a sign of the repression of the female;[1] this charming pastoral also signifies something characteristic of the relations between Indian and White in the nineteenth century. Of course no narrative, especially one so plain and direct, really characterizes so intricate a cultural complex as the relations between races, just as no book, however distended, is really definitive.

The story of Pocahontas does not cut a particularly wide swath; but it does go deep and, when seen in the synchronic context of similar narratives, reveals much about white men and red women in early America, a revelation whose pertinence has not faded. This essay examines stories of the type that have clustered around Pocahontas and Smith, all of which appear to be descriptive of interracial relations and which are the projections of Caucasian, male attitudes toward Indians generally, not only Indian women.

To those stories of the Indian princess who rescues the white stranger I have appended—for the analytic purposes of this paper; they rarely appear together in oral tradition—those tales describing narrow escapes from Indians. The focus of this essay is upon the tale of the white man captured by racial aliens in a strange land who is freed or rescued from death by the local princess (or some other beautiful maiden who happens to be handy); in a slight variation of this scenario the man simply falls in love with the native woman but must regretfully leave her when he is obliged to go home. Something of the "boy meets girl" formula is recapitulated, but this cycle ends upon the motif of "boy loses girl." The story I want to dissect is by far most popularly known in the Pocahontas/John Smith version, though it has been the basis of narratives in epic, song, and romance, even spy novels and Greek myth.

Stories about captivity by the Indians and the escape from them, or else the narrow evasion of capture, are among the oldest and most popular of Indian stories. *A True History of the Captivity and Restoration of Mrs. Mary Rowlandson* dates from 1682; and the recent series *Narratives of North American Indian Captivities,* edited by Washburn, numbers 111 volumes, and includes "only the most important variants," more than three hundred.[2] It is, to import an arctic metaphor, the tip of the iceberg.

Many writers would have it that the Indians were dirty, stupid, lazy, given to alcoholism—all traits of any peripheral group as viewed from the center. The Irish and other immigrant groups were similarly characterized in the last century in America, the Blacks in ours, and so on. On a field trip in Montana, I was lectured on the streets of Hardin by a white man who sought to warn me of the coming dangers of the Crow peril. The Indians too were "dirty" and "lazy," and "stupid," and spent most of their time making babies and collecting welfare instead of working honestly. This last-mentioned trait of peripheral groups, their alleged sexual capacities, has even been asserted by a friendly source. From the "Dear Abby" syndicated column (printed in the Bloomington, Indiana, *Herald-Telephone* and copied in the *Folklore Newsletter* of 26 April 1976), the following item was taken: "I have lived with a Mandan Indian for five years, and I wouldn't trade him for FIVE white lovers. He is the greatest! LINDA IN MARYLAND."

But the "savagery" of the Indians frightened whites most. Most savagely brutal and cruel was their practice of killing infants, and in a particularly violent way: they bashed their brains out against a tree or rock. An early account from Virginia in 1786 is from Mary Moore, temporarily a captive of Indians, whose infant sister was "fretful" from a cut cheek: "irritated by its crying, a savage seized it, and dashing its head against a tree, tossed it into the bushes."[3] Such stories were told many times about Indians, not only on the Eastern seaboard, but on the plains at least as often. It was what the "savages" did to captive infants, often simply for their own cruel amusement. What other act better demonstrated their barbarity than this atrocity against innocent, defenseless creatures? I, and many of my readers, I am sure, have heard similar stories of Germans killing Belgian babies in the First World War and Yugoslavian babies in the Second and of Japanese killing Chinese babies or the children of American missionaries. In these recent updated versions, the baby is not bashed but bayonetted or sabred or otherwise impaled. An indicted war criminal in Adam Hall's *The Quiller Memorandum* is accused of similarly "spitting" Jewish infants in a concentration camp.[4] The story has proved very effective in imputing barbarism to an enemy.

These same treacherous and barbaric Indians, then, were the scourge of many frontier people, particularly the relatively defenseless tenderfoot and the innately weak and innocent woman. When an Indian attacks a frontiersman or a soldier or any man capable of defending himself, we have a different kind of narrative. But in the atrocity stories a woman, child, or tenderfoot as victim is mandatory. The most explicit icon of the defenseless pioneer/victim that I have turned up comes from Edward Wheeler's dime novel, *Deadwood Dick, The Prince of The Road,* in which the young woman captive of Sitting Bull is bound to a stake, stripped naked above the waist, "and upon her snow white back were numerous welts from which trickled diminutive rivulets of crimson. Her head was dropped against the stake to which she was bound, and she was evidently insensible."[5]

Sarah Cummins, early Oregon pioneer and one of the members of the "Lost Wagon Train," remembered an incident on the trail in which one of her father's hired men (not everyone roughed it while in transit!) went to round up a laggard cow and its calf and found himself confronting several Indians. The man, Marion Poe, rode over to them—they were on foot—and while he was trying to make friendly conversation one of the Indians seized the bridle while two others slipped his feet out of the stirrups, and unbuckled the straps. They were about to pull him from his horse when Sarah's father, apparently used to command wherever he was, rode up and with his blacksnake whip sent Poe's horse scurrying away, and then cowed the Indians while Poe raced back to the safety of the wagon.[6]

The major narrative elements of the "standard" close encounter story are present in the Cummins fable: the innocent tenderfoot, the treacherous and evil-intending Indians (who, though this detail is not mentioned, Cummins implies were at first friendly towards Poe), and the narrow escape itself, brought about by the superiority of the white man.

John Lemmon, Sarah Cummins's father, used the threat of force to escape from possible Indian capture; overpowering Indians was a favorite theme of Westerners, particularly mountain men and soldiers. In Custer's *Wild Life on the Plains* a very easy rescue of two white girls is effected when the cavalry simply gives chase to their Indian captors. The red men had shortly before captured the girls during a raid, but the appearance of and pursuit by the cavalry forced them to leave their prisoners behind in order to flee the faster.[7] Guile and knowledge of the ways of the land enabled Daniel Boone, on one occasion, to rescue his young daughter, Jemima, and two friends. Indians surprised the Boone camp and made off with the girls, according to one popular biographical account. Boone recovered his composure after they had left, then set out immediately with several friends to track them down. A day and a half later he came upon the Indians' camp and after proper preparation attacked by surprise. In the confusion and flight of the enemy, the three girls were saved.[8]

White men are superior once more. The other side of that evaluation holds that the Indians are inferior, and one of the Western ways in which that quality is shown is through stories in which a white prisoner is returned through bartering with the red captors. The always imaginative James O. Pattie recalls bargaining with the Indians who had taken a young child prisoner after killing and scalping its mother and were about to burn the child alive. Pattie was well reinforced with armed men; and the threat implied by their presence may have further encouraged the Indians to accept several yards of a bright red cloth in exchange for their captive.[9] In this instance the message is somewhat ambiguous; the Indians are usually satisfied to settle for some inexpensive merchandise, showing how foolish they were in bartering and (or?) how cheaply they valued human life.

Many captivity stories terminate when the prisoners escape on their own. This type of narrative has not only found favor in a Western setting but is a staple of many adventure stories and movies, expandable to encompass civilian prisons (*Escape From Alcatraz*) and military (*The Great Escape* and even the classic *Grand Illusion*). In nearly all of these stories the captors are diminished by contrast with the resourcefulness and quick-wittedness of the escapees, though a good writer/director will make the guards as competent as possible, to make the escape all the harder and more thrilling. Escapes on TV's "Hogan's Heroes" are ridiculously simple, and the German guards are buffoons; one wonders how the allied servicemen were ever captured in the first place. In *The Bridge on the River Kwai* the escape is shown to be a (realistically) difficult undertaking, and the escapee gains in stature when he is successful. At the end of *The Great Escape,* nearly all of the prisoners are recaptured and shot, but our estimation of them has increased because of their heroic attempts.

Stewart White describes the capture of the two young Linn brothers by Indians along the Ohio frontier. The youths were camping out alone when taken by red men. Forced to live among the Indians for some time, the brothers gradually built up the Indians' confidence in them, such deception being acceptable on the part of whites in these situations—as distinguished from the Indian's "treachery" when allegedly professing peace before striking. Then, one day, while fishing with several of the tribe, they bolted for freedom, outrunning their captors to a raft on which they crossed the Ohio into present-day Kentucky.[10] The wily Indians had been tricked and then out-legged by the more wily and speedier white boys.

The cycle of stories that will be the major interest of this chapter is thematically related to tales of escape and occasionally may be found combined with tales of escape. But when the escape from the hostile forces is effected by the daughter of the chief/Sultan/king, that is an escape story of a different kind and message content. The cycle begins with the stranger in an alien and hostile land. He is captured; if he escapes we have tales of the kind just discussed. If he doesn't we may have a salvation story best known to us when Pocahontas is the savior. If the narrative doesn't end here, the next episode finds the man leaving his rescuer and her people to go home. The maiden may then go in search of him; or he may become wistful and lonely and seek to join her; or she will kill herself out of grief for her departed.

One of the two pivotal characters is the male stranger in a strange land. How he got there varies; he may have lost his way, he may have gone there on purpose, he may have been captured and taken to this alien country, he may have been sent there by the army, or he may have gone there on vacation.

Cuchulainn is in the Otherworld voluntarily, as are other heroes and gods, not only in Celtic mythology. William Butler Yeats has his poetic Aengus wander there in search of the land of the golden apples of the sun and the silver apples of the moon. Ulysses is washed ashore after yet another mishap at sea. In one of the most popular of *The English and Scottish Popular Ballads,* young Beichan is captured by Moors or Turks when in their country and imprisoned when he refuses to renounce his Christianity (Child 53). The lonesome British soldier in Kipling's "On The Road To Mandalay," had been assigned a long way from his English home. We don't know why the speaker in the popular song "Jamaica Farewell" (well, it used to be popular) is in Jamaica, but we know, through Harry Belafonte's voice, that he regrets having to leave his little girl in Kingston town; less dramatically, she has not saved his life. A stranger in a strange land, too, is James Bond who, having canoed to the guano island of Dr. No (as in "yes") finds that close behind is the dark-skinned and in other ways exotic beauty, Honey Chile.

The other pivotal character is the beautiful pagan princess who rescues the stranger: Pocahontas is the best known example, but Westerners have been saved by other Indian women, for instance, Mo-na-se-tah and Umentucken; Beichan is saved by Susan Pie (there are various renderings of her name); and the hero of the medieval romance *Launfal* (and its French original) falls in love with the enchanted maid in the woods, Tryamour. The motif is so common in medieval romance that the princess-rescuer has been given the title "The Moslem Princess." She saves the stranger from death by throwing herself upon his body, intervening between him and poised weapons. Umentucken shows her attractive mountain man where his horse has been hidden and helps him out of the tent where he is being held. In most versions, Susan Pie steals the keys to young Beichan's cell; in others she also gives him food and money; in still others, a ship. Mo-na-se-tah's love is tested most urgently only after her lover, General George Custer, is dead; said to have been his lover after he captured her and several of her tribe at the Washita, she is alleged to have saved his body from mutilation by her coup-counting tribesmen at the Little Bighorn. Nausicaä revives the soggy Ulysses on the shore; while other maidens do not save their man, but are nevertheless loved by them: Mandalay's "Burma Girl," the "little girl in Kingston town," the "Little Mohee." Honey Chile's role is more active than these, but not so active as to take the initiative of rescue and of Dr. No's destruction from Bond. She participates in the thwarting of No's evil plans, but mainly at Bond's direction.

Then love rears its turbulent countenance; the beauty of "The Little Mohee"[11] (a "fair Indian lass") and her simple, unwavering faithfulness, her naive openness, is compelling:

> As I sat amusing myself on the grass
> Oh, who did I spy but a young Indian lass!
>
> She came and sat by me, took hold of my hand
> And said, 'you're a stranger and in a strange land.'
>
> 'But if you will follow you're welcome to come
> And dwell in the cottage where I call it my home.'
>
> * * * * *
>
> She asked me to marry and offered her hand,
> Saying, 'My father's the chieftain all over this land.'

What man could refuse! Our hero can: "I have a dear sweet-heart in my own countree," he says, thus establishing *his* integrity; "I will not forsake her, I know she loves me/Her heart is as true as any Mohee." And so, early one morning in May, he sails for home and his dear loved one. The last time that he saw his little Mohee she "knelt on the strand"; and as his boat passed her, he says, "she waved me her hand," calling to him, "when you get over with the girl that you love,/Oh, remember the Mohee in the cocoanut grove." The story's end is inevitable; it will not work out with the girl back home that he loves, but by then it will be too late, too late to find the happiness that might have been his with the little Mohee. At home friends and relations were around him once more, his sweetheart and many others besides, yet the speaker complains, "not one did I see/That really did compare with my little Mohee."

> And the girl I had trusted had proved untrue to me,
> So I says: 'I'll turn my courses back over the sea.'
>
> 'I'll turn my courses and backward I'll flee,
> I'll go and spend my days with the little Mohee.'

Perhaps he will be able to return to his other, more reliable love in her strange land, perhaps not; his yearning, whose fulfillment we will never know about, stimulates those feelings which are themselves the message of this little ballad.

Kipling's soldier in London, yearning for the old Moulmein pagoda, had the same feelings about his Burma girl who, he sings, is "a-settin' and I know she thinks o' me"; and Harry Belafonte's head is down, *his* heart is turning around/Because *he* left a little girl in Kingston town."

The plight of the Tommy in "Mandalay," at the moment of the poem a bank clerk in London, is pathetic. He has been sent "home" from his military service, sent away from his Burmese girl, Supiyaw-lat, and he despises the life he now must live:[12]

But that's all shove be'ind me—long ago an' fur away,
An' there ain't no 'busses runnin' from the Bank to Mandalay;
An' I'm learnin' 'ere in London what the ten-year soldier tells:
'If you've 'eard the East a-callin', you won't never 'eed naught else.
   No! you won't 'eed nothin' else
   But them spicy garlic smells
   An' the sunshine an' the palm-trees an' the tinkly temple-bells;
    On the road to Mandalay . . .

I am sick o' wastin' leather on these gritty pavin' stones,
An' the blasted Henglish drizzle wakes the fever in my bones;
Tho' I walks with fifty 'ousemaids outer Chelsea to the Strand,
An' they talks a lot of lovin', but wot do they understand?
   Beefy face an' grubby 'and—
   Law! wot do they understand?
   I've a neater, sweeter maiden in a cleaner, greener land!
   On the road to Mandalay . . .

In "Young Beichan" the lord ungraciously leaves his Susan Pie behind and in several years' time is ready to marry another, having forgotten the girl who once saved his life and to whom he pledged his love. In medieval romance Dame Tryamour enjoins Sir Launfal never to mention her name; when he does, inevitably, she rejoins him, briefly, to retrieve tokens she had given him, and then he must begin a search for her. This narrative, and the French lai from which it surely derives, are intimately related to the traditional folktale, "The Man On a Quest For His Lost Bride" (Aarne-Thompson type 400); almost invariably it contains the motif of "The Forgotten Fiancé" and is in some way related to the twelfth-century romance of Chretien de Troyes, *Yvain,* which also describes a marriage to an Otherworld lady, a departure from home, a broken vow made to a lady (here, not to stay away beyond a certain time), and a quest to regain her after she angrily breaks off with him. As a folktale the story is extremely popular and has been found throughout Europe and parts of Asia.

Before the story of "The Moslem Princess" is concluded, it should be noticed from what we have already said that these stories, in their various forms and details, are ideal receptacles for male fantasy projections. The Mohee/Umentucken/Nausicaä figure does all of the faithful loving and gets little besides grief for it. She has initially rescued him (Pocahontas, Susan Pie, Nausicaä) or has given him her love for no other reason than that she at once loved him (Mohee, the Burma girl, Honey Chile). And that love is as pure and as wholesomely naive as the land she comes from is free of the corruption of civilization. She loves Beichan/John Smith/Milton Sublette, etc., openly, immediately, and freely. She makes no demands on him. Her uncomplicated love, so removed from what erotic relations between men and women really are with their inevitable give-and-take, is what "every" man desires—she is a "paper doll" he can call his own, a dolly other fellows cannot steal—and desires all the more because he cannot have such a love in this world.

As a demonstration of the intensity of her love, the heroine is willing to give up everything else that is dear to her in life. Susan Pie, in the Child 53 A verison, stanza 10, "turned her back on her ain country"; she is leaving home, literally, but in following her Christian lover and leaving her pagan home and faith, she is also turning her back on those aspects symbolically. Usually the "Moslem Princess" changes her religious ways as well and adopts the faith of her lover. Kipling's Tommy recalls those days,

An' I seed her first a-smokin' of a whackin' white cheroot,
An' a wastin' Christian kisses on an 'eathen idol's foot:
  Bloomin' idol made o' mud—
  Wot they called the Great Gawd Budd—
  Plucky lot she cared for idols when I kissed 'er where she stud!
On the road to Mandalay . . .

The most "literary" of these ladies is Puccini's Cho-Cho-San, "Madame Butterfly," who gave up her religion, was disowned by her family, and was willing to leave Japan to adopt the ways of an American housewife, all for the love of American Navy Lieutenant Pinkerton. He, unfeeling cad, returns home to marry his American sweetheart, but when he comes to Japan to claim the child he has fathered on Cho-Cho-San, she takes the one important thing it is still within her power to destroy: her own life.

Another aspect of the fantasy is that despite the sacrifices the woman has made for the man, no matter how well she has loved or treated him, even though she has saved his life, he often chooses to leave her and, like young Beichan, to marry another. Or he simply chooses to leave her, like Ulysses; or he is sent away, like Kipling's "Tommy." In the first two instances the man is afforded that freedom of emotion and movement. Like James Bond, he has a career to follow, and the dusky lass will simply not do in cultivated circles. In the medieval stories, when she leaves him (*Sir Launfal* and *Yvain*), he has been egregiously at fault, and he eventually regains her love —in the former romance relatively easily. But in many more cases the woman remains faithful while the man does as he wishes.

For the man the time abroad is an escape from his society (from the "blasted Henglish drizzle") a society that for one reason or another discomforts him, that he really cannot cope with. The other world is an outlet: "If you've 'eard the East a-callin', you won't never 'eed naught else." The Burma girl is a simple wish-fulfillment, as is Umentucken, in the spheres of both ego gratification ("there" he can be important, and loved) and sexual gratification, not that they are unrelated. "The Moslem Princess" is usually that—from the nobility of her people, so that the man, who descends from much humbler folk in his own society, has the added flattery of being loved by the daughter of a Sultan or Crow chief.

Sometimes the woman's great love is demonstrated by her decision to search for her lover after he has betrayed her—Susan Pie seeks out her betrothed, and is willing to take him back even after she finds him about to wed another. The more common element in this cycle is for the man, now separated from his princess, either to pine away for the old days when they were lovers ("Mandalay," "Little Mohee," or the girl in Kingston) or to go in search of her, as in *Yvain, Launfal,* and the Sublette/Umentucken story. Her conversion to his religion, as in the case of Pocahontas, is further evidence of her devotion. Her side of the relationship is characterized by faithfulness, an unwavering love, and a willingness to sacrifice; in a number of versions of this story the man is free to leave if he wishes; like Ulysses, he may simply want to move on, or like Beichan, he may want to marry another. To the credit of the Americans, after Sublette escapes he returns to the tribe of Umentucken and negotiates with her father for his daughter's hand. (I don't understand how a man once condemned to death by Indians would be allowed, shortly afterwards, to marry a chief's daughter, but my credulity is not the issue. Sublette does it, the Crows do it, Umentucken does it; and that, as a narrative, is what counts.)

After the moment of their falling in love, the narrative takes one of three courses. The first has already been mentioned: the man returns to his home and either forgets about this princess or yearns pathetically for her. If the latter is the case, he has the further option of trying to find her, like the hero in folktales of the type 400, like Yvain, like Sublette. In all cases he will succeed, and they will most likely live happily ever after. A second option terminates the narrative almost immediately after the Pocahontas figure has saved her John Smith (or Nausicaä her Ulysses, or Mo-na-se-tah the remains of Custer), and though we know, for instance, that there is more to come in the Pocahontas narrative (her marriage to John Rolfe, for instance), the tale can be completed at the moment of the rescue, which provides a natural terminus to the story and is usually related that way. Thirdly, the lady may destroy herself because her lover has been unfaithful in one way or another. Such is the legendary end of hundreds of "lover's leaps" victims around the country, said to have been the site of the suicide of an Indian maiden for the unrequited love of her inaccessible white lover. It is, with the greatest fanfare, the fate of Cho-Cho-San. Not irrelevantly, those suicide legends appear most frequently in the nineteenth century.

The motifs and their relationship within this cycle can be more clearly shown visually in the following diagram:

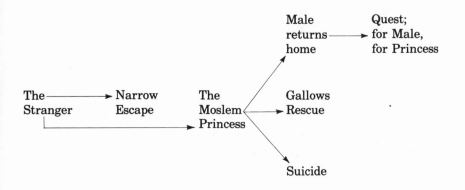

The use of two arrows emanating from "The Stranger" is meant to allow for the two most likely possibilities: the "Stranger" has a narrow escape (quite apart from the end he will achieve with the aid of the "Princess") or a close call; or, he will meet the "Princess." The pivotal action in all these stories is the meeting of these two who will shortly, if not immediately, become lovers, though that "love" takes different forms and implies different degrees of intimacy. In the second option—the man is rescued by the woman when death is imminent ("The Gallows Rescue")—the meeting and the rescue may be simultaneous. A further possibility allows the "Stranger" to return home, in which event a quest will follow. The first option mandates that the male depart for other areas—"home" is vaguely defined here—but wherever that is, its purpose in the narrative is to separate the lovers so as to pose a dramatic problem. Once apart, he will quest for her (*Yvain*, Type 400, etc.) or she for him ("Bei-chan"). Their reunion constitutes the climax of the story. A third option concludes with the "Princess's" self-destruction.

Mo-na-se-tah's role in this cycle has been discussed at length in *Custer and The Epic of Defeat*, [13] and so may be briefly summarized now. Those aspects of the story of her relations, alleged or actual, with Custer that do not conform to the paradigm are those which have been shaped by historical knowledge so well-known that they can not be disregarded. She is said to have first met Custer when he captured her and many other noncombatants during the raid on Black Kettle's village on the Washita. The folklore about the Little Bighorn has it that when she discovered his body on "Custer Ridge," she protected it from mutilation by her tribesmen. The "Gallows Rescue" here obviously takes quite a different form, the rescue being not from death but from disfigurement after death. The constant is the expressed love of the "Princess" at the risk of jeopardizing her standing among her own people.

Custer's body has long been thought to have been left uncut by the conquering Sioux and Cheyenne warriors at the Little Bighorn. This understanding has led to various interpretations: that the Sioux would not mutilate a truly brave fallen foe; that Custer had committed suicide and to touch his body would be bad medicine; that Mo-na-se-tah had saved him this posthumous humiliation. Recently, however, Mr. John Carroll, expert on Custeriana and author of several books on the subject, told me (in a private conversation) that Custer's body really was slashed as destructively as the others but that this distressing detail was kept discreetly quiet to spare Mrs. Custer's feelings. If so, the officers and men of the burial detail were party to the conspiracy; and once Custer's body had been interred, mutilation could not be demonstrated one way or the other. Carroll, of course, cannot be certain—he is repeating what he heard while visiting the Custer Battlefield National Monument for the Little Bighorn Centennial in 1976. The story might even be correct; we will never know.

The "Green River Pocahontas," as Isaac Russell and Howard R. Driggs call her,[14] was the Crow lass, Umentucken, whose name means "The Mountain Lamb." She was, of course, as beautiful as she was exotic, and as devoted, as develops later on in the story. At the beginning of the narrative Milton Sublette (the "Stranger") has been stabbed in a fight with an Indian (of his own trapping party?) in the Bear River country and improbably left by the other trappers to die as they moved on, eager for an early chance at pelts in their spring hunt. Trapper Joe Meek stayed with Sublette or was "left" with him to bury him, Russell and Driggs guess, and to make and mark the grave.

But as heroes tend to do—even pivotal characters in a wide variety of narratives—Milton Sublette recovered (he was the brother of William, after all). After forty days' convalescence he and Meek began a slow ride toward a trapper's rendezvous at Pierre's Hole. A party of Crow Indians appeared, threateningly, in the distance, and the two trappers, correctly perceiving their danger, had but seconds to escape. In another direction they saw, happily, the silhouette of a Crow Medicine Lodge. Outracing their pursuers to the lodge, Meek and Sublette huddled inside while the Crows outside pondered the next turn of events: how to get at the white men without violating the sanctity of the lodge.

While the braves were in the midst of these deliberations, Umentucken slipped unnoticed into the lodge, a remarkable feat in itself, and told the whites where their horses were being held (again, remarkably, nearby and without guards); she showed Meek and Sublette how to get through the lodge's buffalo-skin covering without being seen, and they were then able—miracle upon miracle—to ride away without drawing attention to themselves.

But they left a part of themselves behind. As Russell and Driggs would have it, "two white men had lost their hearts—and to the same dusky lass of the mountains. They dreamed of their beautiful deliverer and wished, each for himself, that he might bear her away to be his own forever." If Chaucer were working this tale, we would have a different complicating action, probably something like the scenario of the *Knight's Tale:* in the Rockies, the two fellow trappers do not fight over the love of a woman, or at least we are given no hint of this. This is Milton's story; and we learn that shortly, under circumstances no less extraordinary than what has already transpired, Sublette sued for her hand to her father, the Crow chieftain. According to Indian custom, he gave a lavish gift to the father of the bride, here beads and scarlet cloth, "to make his bride the most beautifully dressed girl among all the mountain clans."

Little that brings happiness lasts forever. In 1835 Sublette fell victim to an old wound—the original stab-wound that led him to Umentucken's village?—and he decided to go to the East for medical treatment. He died a short while later, at Fort William, and after a respectful period Joe Meek visited "The Mountain Lamb" and became her "ardent wooer." This courtship was to be her death. Meek gave her expensive gifts that soon aroused the jealousy of squaws who, green-eyed, watched her comings and goings. With the inexorable precision of classical drama, those squaws chided their husbands, and courters, several of whom one day raided Meek's camp and shot Umentucken with an arrow—"a sacrifice to the red man's jealousy." Indians often killed with hatchet and war club; an arrow is far more romantically acceptable. Unless one has been wounded by an arrow or seen such wounds, it may seem a romantic way to die, at least for a beautiful Indian lass of the mountains. In an appropriately brutal retaliation, Meek later killed a Bannock brave with a bullet from his rifle. The Stranger in a Strange Land, the Moslem Princess, the Gallows Rescue, the Return "Home," the Quest for the bride (to be); all the elements, in Rocky Mountain variations of the nineteenth century, are in the "Green River Pocahontas" story of Sublette and Umentucken, with the added portion of Meek's love and the maiden's pathetic death. This is a tale in which both men get their girl, and neither has broken his (unstated) vows of friendship to the other. Conflict is with the bad guys only; Sublette dies off-stage, without violence, and Umentucken's death is made to seem almost a beautiful thing. Meek's nobility, and the justice of his vengeance, are almost enough to foreground him as the pivotal character. The setting, however, Sublette's struggle for life and then for the hand of Umentucken, make him the character of our prime interest. But no matter; these details are only the surface materials of the narrative's deep structure.

It is a story, in recapitulation, of male fantasy gratification, operating sequentially throughout several episodes which are multiforms of the same, or very similar, assumptions: a woman's beauty is paramount, her chastity and loyalty to the "right" man is an implicit given, and she is the man's property to leave or to desert. Caucasians are, in these stories, superior to individuals of other races—Sublette and Meek could outride and out-think their Indian antagonists—and they are irresistible to women of other races. The Indians, to turn to the other side of this story's implied message, are so driven by their passions that they would murder a beautiful, innocent "lass," one of their own, to silence a nagging lover's tongue. In the last act, they get the punishment they deserve.

The binary pairs are male/female, white/non-white, and Christian/pagan. Yvain's Lady of the Fountain and Launfal's Tryamour are not racially "other," but they are not of this world. While in a number of the versions the Christian aspect of the man's character is stressed, in the Rockies it is the race of Sublette and Meek. In the various confrontations presented above, some win and some lose, and the binary composition of these stories heightens the aspect of competition. White Christian males are the winners; in stories of quite another kind, they will defeat and thus show their superiority to Indian men. In the cycle of Pocahontas/Umentucken the inferiority of Indian men is implied—as is the inferior status of their women, whose main contribution to the story is to save the man— the net result being a strong statement about other races in general. The story of Milton Sublette and Umentucken is no simple tale of love.

The White Steed
of the Prairies

I N *Songs of the Great West,* the Fifes include a poem by a "J. Barber," "The White Steed of the Prairies."[1] The subject seems unlikely only to people who know little about Western history, for few Western legends are better known, and few are so full of the spirit of what the West meant more than a century ago. A sampling of Barber's poem—stanzas 1, 4, 6, and 8—expresses all those qualities of speed, wild beauty, and strength for which the white steed was famed all over the West:

> Mount, mount for the chase! let your lassos be strong,
> And forget not sharp spur and tough buffalo thong;
> For the quarry ye seek hath oft baffled, I ween,
> Steeds swift as your own, backed by hunters as keen.
>
> Ye may know him at once, though a herd be in sight,
> As he moves o'er the plain like a creature of light—
> His mane streaming forth from his beautiful form
> Like the drift from a wave that has burst in the storm.
>
> Much gold for his guerdon, promotion and fame,
> Wait the hunter who captures that fleet-footed game;
> Let them bid for his freedom, unbridled, unshod,
> He will roam till he dies through these pastures of God.
>
> His fields have no fence save the mountain and sky;
> His drink the snow-capped Cordilleras supply;
> 'Mid the grandeur of nature sole monarch is he,
> And his gallant heart swells with the pride of the free.

In 1980 a mail-order house in Connecticut offered (for only $3) an eight-foot-square lithograph called "Hoofbeats on the Mesa." The original, by a "Lumen Winter," said the advertising copy, caught an "untamed stallion and his four mares" in "a magic moment, almost ghost-like in the pale moonlight." A muscular white stallion prances in the foreground; the other four horses, at differing intervals in the distance. But if there is any doubt about which stallion is intended, we are told that "somewhere atop a Western mesa" this stallion and his mares "still roam free." We must guess at what "almost ghost-like" is meant to suggest; that they are still untamed and roaming free makes the issue clear. The concept, if not the precise identification, is the same as thousands of Westerners and visitors to the West have heard. Now anyone can have, for only three dollars, a 24" x 48" lithograph of the White Steed, to be the "focus of all eyes," guaranteed to be exclaimed over by friends.[2]

Such is the fame of the White Steed (or Stallion, or Mustang) of the Prairies. Washington Irving was the first American writer to write an account of him. Irving's account, published in 1835, formed a part of *A Tour on the Prairies,* a chronicle of the author's journey in 1832 through what is now central Oklahoma. In the afternoon of October 21, 1832, Irving saw his first wild horse on the prairie:

> At sight of us he stopped short, gazed at us for an instant with surprise, then tossing up his head, trotted off in fine style, glancing at us first over one shoulder, then over the other, his ample mane and tail streaming in the wind. . . .
>
> It was the first time I had ever seen a horse scouring his native wilderness in all the pride and freedom of his nature.[3]

And, as was the practice of the skilled, trained writer of his day —as was Irving's wont—he moralized on the episode, in this event comparing the proud, free horse with others less fortunate: "How different from the poor, mutilated, harnessed, checked, reined-up victim of luxury, caprice and avarice, in our cities!"[4]

Irving did a great deal of moralizing on that trip, and much of it contrasted life in the wilds (he was, after all, on the open prairie) with the regulated life in the cities—the millenia-old theme of the pastoral. On encountering a young Osage man, Irving shortly after noted that

> such is the glorious independence of man in a savage state. This youth [the Osage], with his rifle, his blanket, and his horse, was ready at a moment's warning to rove the world. . . . We are a society of slaves, not so much to others as to ourselves. . . .[5]

Irving had recently returned from several years abroad in the urban capitals of Europe and had had much time to reflect on "civilized" society. That he chose to continue living in the city, that his observations were largely inspired by a literary and philosophic tradition, is beside the point here. For whatever reason, by whatever impulse, the moralizing tendency induced him to make observations that would not occur to others, even to see things that his less reflective contemporaries did not. One of his companions, Henry Leavitt Ellsworth, recorded the encounter with the horse that so enthralled Irving and triggered his philosophizing; where Irving had seen in the encounter an icon of great conflicts in nineteenth-century life, Ellsworth merely evaluates a fine piece of horseflesh:

> ... the Wild horse was a beautiful iron grey—well made and had a most lofty carriage. ... he might easily have been shot down but none wished to destroy so fine an animal. ...[6]

Irving also mused upon another mustang of the plains that a member of his party captured:

> I could not but look with compassion upon this fine young animal, whose whole course of existence had been so suddenly reversed. From being a denizen of these vast pastures, ranging at will from plain to plain and mead to mead, cropping of every herb and flower, and drinking of every stream, he was suddenly reduced to perpetual and painful servitude, to pass his life under the harness and the curb, amid, perhaps, the din and dust and drudgery of cities. ... one day, a prince of the prairies—the next day, a pack-horse.[7]

When Irving writes about first hearing of the White Steed, he does not immediately moralize about that horse; yet from what he has said of other prairie mustangs, his meaning is clear. The few words that Irving does devote to this wonder-horse praise its speed, endurance, and passion for its freedom. The idea that the White Stallion is the legendary embodiment of the Westerner's craving for and admiration of freedom, his fear and loathing of being fenced in, is found on these pages, however much earlier the idea may have occurred to others. Irving does not see the White Stallion prancing along on the horizon; he has only heard such tales as the following:

> There were several anecdotes of a famous gray horse, which has ranged the prairies of this neighborhood for six or seven years, setting at naught every attempt of the hunters to capture him. They say he can pace and rack (or amble) faster than the fleetest horses can run.[8]

Nearly all of the elements of the legend that will later emerge full-blown are embedded in this succinct passage. Nevertheless, so eminent an authority on the Southwest and its traditions as Walter Prescott Webb thought that an account of the Steed in George Wilkins Kendall's *Narrative of the Texan Sante Fe Expedition* was the most influential. Kendall traveled to the West in 1841, several years after Irving, but his account, published in 1844, is much richer. The legend has grown to maturity. In Kendall's *Narrative,* as in Irving's, such tales are heard when the men are relaxing:

> Many were the stories told that night in camp, by some of the old hunters, of a large white horse that had often been seen in the vicinity of the Cross Timbers. . . . That many of these stories were either apocryphal or marvelously garnished, I have little doubt. . . . as the camp stories ran, he has never been known to gallop or trot, but paces faster than any horse that has been sent out after him can run; and so game and untiring is the "White Steed of the Prairies," for he is well known to hunters and trappers by that name, that he has tired down no less than three race-nags, sent expressly to catch him. . . . Large sums of money have been offered for his capture, and the attempt has been frequently made; but he still roams his native prairies in freedom, solitary and alone. The fact of his being always found with no other horse in company is accounted for, by an old hunter, on the ground that he is too proud to be seen with those of his class, being an animal far superior in form and action to any of his brothers. This I put down as rank embellishment.[9]

In that same year other writers published accounts of their experiences with this marvelous beast, and one is hard put to say which is the most influential, or the first. In 1844 Josiah Gregg's *Commerce of the Prairies* mentions the horse, and also at some length. Like Kendall, Gregg expresses doubts over certain of the more extravagant claims and descriptions; yet he seems to believe, or at least to half-believe, in the White Steed and to want his readers to believe also.

> The beauty of the mustang is proverbial. One in particular has been celebrated by hunters, of which marvelous stories are told. He has been represented as a medium-sized stallion of perfect symmetry, milk-white, save a pair of black ears—a natural "pacer," and so fleet, it has been said, as to leave far behind every horse that had been tried in pursuit of him, without breaking his "pace." But I infer that this story is somewhat mythical, from the difficulty which one finds in fixing the abode of its equine hero. He is familiarly known, by common report, all

over the great Prairies. The trapper celebrates him in the vicinity of the northern Rocky Mountains; the hunter, on the Arkansas, or in the midst of the Plains; while others have him pacing at the rate of half a mile a minute on the borders of Texas. It is hardly a matter of surprise, then, that a creature of such an ubiquitary existence should never have been caught.[10]

We know from Irving's account that at least ten years before the Kendall and Gregg reports of the White Stallion, he was famous in the area. Descriptions vary little, then as now. Sometimes he is the leader of his herd, sometimes he is accompanied only by his mares, sometimes he is alone. Sometimes he is grey instead of white. But always he is indefatigable, tremendously strong, and eerily swift: he can "pace" more rapidly than other horses can gallop. But most important of all, in both Irving's interpretation and mine, he is free: he can never be captured, he roams the plains at will—they are "his" —and he is everywhere in lands on which "civilization," technological civilization, has not encroached. Men try to subdue and enthrall him, but always he remains free.

He means different things to different men, as we shall see; in *Moby-Dick* (first published in 1851), there is a chapter on "The Whiteness of the Whale." To Melville the stallion's color has an "elusive something in the innermost idea of this hue, which strikes more of panic to the soul than that redness which affrights in blood."[11] For Melville, the White Steed is the terrestrial counterpart of the white whale.

Most famous in our Western annals and Indian traditions is that of the White Steed of the Prairies; a magnificent milk-white charger, large-eyed, small-headed, bluff-chested, and with the dignity of a thousand monarchs in his lofty, overscorning carriage. He was the elected Xerxes of vast herds of wild horses. . . . At their flaming head he westward trooped it like that chosen star which every evening leads on the hosts of light. The flashing cascade of his mane, the curving comet of his tail, invested him with housings more resplendent than gold and silver-beaters could have furnished him. A most imperial and archangelical apparition of that unfallen, western world, which to the eyes of the old trappers and hunters revived the glories of those primeval times when Adam walked majestic as a god, bluff-bowed and fearless as this mighty steed. . . . in whatever aspect he presented himself, always to the bravest Indians he was the object of trembling reverence and awe. Nor can it be questioned from what stands on legendary record of the noble horse, that it was his spiritual whiteness chiefly, which so clothed him with divineness; and that this divineness had that in it which, though commanding worship, at the same time enforced a certain nameless terror.[12]

We have come to understand Melville's symbolic perceptions of ordinary events; in the passage above, his reading is metaphysical. Of course, white horses, not being supernaturally rare, would not enforce quite as much nameless terror as white whales; and Melville would have little idea what trembling reverence and awe the Native American would experience upon being presented with it. The important fact for us is that Melville had heard of the Steed, by the time of the publication of *Moby-Dick,* though he feels it necessary to explain many of his attributes to an audience that may be ignorant of him. This interpretation is peculiarly Melville's; freedom is not an aspect of the stallion' character, unless we extrapolate his freedom from his "divineness." The Steed was not only born free, he is (here) a symbol of the unfallen world; Melville's interpretation is unique.

Texan Walter Prescott Webb had quite another idea about the Steed's "meaning," an idea based on his deep knowledge of horses and horsemen. Webb offers an historical, evolutionary thesis about the genesis of the legend. Horses had been indigenous to North America more than 30,000 years ago, but had long been extinct on this continent when the Spanish reintroduced them in the sixteenth century. Some were stolen by Indians; others escaped into the wild. By the eighteenth century they were known to travel in herds in the West, each group led by a stallion preeminent for his speed, strength, and courage.[13] Webb insists that the herd leader "actually herded them, controlled them, dominated them," and that the leader "had to be wise and wary as well." These facts of herd life were well known to plainsmen; and they therefore desired to capture, to subdue, and to possess the stallion leader—not only the White Stallion, but the leader of any mustang herd.

Webb's rationale is sociologically based. The West of the eighteenth and nineteenth centuries was predominantly a horse culture, a society in which—as Webb put it—a man was "little better" than his horse. He who captured a mustang leader became instantly more of a man, actually—in the everyday transactions of living on the plains—as well as psychologically. But at this point in his argument Webb implies that the hunt for the herd chieftain became a philosophical quest. The herds always had leaders, but the quality of leadership is evanescent: it "could never be caught—it resided in the herd." And so, Webb thinks, the object of desire became that quality of leadership, and thus the hunt for the mustang leader became (becomes) the quest for the object of one's innermost desires, and thus a seeking for the unattainable.

From the plainsmen's questing for incorporeal qualities grew the legend of the White Steed, "that superb horse, a super-horse that had all the desirable and unusual qualities, all the speed, all the endurance, all the beauty that imagination could give him. Since he had all these attributes, everybody wanted him, but nobody could take him. He was ubiquitous, ethereal, a mere ideal, a phantom of the plainsman's mind, and he ranged from Canada to Mexico."[14]

If the "story" of the White Stallion were a literary text, we would attempt to determine, as best we could and as much as that were possible, the author's intentions. The same principles are not applicable in precisely the same ways when the text is folkloric or popular. If there ever was one author of a folk legend, he is probably unknown to us; that is certainly the case with the White Stallion accounts. But as with the interpretation of literary texts, the understanding of the meaning of the legend may justifiably signify several values; it has no "central," controlling meaning, because it genuinely "belongs" to each of those active bearers of it. Webb's understanding of the White Stallion is no more or less valid than that of any bearer, but the folklorist will be more seriously interested in any version of the story as it occurs in an authentic oral tradition. The oral currency of Webb's analyses is not given, and we are not told whether his ideas are his own entirely or in part derived from Texans who had seen or heard stories about the Steed. Though he is Texan himself and though he comes from an established Texas tradition, his interpretation has not been demonstrated to be based on any more authentically oral source than Washington Irving's.

The Easterner's admiration of the Stallion as a "denizen of these vast pastures" who ranges at will from "mead to mead, cropping of every herb and flower, and drinking of every stream" and as such the embodiment and therefore the signifier of freedom and independence, is not unique: it is characteristic of Irving's personal philosophy and of much of the elitist sentiments of his day, but many plainsmen seem to have had many of the same feelings about the Stallion, if observers Kendall and Gregg are also to be believed. Webb stated, in 1924, the year he wrote his short note on the White

Stallion, that stories about this wonder-horse were even then in short supply. But the reasons he gave could also be used to justify an interpretation of the Steed as symbol of freedom and independence; noting that the legend has almost died out, he continued,

> One can pick it up now only from the older generation, from those who have recollections of the open country when Texas was held together by rawhide and dominated by horsemen. . . . There is no room for the White Steed of the Prairies in a country where horses are no longer wild and free.[15]

As man is more confined and restrained, the White Steed is seldom seen.

Robert Denhardt has written that "all" of the early travelers on the plains heard at one time or another of the White Steed and that hunts were organized to capture him. It was "every youth's dream," he writes, "to capture and tame the White Steed for his own,"[16] a narrative notion which is similar to the plot of the recent movie *The Black Stallion*. Frederick Whittaker's dime novel, *The Mustang Hunters*, fictionalized this fantasy for nineteenth-century Eastern readers.

But (nearly) all attempts to capture him end in the hunter's frustration. As Phil Stong tells one story,[17] the Steed was forced into a horseshoe-shaped arroyo by nearly one hundred pursuers but still could not be captured. Seemingly hopelessly trapped, the White Stallion galloped back and forth until one after another of the pursuing horses gave up from exhaustion. Then, as if in contempt, the Stallion paced up the sides of the escarpment previously thought unclimbable.

When the Steed does die, the accounts stress his defiance of his captors and his choosing to die rather than live in captivity. J. Frank Dobie collected a tale in the late 1930s[18] that relates how the Stallion was hunted relentlessly yet always managed to pace away from those in pursuit. In the arid country of Texas, between the Nueces and the Rio Grande, he was greatly weakened from lack of water. At a boxed waterhole he was cornered by a cowboy, who had the wind in his favor, Dobie's informant assures us, but jaded as the Stallion was it still took two more vaqueros to rope him. Staked to the parched land within reach of a water trough, the Stallion refused to eat or drink, preferring death to a life under a saddle or in a corral. He died several days later.

In another tale of this sort, the captured Stallion simply, though the tale is told with more romantic effusion, dies "of a broken heart."[19]

The Stallion is like the land, wild and untamed. And so, as they sought to colonize, to civilize the land west of the Mississippi in the nineteenth century, men sought to capture, subdue, and tame the Stallion. The Stallion is close to nature, pacing at will in the open country, and as Americans have for more than one century sought to harness nature's great powers, so was there a passion to corral this great mustang of the wild.

The Steed exudes power and, as Freud often argued, sexual power as well. His well-muscled body, flashing cascade of mane, his legendary swiftness, all express these qualities. When he is in good health he outpaces all other gallopers; and only when he is greatly weakened can men—and then it takes several of them—capture him. His pacing—an attribute ascribed to him with great frequency —is a manifestation of his strength. One of my students, Ms. Elizabeth Lawrence,[20] has reminded me that a "pace" is usually an unnatural gait, one that is only learned by a horse after intensive training. To execute this gait the horse must co-ordinate his legs on each side of his body to move in unison, rather than move those on opposite sides, as in a "natural" trot. Most riders have difficulty when astride pacing horses, and the gait is used mainly for harness racers. Nevertheless, it is a visually graceful movement and that fact, in addition to its normally being a slower gait than a gallop, may account for its persistent attribution to the Stallion.

And, of course, he is white. It is no coincidence that the Lone Ranger's mighty stallion, "Silver," is also white. His color signifies his special qualities; the Navajos also thought so—of white horses in general, not the fictional "Silver," of course.[21] Navajo gods of the sun and moon ride pure white horses, and a man who owns such a horse believes that it brings good luck. Black Elk, an Oglala Sioux, had a vision of a dozen snowy horses, whose hue designated the north, that region from whence great white cleansing winds are born. And Black Elk's visionary steeds were as strong as they were beautiful.[22]

The Stallion is also capable of kindness to humans. Dobie includes a version of the "Little Gretchen" story in his *Life on the Open Range*.[23] Frequently told and widely distributed, this tale centers around a small girl, "Gretchen," going west in a wagon train. She was tied onto an old mare, which strayed away from the train.

Suddenly the White Stallion appeared and led Gretchen's mare to his own herd. When the small girl's frightened cries made her plight clear, the Stallion bit through the ropes securing her to her mare and, taking the collar of her dress in his mouth, lifted her to the ground. After she had rested, the Stallion lifted Gretchen back onto her mare, and sent horse and rider back to the girl's family. In later years Gretchen proudly bared the scars left inadvertently by the Steed's teeth to her doubting grandchildren. In 1980 an acquaintance in Seattle, Washington, told me that she remembered the "Little Gretchen" story very well, not from having heard it related orally but from having read a version of it in *Reader's Digest*. Since that encounter in print, Mrs. Suzanne Rahn has retold the story several times, thus adding to its oral currency. Mrs. Rahn is at present writing her Ph.D. dissertation on children's literature.

Ingratiating as is the "Little Gretchen" story, it is merely a sidelight in the White Steed cycle. In the main the Stallion stories are not about children lost on the prairies, but about the love of being free and alone in the wild, about being independent. And they are about our attempts to shape the forces of nature, so wild and seemingly random, to our orderly, logical, hierarchical, purposive aims. As Rufus Steele exuberantly put it,

> You can talk about your Patrick Henrys and your George Washingtons; you can warble about your country 'tis of thee,' the Star Spangled Banner and our own red white and blue; but the upright tail of a mustang that wore cinches for years and then got back to the great unfenced will continue to fan the atmosphere as the true banner of freedom that never does come down.[24]

As any cattleman will tell you, the hardest horse of all to rope is a formerly docile and well-behaved mustang that has once gotten a taste of freedom.

The love of freedom and unfettered independence is not unique to the American West, yet it is characteristic of those men and women who, during the last two centuries were its colonizing pioneers. The locale of the legends of the White Stallion of the Prairies is the American plains, from Mexico to Canada; the horse and the legend are primarily American (the Steed does not appear in any folk-motif index), however universal the message. In that respect, they are like the popular legends of Custer's Last Stand as they were created in the decades after the battle; each of the details in the popular perception and account of the battle is a rephrasing of the belief that Custer and his men were brave. The locale is the Dakota Territory, the year is 1876, but the message—bravery—is not just for one time and one place only; it too is a universal.

In contrast are those oral and popular tales which rose out of or accreted to the activities in the Mother Lode and Comstock Lode regions—and many other mineral mining areas as well. Many of these tales, especially ones in which a prospector sells out his claim or his vein footage after extracting a few hundred or thousand dollars worth of "color" only to have the subsequent owner take out many times that amount, are more local. Not only do they take place in specific Western American towns (or near mines) and are placed in chronological historical contexts, but they express characteristic American attitudes: the mineral wealth of the West is inexhaustible. There is nothing foolish about selling out one's claim early because more wealth can easily be found in any of a dozen other, accessible places. In the American grain, tales told about the mountain men proclaim the beauty of the American landscape or praise the mountain man's ability to cope with the dangers of Western weather, animals, and Indians.

The narratives of the Overland Trail are customarily said to constitute one of the few original American literary genres. Yet the qualities that most of these narratives extol—endurance, patience, and persistence—are not limited to that area west of the Mississippi River. Nor is the love of freedom and independence an American monopoly. But their symbolic expression, their place and time, the dramatis personae, conspire to make the legends of "The Pacing Steed of the Prairies" a body of narratives that express an attitude characteristically American.

NOTES

INTRODUCTION

1. R. W. B. Lewis, *The American Adam: Innocence, Tragedy, and Tradition in the Nineteenth Century* (Chicago: The University of Chicago Press, 1975), pp. 1–4.

2. James Carey, "Communication and Culture," *Communication Research* 2 (April 1975): 177; this was pointed out to me by Professor Horace Newcomb of the University of Texas.

3. Henry Nash Smith, *Virgin Land: The American West as Symbol and Myth* (Cambridge: Harvard University Press, 1978), pp. viii–ix.

4. Richard Dorson, *American Folklore and the Historian* (Chicago: The University of Chicago Press, 1971), pp. 91–92.

5. Ray Allen Billington, *America's Frontier Heritage* (Albuquerque: University of New Mexico Press, 1974), pp. 62–67. Much to the great sadness of all who knew him, Professor Billington died in March of 1981.

6. A commonly expressed observation; this citation is from Billington, p. 216.

7. Leo Marx, *The Machine in The Garden* (New York: Oxford University Press, 1979).

MOUNTAIN MEN NARRATIVES

1. Charles Francis Adams, *What Jim Bridger and I Saw at Yellowstone National Park,* publisher and place of publication are not apparent. The date is probably 1913. Accession number at the Henry E. Huntington Library is 381882. The passage cited here is on p. 6.

2. Hiram Martin Chittenden, *Yellowstone National Park* (Stanford: Stanford University Press, 1933), pp. 42–43.

3. George Frederick Ruxton, *Life in The Far West,* ed. Leroy R. Hafen (Norman: University of Oklahoma Press, 1951), pp. 7–9.

4. J. Frank Dobie, *Tales of Old Time Texas* (Boston: Little, Brown, 1955), p. 184.

5. Chittenden, p. 45.

6. Gene Caesar, *King of the Mountain Men* (New York: E. P. Dutton, 1961), p. 14.

7. Adams, p. 7.

8. Stanley Vestal, *Kit Carson; Happy Warrior of the Old West* (Boston: Houghton Mifflin, 1928), p. 143.

9. James Dougherty, *Their Weight in Wildcats* (Boston: Houghton Mifflin, 1936), pp. 143–44.

10. Chittenden, p. 43.

11. Caesar, pp. 13–14.

12. Mody C. Boatright, *Folk Laughter on the American Frontier* (New York: Macmillan, 1949), pp. 75–76.

13. Ibid., p. 156.

14. Ibid., pp. 163–164.

15. Ibid., p. 53.

16. Ibid., p. 162.

17. Chittenden, pp. 25–27.

18. Thomas D. Bonner, *The Life and Adventures of James P. Beckwourth* (Lincoln: University of Nebraska Press, 1972 reprint), p. 124.

19. Oliver G. Swan, *Frontier Days* (Philadelphia: Macrae Smith, 1928), p. 29.

20. Dobie, p. 48.

21. James Monaghan, ed., *The Book of The American West* (New York: Messuer, 1963), pp. 516–17.

22. Swan, p. 26.

23. Dougherty pp. 166–67.

24. Humfreyville, Capt. J. Lee, *Twenty Years Among Our Hostile Indians* (New York: Hunter & Co., 1899), p. 465.

25. Vestal, *Kit Carson,* p. 145.

26. Ibid.

27. Caesar, p. 292.

28. Joaquin Miller, *True Bear Stories* (Portland, Oregon: Binfords and Mort, 1949), pp. 54, 96.

29. John Q. Anderson, ed., *Tales of Frontier Texas* (Dallas: Southern Methodist University Press, 1966), p. 224.

30. Edward S. Ellis, *Bill Biddon, Trapper; Or, Life in the Northwest* (New York: Beadle & Co., 1860), p. 74.

31. Ibid.

32. Franklin J. Meine, ed., *The Crockett Almanacks: Nashville Series, 1835–1838* (Chicago: The Caxton Club, 1955), pp. 65, 22, 94, 131.

33. Stanley Vestal, *Jim Bridger* (New York: William Marrow & Co., 1946), pp. 206–7.

34. J. Cecil Alter, *Jim Bridger* (Norman: University of Oklahoma Press, 1962), p. 287.

35. Caesar, p. 13.

36. Ibid., p. 121.

37. Francis F. Victor, *The River of the West* (Hartford: Columbian Book Co., 1870), p. 366.

38. Vestal, *Jim Bridger,* p. 206.

39. Caesar, p. 121.

40. Neill Compton Wilson, *Silver Stampede; The Career of Death Valley's Hell-Camp, Old Panamint* (New York: Macmillan, 1937), pp. 90–91.

41. Nolie Mumey, *The Life of Jim Baker 1818–1898* (Denver: The World Press, 1931), pp. 173, 116.

42. "Recollections of Taylor Pennock," *Annals of Wyoming* 6 (1929): 219.

43. Ray Allen Billington, *The Far Western Frontier: 1830–1860* (New York: Harper and Row, 1962), p. 49.

44. Mumey, p. 166.

45. Caesar, pp. 263, 260, 262.

46. Boatright, p. 100.

47. Caesar, pp. 173–74.

48. Lansford Warren Hastings, *The Emigrant's Guide to Oregon and California* (Cincinnati: G. Conclin, 1845), p. 21.

PROSPECTORS AND THEIR GOLD

1. Privately published by Samuel C. Upham in Philadelphia, 1878, in the manuscript collection of the Huntington Library, p. 468.

2. Collected in Levette Jay Davidson, "Songs of The Rocky Mt. Frontier," *California Folklore Quarterly* 2 (1943): 92.

3. Eleanora Black and Sidney Robertson, eds., *The Gold Rush Song Book* (San Francisco: The Colt Press, 1940), pp. 2–3.

4. Austin and Alta Fife, *Ballads of The Great West* (Palo Alto: American West Publishing Co., 1970), pp. 61–62.

5. *Alta California,* 15 January 1859, p. 2; St. Louis *Republican,* 5 February 1859, p. 3; *Alta California,* 26 March 1859, p. 7; 16 April 1859, p. 7.

6. *Alta California,* 15 November 1859, p. 1.

7. Lucius Beebe and Charles Clegg, *U.S. West: The Saga of Wells Fargo* (New York: E. P. Dutton, 1949), p. 161. The story is widespread.

8. Much has been written—and spoken—about this most famous of lost mine stories, never to a bigger audience than the NBC presentation of 22 December 1977 in the "In Search of . . ." series.

9. Wayland D. Hand, "California Miners' Folklore: Above Ground," *California Folklore Quarterly* 1 (1942): 40

10. Bob Lee, *Lost Mines and Buried Treasures of San Diego County* (Ramon, California: Ballena Press, 1973), pp. 21–22.

11. Hand, p. 27.

12. J. Frank Dobie, *Coronado's Children* (New York: Grosset and Dunlap, 1930), pp. 187–88.

13. Ibid., pp. 209–14.

14. Ibid., pp. 246–47.

15. Ibid., pp. 161–62.

16. John B. Marshall and Temple H. Cornelius, *Golden Treasures of the San Juan* (Denver: Alan Swallow, 1961), pp. 11, 17.

17. Frank Robertson, "Some Lost Mines of California," *Western Folklore* 10 (1951): 31.

18. Dobie, p. 259.

19. Ibid., p. 238.

20. Robertson, p. 27.

21. Marshall and Cornelius, p. 22.

22. Ibid., p. 21.

23. George M. Foster, *Tzintzuntzan: Mexican Peasants in a Changing World* (Boston: Little, Brown, 1967).

24. Neill Compton Wilson, *Silver Stampede* (New York: Macmillan, 1937), p. 8.

25. This tale has been frequently repeated, often in print.

26. John Greenway, ed., *Folklore of The Great West* (Palo Alto: American West Publishing Co., 1969), p. 294.

27. Told me by Dr. Judith Siegel of Seattle, Washington, whose father prospected in the region.

28. William S. Greever, *Bonanza West* (Norman: University of Oklahoma Press, 1963), pp. 91ff. Also Lucius Beebe, *Comstock Commotion* (Stanford: Stanford University Press, 1954), p. 28.

29. *Alta California,* 5 February 1859, p. 7; 5 November 1859, p. 1.

30. J. H. Beadle, *Western Wilds, and The Men Who Redeem Them* (Detroit: J. C. Chilton Publishing Co., 1877), p. 577.

31. Wilson, p. 229.

32. Interview with "Shorty, Mine Peddler," in "Tales of The Pioneers," *Pony Express Courier,* January 1939, p. 14.

33. Hundreds of stories have circulated orally and in print about this famous Virginia City character; in April of 1946, the rejuvenated *Territorial Enterprise* printed a brief biography of her, taken almost entirely from oral sources.

34. Warren Loose, *Bodie Bonanza* (New York: Exposition Press, 1971), p. 66.

35. Wilson, p. 90.

36. Loose, p. 17.

37. *Pony Express Courier,* September 1937, p. 6.

38. Levette J. Davidson, "Songs of The Rocky Mt. Frontier," *California Folklore Quarterly* 2 (1943): 97.

39. Beebe and Clegg, pp. 104ff., recount many Virginia City legends.

40. Ibid., p. 110.

41. These tales are extremely popular; those used here are from Hand, pp. 24–46; Dobie, pp. 208ff; Greenway, pp. 290–94.

42. Hand, pp. 36–37.

43. Ibid., pp. 37–38.

44. Margaret Sheffield Allen collected and analyzed analogous tales from the oil fields of Pennsylvania.

45. In the speech cited in note 1, p. 467.

46. *Pony Express Courier,* March 1938, p. 3.

47. Collected in Davidson, p. 96. Stanzas 3 and 4 are quoted here.

48. *Territorial Enterprise* quoted in Placerville *Daily News,* 27 September 1862, p. 3; *Alta California,* 5 November 1859, p. 1; 22 January 1859, p. 4.

49. The quantification of the Orrum-Bowers fortune and spree was supplied by Beebe and Clegg, pp. 98ff.

50. Ibid., p. 579.

51. *Territorial Enterprise,* 10 April 1946, p. 3.

52. Beebe and Clegg, p. 205.

NARRATIVES OF THE OVERLAND TRAIL

1. David Morris Potter, *Trail To California: The Overland Journey of Vincent Geiger and Waherman Bryarly* (New Haven: Yale University Press, 1967), p. 96.

2. Ibid.

3. John Francis McDermott, ed. *An Artist on the Overland Trail: The 1849 Diary and Sketches of James F. Wilkins* (San Marino, California: The Huntington Library, 1968), pp. 37–38.

4. This essay is not an attempt to duplicate Archer Butler Hulbert, *The Forty-Niners; The Chronicle of the California Trail* (Boston: Little, Brown, 1949), which is a fictionalized rendering of a great many trail episodes.

5. C. W. Smith, *Journal of a Trip to California—Across the Continent, ... in 1850* (Fairfield, Washington: Ye Galleon Press, 1974), p. 77; entry for July 26, 1950.

6. Pages 1 and 2 of diary in Bancroft Library.

7. Clarence Booth Bagley, *The Acquisition and Pioneering of Old Oregon* (Seattle: Argus Print, 1924), pp. 17–18.

8. Luella Dickenson, *Reminiscences of a Trip Across the Plains in 1846 and Early Days in California* (San Francisco: Whitaker and Ray, 1904), p. 9.

9. Diary entry for 30 June, 1852, Edgerley Woodman Todd, *A Doctor on the California Trail* (Denver: Old West Publishing Co., 1971), p. 60.

10. Bagley, p. 23.

11. James Bennett, *Overland Journey to California* (New Harmony, Indiana: New Harmony Times Print, 1906), p. 16.

12. Elisha Brooks, *A Pioneer Mother of California* (San Francisco: Harr Wagner Publishing Co., 1922), p. 17.

13. Ted Hinckley and Caryl Hinckley, "Overland From St. Louis to the California Gold Field in 1849: The Diary of Joseph Waring Berrien," *Indiana Magazine of History* 56 (1960): 339.

14. Mary Searles Heuer et al., eds., *The Diary of a Pioneer and Other Papers* (Privately printed in San Francisco, 1940), p. 23.

15. James Abbey, "California—A Trip Across the Plains," *The Magazine of History* 46 (1933): 113–14.

16. Joel Barnett, *A Long Trip in a Prairie Schooner* (Whittier, California: Western Stationers Co., 1928), p. 37.

17. Heuer et al., p. 39.

18. Randall Henry Hewitt, *Across The Plains and Over The Divide* (New York: Broadway Publishing Co., 1906), p. 38.

19. Bennett, p. 14.

20. Hinckley and Hinckley, p. 303.

21. Smith, pp. 37–38.

22. Carlisle Stewart Abbott, *Recollections of a California Pioneer* (New York: The Neale Publishing Co., 1917), pp. 36–37.

23. Smith, p. 31.

24. Hinckley and Hinckley, p. 300.

25. Todd, p. 41.

26. Abbey, p. 112.

27. Smith, pp. 34–35.

28. Hewitt, p. 198.

29. Abbey, p. 148.

30. Todd, p. 62.

31. Hewitt, p. 89.

32. Brooks, pp. 20–21.

33. Ward G. Dewitt and Florence Stark Dewitt, eds., *Prairie Schooner Lady* (Los Angeles: Westernlore Press, 1959), pp. 119–120.

34. Cornelius Cole, *Memoirs of Cornelius Cole* (New York: McLaughlin Bros., 1908), p. 30.

35. Helen E. Clark and Calvin Perry Clark, *Two Diaries* (Denver: Denver Public Library, 1962), pp. 17–18.

36. Brooks, p. 15.

37. Ibid., pp. 14–15.

38. Clark and Clark, p. 11.

39. Dewitt and Dewitt, p. 134 (entry for 20 August 1853).

40. Hinckley and Hinckley, p. 341.

41. Francis Coleman Rosenberger, *Journey To The Gold Fields: The Diary of Zirkle D. Robinson* (Iowa City: The Prairie Press, 1966), p. 11; Abbey, p. 151; McDermott, pp. 71–72.

42. Abbey, p. 160.

43. Cole, p. 52.

44. Brooks, p. 34.

45. Dickenson, pp. 30–31; Abbey, p. 160.

46. Todd, p. 57.

THE HANDCART ODYSSEY

1. Quoted in LeRoy R. and Ann W. Hafen, *Handcarts to Zion* (Glendale: Arthur H. Clark Co., 1960), pp. 35–36.

2. Ibid., p. 40.

3. Cited in John Greenway, *Folklore of the Great West* (Palo Alto: American West Publishing Co., 1969), p. 252.

4. Quoted in Hafen, p. 275.

5. Ibid., p. 276.

6. Ibid., p. 274.

7. Ibid., pp. 53–55.

8. Ibid., p. 16.

9. Both diaries can be found in Hafen, pp. 60ff.

10. *Millennial Star* 18 (1856): 637.

11. Greenway, pp. 252–53.

12. Quoted in Hafen, entry for August 3.

13. Ibid., pp. 102–3.

14. Ibid., pp. 76–77.

15. Greenway, p. 254.

16. Hafen, p. 195.

17. Wallace Stegner, "Ordeal by Handcart," *Colliers,* 6 July 1956, pp. 78–85; quoted in Hafen, p. 141.

CUSTER'S LAST STAND

1. A catalogue of the illustrations is found in Don Russell, *Custer's List* (Fort Worth, Texas: Amon Carter Museum of Western Art, 1969); the best (but nevertheless inadequate) bibliography is Fred Dustin's, most conveniently found in William A. Graham, *The Custer Myth* (New York: Bonanza Books, 1953), pp. 383–405.

2. These legends are discussed in Bruce A. Rosenberg, "Custer: The Legend of the Martyred Hero in America," *Journal of the Folklore Institute* 9 (Fall 1972): 110–32.

3. "The Revenge of Rain-in-the-Face," collected in *The Complete Poetical Works of Henry Wadsworth Longfellow* (Boston: Houghton Mifflin, 1880), p. 272.

4. Robert M. Utley, *Custer and the Great Controversy* (Los Angeles: Westernlore Press, 1962), pp. 135–45.

5. In *Heroic Song and Heroic Legend,* trans. B. J. Timmer (London: Oxford University Press, 1963), pp. 240–41.

6. See Rosenberg, pp. 124–25.

7. "Custer's Last Battle." *The Penn Monthly* (September, 1877): 698.

8. *Chicago Tribune,* 8 July 1876, p. 5.

9. Ibid., 19 July 1876, p. 1.

10. Ibid., 7 July 1876, p. 2.

11. *New York Herald,* 12 July 1876, p. 6.

12. Ibid., 13 July 1876, p. 5.

13. *Custer's Immortality* (New York: New York Evening Post Steam Presses, 1876), p. 11.

14. Ibid., p. 70.

15. "Custer's Farewell," in *Once Their Home; or Our Legacy From the Dakotahs* (Chicago: Donohue and Henneberry, 1891), 253–54. Only stanzas 4 and 6 are reprinted here.

16. *Custer; and Other Poems* (Chicago: W. B. Conkey Co., 1896), bk. III, p. xxxii.

17. Fred S. Kaufman, *Custer Passed Our Way* (Aberdeen, S.D.: North Plains Press, 1971), p. 353.

18. As defined by Stith Thompson, *The Folktale* (New York: The Dryden Press, 1946), p. 8.

19. I have intentionally avoided counting up "points" as Raglan did because point-counting might give the impression that some heroes are

"better" than others because their legends are more "complete" or that it is possible to determine the type of the legend by some precise mathematical formulation.

20. Joseph Bedier, ed., *Chanson de Roland,* 2 vols. (Paris: H. Piazza, 1927–28); a convenient translation is that by Patricia Terry, *The Song of Roland* (Indianapolis: Bobbs-Merrill, 1965). Roland's stand is described in lines 841–2396.

21. Edmund Brock, ed., *Morte Arthure,* Early English Texts Society No. 8 (London: N. Trübner and Co., 1865); the death of Gawain occurs between lines 3724 and 3863. John Gardner has recently translated the entire poem in *The Alliterative Morte Arthure,* a volume of Middle English poems published by the Southern Illinois University Press (Carbondale, 1971).

22. George Rawlinson, ed., *The History of Herodotus,* Vol. 2, (London: J. M. Dent & Sons, 1933), pp. 210–11.

23. E. V. Gordon, ed., *The Battle of Maldon* (New York: Barnes and Noble, 1976).

24. George Clark, "The Battle of Maldon: A Heroic Poem," *Speculum* 43 (January 1965), 56–57.

25. See Helen Rootham, tr., *Kóssovo: Heroic Songs of the Serbs* (Boston: Houghton Mifflin, 1920), and Sir John Bowring, tr., *Servian Popular Poetry* (London: privately printed, 1827).

26. The folklore about the fall of Constantinople was given to me by Prof. Constantine A. Patrides of the English Department of the University of York, one of whose sources was an anonymous anthology entitled *Konstantinoupolis kai Hagia Saphia* (Athens, n.d.).

27. Steven Runciman, *The Fall of Constantinople, 1453* (Cambridge: The University Press, 1965).

28. Pictures in nineteenth-century illustrated children's histories show the gate on a hill. I saw the books on display in the Wiener Stadt historische Museum but did not get bibliographical information about them.

29. Prof. Constantine Patrides has written to me about a popular poem by George Zalokostas which specifies this force of the enemy, but I have no bibliographical data.

30. In the *Hrolfssaga Kraki,* but fragments of his "life" are to be found in several places. See Gwyn Jones, *Kings, Beasts, and Heroes* (London: Oxford University Press, 1972), pp. 128–37, for a convenient summary.

31. Kent Ladd Steckmesser, *The Western Hero in History and Legend* (Norman: University of Oklahoma Press, 1965), pp. 199–200.

32. W. R. Paton, tr., *The Histories,* Vol. 1 (Cambridge: Harvard University Press, 1955), pp. 189–91, 235.

THE PONY EXPRESS

1. "Roughing It," in *The Works of Mark Twain,* Vol. 2 (Berkeley and Los Angeles: University of California Press, 1972), p. 82.

2. Arthur Chapman, *The Pony Express* (New York; G. P. Putnam's, 1932), pp. 214–15.

3. *Pony Express Courier,* November 1934, p. 11.

4. Twain, p. 83.

5. Chapman, pp. 216–17.

6. *PEC,* February 1935, p. 11; and October 1934, p. 4.

7. *PEC,* 23 April 1860, p. 3.

8. *PEC,* August 1934, p. 15.

9. *PEC,* January 1935, p. 23.

10. *PEC,* July 1934, p. 1.

11. Fred Reinfeld, *Pony Express* (New York: Collier Books, 1966), pp. 91–93.

12. Esoteric lore—that which was current among the riders, attendants, keepers, etc., and told about themselves—would probably have been more varied, less dramatic and heroic, and thus would have revealed much more about what the hired personnel felt about their occupations.

13. Reinfeld, pp. 93–94.

14. *PEC,* Dec. 1934, p. 13.

15. Chapman, p. 298.

16. Reinfeld, p. 94.

17. *PEC,* April 1937, p. 12.

18. Reinfeld, p. 79.

19. Ibid.

20. Prentiss Ingraham, *Buffalo Bill, From Boyhood to Manhood* (New York: Beadle and Adams, 1884), pp. 17–18.

21. Frank Glines Patchin, *The Pony Rider Boys in New Mexico* (Philadelphia: M. Altemus, 1910), pp. 300–301, 314.

22. Chapman, pp. 124–124.

23. Ibid., p. 133.

24. Ibid., pp. 229–30.

25. Ibid., p. 204.

26. Reinfeld, pp. 77–8.

27. From *Hutching's California Magazine,* reprinted in *PEC,* December 1936, p. 9.

THE RACE OF THE *NATCHEZ* AND THE *ROBERT E. LEE*

1. These details, as well as those of the great race and the contesting personnel, are well known and have been published in a great many places; used here was Roy L. Barkhau, *The Great Steamboat Race Between the Natchez and the Rob't E. Lee* (Cincinnati: Steamship Historical Society of America, 1962) p. 12, given me by the Marketing Services Department of the Delta Queen Steamboat Company.

2. Quoted in Barkhau, p. 17.

3. Barkhau, p. 12.

4. New Orleans *Times-Picayune,* 6/30/70, p. 1.

5. In a front-page essay on July 1, 1870.

6. Quoted in Barkhau, p. 16.

7. In an interview in Captain Way's Sewickley, Pennsylvania, home, April, 1975.

8. Datelined Cincinnati, published in the *New York Times,* 7/2/70, p. 1.

9. New Orleans *Times-Picayune,* 7/6/70, p. 1.

10. The elapsed times of each boat at each milestone is usually included in accounts of the race; see Barkhau and Mark Twain's *Roughing It.*

THE TEN-MILE DAY

1. For surveys of the history of the transcontinental railroad see Robert G. Athern, *Union Pacific Country* (Chicago: Rand McNally, 1971) and the popular history by Dee Alexander Brown, *Hear that Lonesome Whistle Blow* (New York: Holt, Rinehart and Winston, 1977).

2. William Francis Bailey, *The Story of the First Trans-continental Railroad* (Fair Oaks, California: W. F. Bailey, 1906), p. 54.

3. Brown, p. 65.

4. Quoted in John Greenway, *Folklore of the Great American West* (Palo Alto: American West Publishing Co., 197), p. 271.

5. Athern, p. 36.

6. Athern, p. 54.

7. Quoted in Athern, p. 62.

8. 28 April 1869, p. 5.

9. Brown, p. 109.

10. Athern, pp. 37–38.

11. Brown, p. 103.

12. Athern, pp. 43–44

13. Brown, pp. 117–19.

14. Quoted in Edwin L. Sabin, *Building the Pacific Railway* (Philadelphia: J. B. Lippincott, 1919), p. 113.

15. Brown, p. 104.

16. See Robert M. Utley, "The Dash to Promontory," *Utah Historical Quarterly* 29 (April 1961): 99–117.

17. Brown, p. 123.

18. Ibid., 123–24.

19. Oscar O. Winthur, *The Transportation Frontier* (New York: Holt, Rinehart and Winston, 1964), p. 111.

20. Sabin, pp. 201–2.

21. Sabin, footnote on p. 202.

22. Sabin, p. 203.

23. Letter of 2 May 1869, in J. R. Perkins, *Trails, Rails and War* (Indianapolis: Bobbs-Merrill, 1929), p. 238.

24. From a syndicated news item in the Chicago *Tribune,* 30 April 1869, p. 1; and the New York *Herald,* same date, p. 7.

25. *Alta California,* 30 April 1869, p. 1.

26. Sacramento *Daily Union,* 30 April 1869, p. 3.

27. Sacramento *Daily Union,* 3 May 1869, p. 4.

28. Issue of 29 May 1869, p. 162.

29. Andrew Nelson of Pittsburgh, Pennsylvania, who has worked summers as a track-layer, recalls how his crew laid down about three-and-one-half miles of track in one day, using modern power-driven automatic equipment, and felt very proud of themselves for it.

THE OUTLAW

1. See Bruce A. Rosenberg, *Custer and the Epic of Defeat* (University Park: Pennsylvania State University Press, 1975).

2. G. W. N., "Wild Bill," *Harper's New Monthly Magazine* 36 (1867), p. 277.

3. Will Hale, *Twenty-four Years a Cowboy and Ranchman in Southern Texas and Old Mexico* (Norman: University of Oklahoma Press, 1959 reprint).

4. There he gave the details of his earlier, "heroic" life to friends in the movie industry and to biographer Stuart Lake, who wrote *Wyatt Earp, Frontier Marshall.*

5. Kent Ladd Steckmesser, *The Western Hero In History and Legend* (Norman: University of Oklahoma Press), pp. 74ff.

6. John A. Lomax and Allan Lomax, *American Ballads and Folk Songs* (New York: Macmillan, 1934), p. 132.

7. Kent Ladd Steckmesser, "Robin Hood and the American Outlaw," *Journal of American Folklore* 79 (1966): 350. For a detailed chronicle of the War, see Maurice Garland Fulton, *History of The Lincoln County War* (Tucson: University of Arizona Press, 1968).

8. Lomax and Lomax, pp. 136–37.

9. *Ibid.,* pp. 137–38; verses 4–6 are cited here.

10. Cited in Steckmesser, *Western Hero,* p. 91.

11. Steckmesser, "Robin Hood," p. 350.

12. *Ibid.,* p. 348.

13. *Ibid.,* p. 353; but also see *Custer and the Epic of Defeat* for similar observations worked out in detail.

14. Austin Fife and Alta Fife, *Ballads of the Great West* (Palo Alto: American West Publishing Co., 1970), pp. 112–13.

15. From the Thorp text of 1908 and 1921, quoted in Fife, pp. 114–115.

16. This synopsis is from the version in Homer Croy, *Jesse James Was My Neighbor* (New York: Duell, Sloan and Pearce, 1949), pp. 100–103; variants also occur in Carl W. Breihan, *The Escapades of Frank and Jesse James* (New York: F. Fell Publisher, 1974), pp. 186–87; Robertus Love, *The Rise and Fall of Jesse James* (New York: G. P. Putnam's Sons, 1926) pp. 289–92; Joseph A. Dacus, *Life and Adventures of Frank and Jesse James* (St. Louis: W. S. Bryan, 1880), p. 271; and William A. Settle, Jr., *Jesse James Was His Name* (Columbia: University of Missouri Press, 1966), pp. 171–72.

17. Collected by John A. Lomax and printed in his *Adventures of a Ballad Hunter* (New York: Macmillan, 1947), pp. 58–59.

18. Francis James Child, ed., *The English and Scottish Popular Ballads,* 5 vols. (Boston: Houghton Mifflin, 1882–98).

19. Robert L. Fish, *Pursuit* (New York: Berkley Publishing Corp., 1978), p. 47.

20. See Steckmesser, "Robin Hood," p. 351

21. *Ibid.,* p. 349.

THE MOSLEM PRINCESS OF THE PRAIRIES

1. See Philip Young, "The Mother of Us All," *Kenyon Review* 24 (1962): 391–441; and Rayna Green, "The Pocahontas Perplex: The Image of Indian Women in American Culture," *Massachusetts Review* 16 (1975): 698–714.

2. Wilcomb E. Washburn, ed., *Narratives of North American Indian Captivities* (New York: Garland Publishing, Inc., 1976).

3. Elizabeth F. Ellett, *The Pioneer Women of the West* (Philadelphia: Porter and Coates, 1873), p. 125.

4. Adam Hall, *The Quiller Memorandum* (New York: Pyramid Books, 1965), p. 29.

5. Edward L. Wheeler, *Deadwood Dick, the Prince of the Road; Or, The Black Rider of the Black Hills* (Cleveland: The Arthur Westbrook Co., 1878), p. 4.

6. Sarah J. Cummins, *Autobiography and Reminiscences* (Cleveland: The Arthur H. Clark Co., 1914), p. 31.

7. George Armstrong Custer, *Wild Life on the Plains and Horrors of Indian Warfare,* ed. Robert M. Fogelson and Richard E. Rubenstein (New York: Arno Press, 1969), p. 146.

8. Stewart Edward White, *Daniel Boone Wilderness Scout* (New York: Doubleday, Page and Co., 1923), pp. 166–69.

9. James O. Pattie, *The Personal Narrative of James O. Pattie,* ed. Timothy Flint (Chicago: The Lakeside Press, 1930), p. 12.

10. White, pp. 13–18.

11. John A. Lomax and Allan Lomax, *American Ballads and Folk Songs* (New York: Macmillan, 1934), pp. 163–65.

12. *Collected Verse of Rudyard Kipling* (London: Hodden and Stoughton, 1912), pp. 369–71.

13. Bruce A. Rosenberg, *Custer and the Epic of Defeat* (University Park: Pennsylvania State University Press, 1975).

14. Issac K. Russell and Howard R. Driggs, *Hidden Heroes of the Rockies* (Yonkers, New York: World Book Co., 1923), pp. 245–51.

THE WHITE STEED OF THE PRAIRIES

1. Austin E. Fife and Alta Fife, *Ballads of the Great West* (Palo Alto: American West Publishing Co., 1970), pp. 87–88.

2. I saw this ad in the March 1, 1980, issue of *TV Guide* for Western Pennsylvania, A-29.

3. Washington Irving, *A Tour on the Prairies,* ed. John Francis McDermott (Norman, Oklahoma: University of Oklahoma Press, 1956), p. 114.

4. Ibid., p. 114.

5. Ibid., p. 34.

6. Henry Leavitt Ellsworth, *Washington Irving on the Prairie,* ed. Stanley T. Williams and Barbara D. Simiso (New York: American Book Co., 1937), p. 85.

7. Irving, p. 122.

8. Ibid., p. 116.

9. George Wilkins Kendall, *Narrative of the Texan Santa Fe Expedition* (New York: Harper and Brothers, 1844), pp. 89–90.

10. Josiah Gregg, *Commerce of the Prairies,* Vol. 2 (Ann Arbor: University Microfilms, Inc., 1966), p. 207; reprint (Xerox) of 1844 edition.

11. Herman Melville, *Moby-Dick* (New York: Random House, 1930), p. 274.

12. Ibid., pp. 275–76.

13. W. P. Webb, "The White Steed of the Prairies," in J. Frank Dobie, *Legends of Texas,* Publications of the Texas Folklore Society, 3 (Dallas: Southern Methodist Press, 1924), 223.

14. Ibid., pp. 223–24.

15. Ibid., p. 226.

16. Robert M. Denhardt, *The Horse of the Americas* (Norman: University of Oklahoma Press, 1975), p. 117.

17. Philip Duffield Stong, *Horses and Americans* (Garden City, N.Y.: Garden City Publishing Co., Inc., 1946), p. 195.

18. J. Frank Dobie, *On The Open Range* (Dallas: Banks Upshaw, 1940), pp. 176–79.

19. Walker D. Wyman, *The Wild Horse of the West* (Lincoln: University of Nebraska Press, 1965), p. 313.

20. Anthropology major graduate student in my course on the "Folklore of the American West" given at Brown University, Spring, 1979.

21. La Verne Harrell Clark, *They Sang for Horses* (Tucson: University of Arizona Press, 1966), p. 22.

22. John G. Neihardt, *Black Elk Speaks* (London: Abacus Press, 1974), p. 28.

23. Dobie, pp. 103–9.

24. Rufus Steele, *Mustangs of the Mesas* (Hollywood, California: Murray and Gee, 1941), p. 188.